INSIDERS' GUIDE® TO
PALM SPRINGS

HELP US KEEP THIS GUIDE UP TO DATE

We would love to hear from you concerning your experiences with this guide and how you feel it could be improved and kept up to date. Please send your comments and suggestions to:

editorial@GlobePequot.com

Thanks for your input, and happy travels!

INSIDERS' GUIDE® TO

PALM SPRINGS

SECOND EDITION

KEN VAN VECHTEN

INSIDERS' GUIDE

GUILFORD, CONNECTICUT
AN IMPRINT OF GLOBE PEQUOT PRESS

All the information in this guidebook is subject to change. We recommend that you call ahead to obtain current information before traveling.

To buy books in quantity for corporate use or incentives, call **(800) 962–0973** or e-mail **premiums@GlobePequot.com.**

INSIDERS' GUIDE ®

Editorial Director, Travel: Amy Lyons
Project Editor: Lynn Zelem
Text design: Sheryl Kober
Maps: XNR Productions, Inc. © Morris Book Publishing, LLC
Layout Artist: Maggie Peterson
Previous edition written by Carolyn Patten

ISSN 1933-2637
ISBN 978-0-7627-5733-6

Printed in the United States of America
10 9 8 7 6 5 4 3 2 1

CONTENTS

Directory of Maps

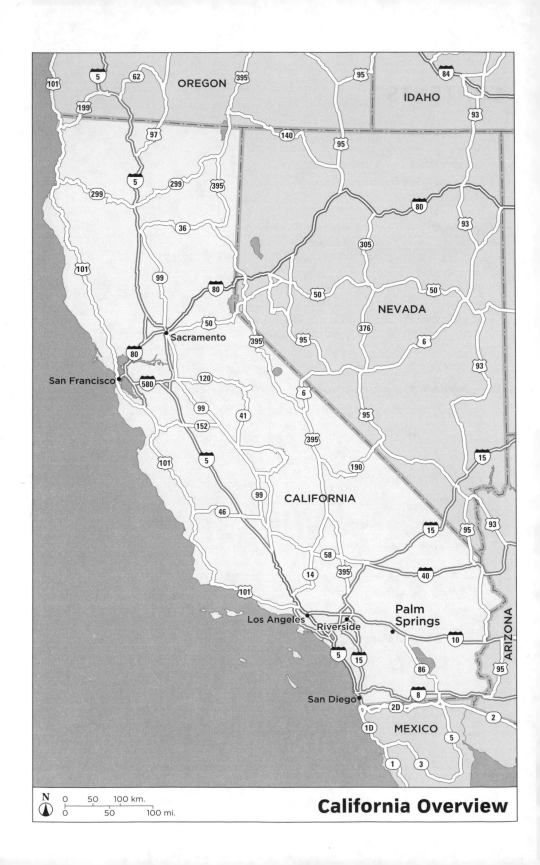

California Overview

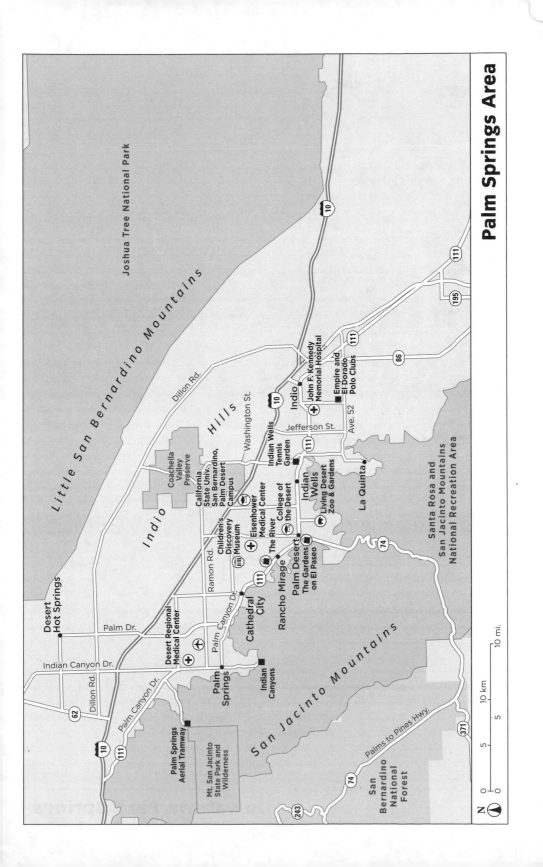

Palm Springs Area

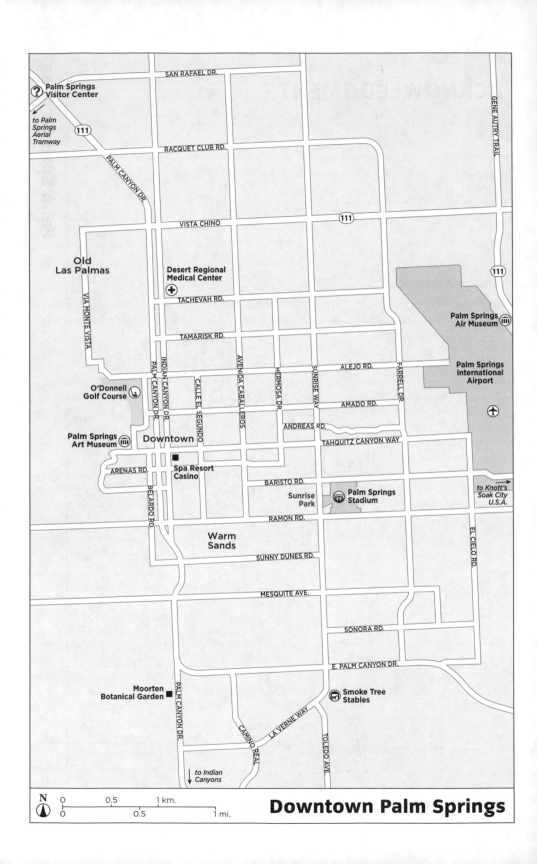

Downtown Palm Springs

Palm Springs Visitor Center

to Palm Springs Aerial Tramway

SAN RAFAEL DR.

RACQUET CLUB RD.

111

PALM CANYON DR.

VISTA CHINO

111

GENE AUTRY TRAIL

111

Old Las Palmas

Desert Regional Medical Center

TACHEVAH RD.

TAMARISK RD.

VIA MONTE VISTA

Palm Springs Air Museum

ALEJO RD.

Palm Springs International Airport

O'Donnell Golf Course

PALM CANYON DR.

INDIAN CANYON DR.

CALLE EL SEGUNDO

AVENIDA CABALLEROS

HERMOSA DR.

SUNRISE WAY

AMADO RD.

FARRELL DR.

Palm Springs Art Museum

Downtown

ANDREAS RD.

TAHQUITZ CANYON WAY

Spa Resort Casino

ARENAS RD.

BARISTO RD.

Sunrise Park

Palm Springs Stadium

to Knott's Soak City U.S.A.

BELARDO RD.

RAMON RD.

Warm Sands

SUNNY DUNES RD.

EL CIELO RD.

MESQUITE AVE.

SONORA RD.

E. PALM CANYON DR.

Moorten Botanical Garden

PALM CANYON DR.

Smoke Tree Stables

CAMINO REAL

LA VERNE WAY

TOLEDO AVE.

to Indian Canyons

N

0   0.5   1 km.
0   0.5   1 mi.

ACKNOWLEDGMENTS

Guidebooks are funny critters. They are the culmination of years of familiarity with a particular area (or subject matter) as set forth by a person who had the time, opportunity and inclination to get to know the locale in question. Travel guides are singularly personal. Yet few of us who share our love of place and experience operate in a vacuum or navigate uncharted waters, literal or figurative; we're not Darwin on the *Beagle* or Odysseus or Polo. We as often as not have someone along for the ride, an indispensable second set of eyes, taste buds, and sensibilities, and then there are those who provide an outside assist.

Leading the last group is Mark Graves of the Palm Springs Desert Resort Communities Convention and Visitors Authority. Mark knows the desert almost as well as he knows what a writer on deadline is facing. He's a tireless advocate for the valley and in a tangible way somewhat responsible for me doing what it is I'm doing today.

This might sound strange, but I also want to give thanks to some folks in Seattle who publish a magazine to which I've contributed for some number of years, and as often as not they let me pontificate about Coachella Valley golf, spa, recreation and the like. That would be Paradigm Communications Group and *Alaska Airlines Magazine*.

Let me say "hi" to someone I've never met: Carolyn Patten. Carolyn wrote the first edition of this book, and her insight and knowledge remain a key part of this edition. Where I have expanded on her particular desert views and experiences, hopefully all will benefit. Where my additions missed any marks, as in all such endeavors, those errors and omissions are solely of my doing.

Closer to the home front, to the friends and family I have in the valley, thanks for all the years of putting a roof over my head.

And to my wife Terri: no one could ask for anyone better with whom to experience the world.

PREFACE

Palm Springs.

Depending on generation and geographic circumstance, "Palm Springs" can conjure up any number of images. For the older crowd, it's the Hollywood playpen of yore, a place where stars and starlets could let down their hair and perhaps even their guard. Young Boomers remember spring break, when Palm Springs featured front-and-center on the list of where to be between semesters, while Generation Xers and Yers might relate to Coachella, the east valley's annual West Coast Woodstock with better sanitation, less wannabe utopianism, and an official ban on drugs. GLBT travelers know it as place of acceptance. Golfers think of Arnie and his Army, Dinah, Duval's 59, and PGA West's Stadium Course—the course tour players refuse to play—even if they've never taken a single divot out of course designer Pete Dye's little shop of joyous horrors. Yet none of that golf lore, not even the Ryder Cups once held in Palm Springs, actually took place in Palm Springs. What's that you say? Indeed. Palm Springs is a city, one of nine in the Coachella Valley, and an iconic one at that, but it's not the only show in town.

Being a lifelong fan of *all* areas of the valley, I lack the Palm Springs-or-else orientation of those who reside or typically cavort not far from the shadow of the San Jacintos. From Indio's music and date festivals to a hidden golf gem beneath the windmills of the far western valley, "Palm Springs" is the Coachella Valley, and it resonates through seasonal ebbs and flows in population and whether the Little San Bernardino Mountains are dusted in snow or the thermo is pushing 120 degrees in the La Quinta Cove. That most visitors refer to the entire area as "Palm Springs" is as much a product of convenience as history; in the gringo era Palm Springs was first in time and first in line and the City of Indian Wells didn't exist so it couldn't build perhaps the most audacious publicly-owned clubhouse in the Great Republic. And when someone asks at work, "So, where you goin' for Easter Break?" does anyone really want to rattle off the jumble of words the local tourism folks understandably use to denote a desert valley comprised of a bunch of cities, a number of unincorporated communities and unlimited stakeholders? I'm plenty comfy noting I'm off to Palm Springs regardless where I'm staying and playing if the alternative is "Palm Springs Desert Resort Communities."

For someone who has never lawfully resided in Palm Springs or anywhere else in the Coachella Valley, I still managed long ago to lose track of the gazillions of calories I've consumed at valley restaurants, the thousands of strokes expended on golf courses (and the hundreds of balls dispatched at far too young of an age), and the scores of hotels, condos, and resorts where I've put in for a week or a night. The family has carved dozens and dozens of Thanksgiving turkeys in Palm Desert and Rancho Mirage and Indian Wells. We've decorated palms and ficus trees with lights and tinsel in anticipation of Santa's arrival. I nearly killed an uncle when the August temps and his meds were a dicey mix on the course, and my wife and I have seen I-10 cloaked in a Fargo-grade whiteout, of sand if not snow, on several occasions.

You see, I'm a native southern Californian and a recovering Oregonian, so for a very long time I've either been pushed to the desert so my body could remember that Gore-Tex is not a natural layer of skin or drawn by the 57.85-mile proximity to my Golden State domicile. I've seen all sides of "Palm Springs" for several decades, so in essence my Palm Springs is your Palm Springs—that of swaying palms and great eats, show times and tee times, spa and dropping coin along El Paseo and at the outlets, chilling poolside in Rancho Mirage and hiking above the tram or across the magical landscapes of Joshua Tree National Park. Ours is the Palm Springs of vacation. I might just be a bit more habitual about it, that's all.

If the picture isn't clear enough, think of Palm Springs as a beam of white light. There's an undeniable brilliance to that light, and uniformity. Now run it through a prism and you get an array of Palm Springses, each aglow in its own unique color. Run those hues back the other way, and …

However you see it, it's all "Palm Springs," and that's all good.

HOW TO USE THIS BOOK

Mr. Peabody and Sherman need not crank too hard on the controls of the WABAC Machine for a Palm Springs time traveler not to recognize much of anything about his or her beloved desert beyond the desert of sand, rock, mountain and Washingtonia filifera, or the indigenous California fan palm. Even by western American standards, the story behind Palm Springs' history is rather short. The Native peoples, the Cahuilla, of course created a material and spiritual life from the land dating back some thousands of years. And as history generally went in the Aridlands, some succession of Spaniards, Mexicans, and Americans followed, typically looking for ways through. Yet permanent American settlement didn't effectively commence until the arrival of the railroad in the late 19th century, all of which begat townships, and from there nascent resorts (1920s) and self-governing municipalities (1930s) began to appear—and fact be told, Indio beat Palm Springs to cityhood by nearly a decade. So by the post-war era, the modern vacation mecca of Palm Springs, even if some of it was 25 miles away in La Quinta, was in full play.

In 2008 visitors numbered about half way between three and four million in number. They, along with a permanent population estimated to hit 500,000 by 2010, can choose from 120 golf courses, 200-plus hotels, a whopping 600 or so eateries, a like number of tennis courts, and more than 40,000 swimming pools. Both of California's university systems have a presence in the desert, and the local community college district is a leader in the state. And the descendents of those first Cahuilla have discovered a new wealth springing up from the ground—casinos.

If it sounds like yesterday became today at the snap of a finger, desert denizens should be commended for wasting little time transforming isolated desert burgs into one of the globe's gotta go destination areas.

But for all this, Palm Springs and its neighbors still retain some quirky small-townness, a sense of being at least somewhat unique in a growing web of growth and prosperity that has erased many of the open spaces that once set each community apart, quite literally. Part of it, of course, is the incredible weather— less than 6 inches of rain every year and 350 days of sunshine. Part of it is the abundance of wilderness that surrounds the desert and offers respite from the hassles of "civilization." Part of it is an amiable built environment that makes the valley a magnet for visitors and businesses, retirees and long-time residents. The Coachella Valley is an easy place to visit and an easy place in which to put down roots.

The *Insiders' Guide to Palm Springs* is designed to be your companion in enjoying this unique desert playground, whether you are here for a few days or a few years or the remainder of your years. This is a book to take with you—keep it in the car, stuff it in your backpack, mark it up, heck, go ahead and get a few wine-glass rings on the cover. It's for you to use and share as you get to know—and we assume love—the many "Palm Springses" in Palm Springs. The chapters are organized thematically, covering everything from hotels and restaurants to relocation and retirement. Each chapter varies a bit in its structure, depending on the content. For example, the Annual Festivals and Events chapter has sections on film festivals, golf tournaments, ongoing events, and annual events by month. The Accommodations chapter lists hotels alphabetically within the categories of resorts, hotels and motels, RV parks, and vacation rentals.

Although the Palm Springs area has nine cities laid out from northwest to southeast—Desert Hot Springs, Palm Springs, Cathedral City, Rancho Mirage, Palm Desert, Indian Wells, La Quinta, Indio, and Coachella—and a number of recognizable unincorporated communities, the book treats the area as a whole. You won't even notice when you move from one city to the next, but you will need to know which city or community you're talking about when you are interested in real estate, schools, and government. When it's important to know, we will always point out these distinctions.

The first few chapters will get you oriented to the area by providing information about history and transportation and giving you a geographic and political overview, plus some insight into local anomalies and "Palm Springs–ese," including that little matter of geographic double-speak in which "Palm Springs" always means the city of Palm Springs, except when it means the valley as a whole.

If you are a visitor, this book will be your resource for locating the best golf courses (and in some instances they are ones where the big boys and girls on tour have played), the best hiking and horseback riding trails, the most entertaining family outings, locales where the glitterati mingle, the best bargains for each season of the year, and all the stuff that makes a guide an indispensible tool. The next few chapters will help you choose among hundreds of excellent hotels, from budget to luxury, and will give you some of the area's best choices for dining out, from low-cost corner gems to spots where Michelin would bestow stars.

The number and variety of golf courses, outdoor tours, cultural and recreational attractions, casinos, spas, nightlife options, and special events can be bewildering; but this *Insiders' Guide* will help you plan a memorable visit at any time of year. Several chapters are devoted to exploring and detailing every possible activity, whatever the season. And we haven't forgotten shopping, with information on everything from designer outlet stores to farmers' markets.

If you're considering making your home in the valley, this book will give you a good overview of the basics—education, medical and health care resources, real estate, parks and recreation, and retirement. For quick reference, information on local governments, safety, media, and local laws and regulations is easy to locate.

Within the chapters, you'll find lots of cross-referencing and even some cross-listings, just to make your search for information easier. One of this book's outstanding features is its many Insider tips—tips that even some locals don't know about—aimed at giving you a comfortable feeling right away. We've also included a number of Close-ups that look at some of the people, places, and events that give Palm Springs its own distinctive personality.

Some basic maps are provided to help you with orientation, but you will probably want to purchase some additional maps to help you navigate neighborhoods and make sure you find that special restaurant in time for your 7 p.m. reservation.

AREA CODES AND LONG-DISTANCE CHARGES

The entire valley has one area code—760—but you may still be charged a toll for calls made within the 760 coverage area, generally if you are calling a number that's 15 miles or more away. You don't need to dial either "1" or "760" anywhere in the valley, but we have included the area code with all phone numbers, just to make it easier when you're using the book outside the desert.

LOOKING AHEAD

Don't just take our word for it. Use this guide to help you explore for yourself the charms of Palm Springs and the Coachella Valley. This beautiful area is always changing, adding new attractions and businesses, closing down others, and expanding existing ones. You may discover some of these changes in your own travels, and we hope you'll let us know those that ought to be reported in future editions. If, in your journey to becoming an Insider, you find you have something to tell us, please send us an e-mail at editorial@GlobePequot.com.

AREA OVERVIEW

One of the many quirks about the Palm Springs area is the variety of ways people describe the collection of cities, and what that can tell you about the person doing the describing. Locals will generally say either "the desert" or "the valley." Those using the "valley" designation are usually year-round residents. People who call the entire area "Palm Springs" are almost always vacationers—if you live here, you quickly learn the political distinctions among cities and the jealous regard each has for its own particular name. To a local, Palm Springs always means the city, not the area. When you hear people saying "The Springs," you can bet that they're from the Los Angeles area and attached to the movie industry in some way, if only in their imaginations. That is except for those who reside in "The Springs," which is one of the many gated golf communities in Rancho Mirage.

People who say "Coachella Valley" fall into two groups. Those who pronounce it correctly (co-chell-a) know their way around the area and those who mispronounce it (co-a-chell-a) have done enough reading to be aware of the proper geographic designation but might not have much time in the saddle here, so to say. One particular term, "down-valley," Is used almost exclusively by Palm Springs residents and dates from the days when there wasn't much of anything to the east of that city.

This sense of place is what defines the politics, culture, and social climate of the valley and each of its cities. When Californians passed Proposition 13 in 1978, property taxes were frozen on each piece of private property until that property was sold (or fundamentally altered), thus choking a huge revenue stream down to a trickle and precipitating then-unforeseen budgetary tomfoolery that befuddles the state and its public agencies to this day. All manner of public projects and services, from roads and schools to prisons and health care, took a big hit. Cities that had counted on a healthy share of property tax revenue found themselves in the red. As a result, sales tax became ever more important to local jurisdictions. But that addiction also had consequences as sales-related revenue fluctuated, the state "raided" the funding source at times, and of

perhaps greatest impact, it led to land-use competition between neighboring cities. Think of the latter as City A cutting a deal with Big Box Retail Z not to locate in City B, though City B very well could pick up the infrastructure impacts of the project without gaining any of the tax benefit. In the valley, each city gets a share of the sales tax generated within its own boundaries, although that amount varies widely from year to year. The one tax that stays within each city and is never shared with the state is the Transient Occupancy Tax (TOT), or hotel tax. Because the valley is primarily a tourist destination, the cities with the most visitors are able not only to stay out of the red but also to flourish. If a city has both a good visitor base and a strong retail trade, the present and the future are rosy indeed; Palm Desert comes to mind. With the valley's largest concentration of retail business and a number of strong convention hotels, the city has a budget that is strong year-in and year-out and a city hall that can provide the parks, recreation, and infrastructure upkeep that make the quality of life there notable in a valley of notable communities.

Palm Springs and Indio, the valley's two oldest cities, have struggled more, historically, than most of the valley's newer cities. Being first in time—as a resort and residential community if not an incorporated city—Palm Springs faces the problems that come with age. It's land-use patterns are fixed, with fewer opportunities for massed, high-ticket development. The city does have a large inventory of hotels, but because they are generally older and smaller than the mega-resorts down-valley, they tend to have a lower room rate and lower occupancy overall, so TOT is affected, in a relative sense. For retailers, the city's location at the western edge of the valley makes it less attractive than Rancho Mirage or Palm Desert, and empty storefronts of both national retailers and local shopkeepers bear testament to that fact. Again, this is in a historic sense, and downtown Palm Springs has been undergoing a spirited renaissance. Indio, which began life as a bustling agricultural city, is the desert's Cousin Eddie, Clark Griswold's affable but down-and-out relative (from the National Lampoon *Vacation* films). Lacking the resort appeal of its sibling cities and a dicey-by-comparison retail base, Indio is challenged to rise above a beer budget and tastes in a Champagne Valley. Located in between Palm Springs and Rancho Mirage, Cathedral City is the valley's "working-class town," with challenges similar to those in Indio—practically no tourism and a light retail base—though it has scored in recent years by luring major auto dealers into town. A strong redevelopment effort has created a downtown core of entertainment and public space out of a previously rundown area, and the city is becoming known for its livable family neighborhoods.

Rancho Mirage—with its high concentration of country clubs, the Eisenhower Medical Center campus, a couple of very upscale hotels, and the new River "retailtainment complex"—is set financially. Indian Wells, between Palm Desert and Indio, is the valley's Bel-Air, a city of residential luxury and some comely golf, to boot.

In the area of master planning, Palm Desert can give the entire valley a good example and lesson on how it's done right. The city's General Plan, a state-mandated document that guides overall development for the next few decades, is noted for its balanced mix of residential, resort, business, and educational land-uses. The city is home to the College of the Desert and branches of California State University and the University of California. Palm Springs has always been the cool Hollywood hangout, even when the façade crumbled and visitors rebelled in the 1970s and 1980s. Now the hipsters and weekenders are back, buying up homes, pouring money into new restaurants and boutiques, filling up hotel rooms, and bringing a sharp air of vitality to the town.

Cathedral City has focused its priorities and is working hard to provide the type of town that will attract and keep young families. Rancho Mirage is hitting a new stride with The River and trendy new restaurants attracting locals and visitors alike. Palm Desert's upward path seems unstoppable, with the new higher-education complex, retail that grows stronger each year, and a commitment to quality-of-life services for its residents.

La Quinta, home from the 1920s on to the area's first true getaway resort, the same-named La Quinta Resort, and Indio are the new hot places to buy a home, as once-empty desert land is fast filling up with year-round residents who want a suburban lifestyle and good bang for their home-buying buck. And Indio has positioned itself as "The Place to Be," adding immensely popular art, music, and equestrian events to its long-time position as the host town for the Riverside County Fair & National Date Festival.

Lots of locals and newcomers lament the changes in the once-sleepy summer resort, arguing that nothing good can come of this explosive growth. Of course, the cities will grow and evolve, but owing to some truly visionary old-timers, the breathtaking combination of pristine desert and mountains around the valley will be preserved for many decades to come.

Back in 1970, several prominent citizens anticipating urban development and wanting to protect the natural desert convinced the Palm Springs Art Museum to establish an interpretive trail and preserve on 360 acres in Palm Desert. That area became today's 1,200-acre Living Desert Wildlife and Botanical Park, the number one open space recreation attraction in the Coachella

Valley. The Living Desert was the inspiration for a wide-ranging open-space plan that regulates development from the San Jacinto Mountains in the west to the Coachella Valley Preserve in the east, extending north to encompass Joshua Tree National Park and south to the Imperial Valley.

Setting up these protected areas has been a complicated endeavor and a stellar example of how different organizations and individuals can work together for a greater good. The Coachella Valley Mountains Conservancy, Friends of the Desert Mountains, Center for Natural Lands Management, the Nature Conservancy, the Wildlands Conservancy, and the Living Desert have worked to purchase and save as wilderness areas several hundred thousand acres of unspoiled desert and mountain land. This land is off-limits to development, ensuring that the valley cities will remain surrounded with natural vistas free of homes, hotels, and businesses. So welcome to the desert … the Coachella Valley … the resort communities … Palm Springs. If it sounds like the valley suffers through an identity crisis, fear not, for in diversity there is richness. And there is no reason all these "separate" communities, snowbirds and lifelong residents, thorny cacti and perfectly manicured golf clubs, Joan and John Q and the richly famous can't just get along nicely, and they nicely do. So come on along. We hope this book will inspire you to explore the many sides of this magical slice of desert. And if you want to call it Palm Springs, why please do so.

Vital Statistics

Population: The Coachella Valley includes nine incorporated cities: Cathedral City, Coachella, Desert Hot Springs, Indian Wells, Indio, La Quinta, Palm Springs, Palm Desert, and Rancho Mirage. Unincorporated areas and towns in the valley include Bermuda Dunes and Thousand Palms in the mid-valley; Indio Hills and Sky Valley to the north; North Palm Springs and Garnet on the west end; Thermal and Mecca to the southeast; and Pinyon Pines and Pinyon Crest in the Santa Rosa Mountains flanking the valley on the south. The Cabazon Band of Mission Indians, Twentynine Palms Band of Mission Indians, Agua Caliente Band of Cahuilla Indians, and the Torres-Martinez tribe each have reservations in the area.

According to the Coachella Valley Association of Government, the valley's population was 422,681 in 2006, projected to hit 501,072 by 2010.

Economy: Tourism is the main industry in the valley, with 3.5 million people visiting in 2008, staying an average of six nights and spending $502 per visitor per day, according to the local convention bureau. Agriculture is #2. The valley is the primary date-growing region in the United States, responsible for more than 90 percent of the nation's crop. Table grapes, chiles, avocados, artichokes, corn, citrus, grain, and cotton are also big products here.

When to go: November and early December are delightful in the desert—the annual lawn and golf course reseeding is all done, the weather is reliably warm and clear, and the tourist season rush has not begun in earnest. From mid-January through early April, the population of the valley doubles as people flock in to enjoy sunny days by the pool and crisp evenings filled with stars. This is the most expensive and crowded time to visit. The "season" begins tapering off in April, and by Memorial Day it's relatively quiet in the desert cities; relatively, for as long-time Coachellians—resident or seasoned visitor—can attest, the summer value season is a lot more heavily populated than it was 20 years ago. Take your pick: lots of action, crowds, and high rollers in the winter; sleepy nights and casual days in the summer; or a near-perfect mix of both in the late fall.

Weather: Daytime temperatures begin topping 100 on a regular basis in June and may stay in the triple digits all the way through October. The Coachella Valley is the beneficiary of the "rain shadow" effect, with the San Jacinto and San Bernardino Mountains acting as shields that block both pollution and rainfall moving inland from the coast. The Palm Springs area is a true desert—less than 6 inches of annual rainfall, most of it in December, January, and February. According to the Palm Springs Desert Resort Communities Convention and Visitors Authority, these are the average daily minimum and maximum temperatures:

Average Daily Minimum/Maximum Temperatures

	Fahrenheit	Celsius
January	44/70	6/21
February	45/75	8/24
March	51/80	11/27
April	56/88	13/31
May	63/95	17/35
June	70/104	21/40
July	76/108	24/42
August	76/107	24/42
September	71/101	22/38
October	61/91	16/33
November	50/78	10/26
December	43/70	6/21

Geography: Most of the desert sits near sea level, with parts of its southeastern corner dropping down to sub-sea range, if not the depths of Death Valley sub-sea range, and several mountain ranges form an enveloping ring. The infamous San Andreas Fault tumbles in from the northwest, trending southeasterly, before turning more southerly by the Salton Sea. If the jumble-rumble of landforms on the north side of the valley aren't a dead giveaway to the fault's existence, look for the bands of green where life-giving water rises to the surface and riparian plants and fan palms long ago pushed toeholds into an otherwise barren environment. In prehistoric times ancient seas rolled in over what today we call Palm Springs and environs, and according to "California Place Names" the valley's name resulted from a cartographer's error following the adoption of the Spanish word for small shell, conchilla, which were and are still found in abundance, as the name for the basin. In a more historic period, a meandering Colorado River spilled into present-day southeastern California—and a portion of Baja—creating a mega-Salton Sea (itself an early 20th-century creation of bad human engineering and big river flows). Ancient Lake Cahuilla betrays itself with a tell-tale bathtub ring easily seen at the foot of the mountains in La Quinta. The Indian Canyons just south of Palm Springs are reputed to be North America's largest natural palm oases, and home to one of only two species of palm that are native to this continent: Washingtonia filifera and Mexico's W. robusta is the other. Additional California fan palm oases can be found in the Indio Hills, Joshua Tree National Park, around the corner down in Anza-Borrego Desert State Park, and other locales in the low desert. The groves of date palms now moving successively southeastward in the valley were originally imported from the Middle East, and they produce the lion's share of this nation's date crop. They also serve as the focal point for the county fair.

Foreign currency exchange: Anderson Travel, with offices 1.5 miles west of the airport and in Indian Wells, offers limited exchange services. In the past Euros and British, Canadian, and Swiss bucks could be exchanged. Please call in advance.
Anderson Travel American Express
1801 East Tahquitz Canyon Way, Suite 101
(760) 325–2001
74-930 Hwy. 111, Indian Wells
(760) 346-8017
www.travelanderson.com

Liquor laws: Alcohol is sold throughout California in bars, restaurants, grocery stores, big-box retailers, membership warehouses, and liquor stores. The legal drinking age is 21.

Smoking: You must be 18 to buy any tobacco products. California law prohibits smoking in all public buildings, restaurants, and bars and on public transportation.

Sales taxes: California's sales tax rate is 8.25 percent on most transactions. Riverside County and the desert cities also impose an additional half-point tax, making the rate 8.75 percent.

Time zone: California observes daylight saving time and is in the Pacific time zone.

GETTING HERE, GETTING AROUND

The city of Palm Springs is located 110 miles east-southeast of Los Angeles and 140 miles north-northeast of San Diego, in the Coachella Valley. Palm Springs and Desert Hot Springs sit at the west end of the valley, southerly and northerly, respectively. The other cities and communities of the valley are mostly laid out in a string heading toward the southeast along the foothills of the San Jacinto and Santa Rosa Mountains. Moving east from Palm Springs, Highway 111 runs right through the middle of the cities of Cathedral City, Rancho Mirage, Palm Desert, Indian Wells, La Quinta, and Indio. The city of Coachella and the communities of Thermal and Mecca are situated beyond Indio. Other unincorporated communities pinch in between the Indio Hills and Little Sen Bernardino mountains to the north. I-10 cuts through the center-line of the valley on its run to Arizona and eventually Jacksonville, FL.

Getting around the valley is a rather straightforward, if not at times time-consuming, proposition. As can happen anywhere, having multiple jurisdictions in charge, and with differing growth curves over time, the various parts of the desert have not always been in lock-step when it comes to traffic circulation. The result is that there are only two major arteries capable of moving cars from the west end of the valley all the way through to the east: I-10 and Highway 111. And because Highway 111 is really the main street in each of these cities, it comes complete with traffic signals and speed limits that work to slow traffic dramatically. I-10 sits relatively far to the north of each city center, so, even though you can drive faster on the Interstate than on Highway 111, the freeway way can only be considered a time-saver if going for a bit of distance, say, from Cathedral City to Indio. Then again, who wouldn't rather keep moving even at the cost of extra miles travelled?

Locals have developed their own shortcuts from place to place, and the effectiveness of each is a function of where from, where to, and when. In recent years the Coachella Valley Association of Governments (CVAG) cooked up a partial solution with its Mid-Valley Parkway, a strand of stitched-together, pre-existing, and constructed surface arterials that generally runs along the

i Palm Canyon Drive in downtown Palm Springs is closed for several blocks each Thursday night for VillageFest, an arts and crafts street fair with live music and other forms of entertainment, food, and a farmers' market. Many downtown shops and galleries stay open late during fest nights. The fun kicks off at 7 p.m. June through September, and at 6 p.m. during shoulder and high seasons. "Doors" close at 10 p.m. Make sure your car is off the street in the festival section by 3 p.m., or it will be towed and you'll have to pay a hefty impound fee plus a parking ticket. The limited-parking zones are clearly noted on curbside signs (www.villagefest.org).

same axis as I-10 and Highway 111, and about halfway between each. It's a decent solution to a problem that should've been diagnosed and treated years back. Like the rest of Southern California, the Palm Springs area is woefully lacking in modern public transportation, though the regional transit agency, SunLine, has multiple bus routes with connecting service throughout the valley. If you're going to be here for any length of time, rent a car and be prepared to take around

45 minutes to drive from Palm Springs to Indian Wells—more if a major event is taking place or seemingly the entire upper part of the Northern Hemisphere seems to have spilled into the valley. Out here we call it the "high season," most of you know it as winter. The best driving tip? Be patient. Remember, it's vacation. Look around. Enjoy the sights. If you're going to work, what's the hurry?

The valley is thick with taxi companies, but unlike urbanized areas their practical affect is nominal, and they aren't cheap. About the only place where you can hail a taxi is at the airport. Otherwise, you must call one of the companies and request a pick up.

Some other quirks: Highway 111 running through Palm Springs is named Palm Canyon Drive on street signs and maps, and a portion of it where the road splits to become one-way is known as Indian Canyon Drive. Some Cathedral City businesses use the Palm Canyon Drive name and others choose to use Highway 111. It's all the same street.

Unless you're really on the lookout, you won't find yourself driving down Highway 111 and then suddenly exclaiming, "Oh, that's where Cat City ends and Rancho Mirage begins" because of some watershed change in architecture or land-use, so it might all look like an urban blur. Some time back CVAG tried to ease the navigational angst by putting numeric signs at nearly 100 intersections along Highway 111, from the start of Palm Springs to the heart of Indio. It's a bueno idea but the signs don't exactly jump out at you. But if you know to look, and you print out a copy of the directory (www.cvag.org/Trans/pdffiles/SignsProject.pdf) you'll be a step up on the guys in the next car over. The convention authority has the directory in its "Ultimate Guide," as well.

Speed limits can vary a bit from spot to spot, so keep an eye on the needle as the locals can be quite vigilant in enforcement. If you're driving slowly and trying to find a street address, stay to the far right and pay attention to your signaling and what's ahead of you. Rush hours in the morning and evening can be particularly busy as local residents try to get to work. And let's be honest

here, the population of the valley explodes from the holidays into late spring, and that means a lot more people on the roads with, er, varying skill sets.

Bike lanes are becoming more common as the various cities work on alternative transportation modes. Bike lanes are always on the far right of the regular lanes. Stay out of these unless you are about to turn right. Never use them for passing or slowing down, and always keep your eyes open for bike riders who may be hard to spot in congested areas. In Palm Desert, golf carts are legally allowed on city streets, but only on very limited parts of Highway 111. In residential areas where golf cart crossings are marked, the carts have the right of way.

AIR TRANSPORTATION

Palm Springs International Airport is located just a few minutes from downtown Palm Springs and is a $40–$75 cab ride from the other valley cities. The airport is regularly served by Allegiant Air, Alaska/Horizon, American, Delta/Delta Connection, and US Airways, and seasonal service is provided by Northwest, Sun Country, United/United Express, and WestJet. Major airports serviced from Palm Springs include several in the Bay Area, Calgary, Dallas/Ft. Worth, Denver, Edmonton, Las Vegas, Los Angeles, Chicago, Phoenix, Portland, Salt Lake City, Seattle, the Twin Cities, and Vancouver. Flights and servicing airlines drop significantly in the summer.

A good alternate airport to PSP is Ontario International Airport, 70 miles west off I–10. Ontario is a major airport with consistent service year-round, and it brings into play carriers that don't service the desert, including Continental. Southwest Airlines also services Ontario and offers its pricing advantage from a number of its hub cities across the nation, including nonstop from Nashville and a number of airports in the West. Shuttle service from Ontario to Palm Springs is available on a prearranged basis and runs about $115 per person for a one-way trip in a shared ride van, and the airport has full rental-car service.

Palm Springs International

PALM SPRINGS INTERNATIONAL AIRPORT (PSP)
3400 East Tahquitz Canyon Way at El Cielo
(760) 318–3800
www.palmspringsairport.com
The airport is a beautifully decorated facility with good food, gift shops and art galleries, comfortable waiting areas, free Wi-Fi, cell phone waiting lot, and a gate-and-exit-convenient baggage claim area adjacent to the rental car concessions. For those accustomed to more frenetic airports, parking is close-at-hand and user-friendly. Parking is $1 for each 20 minutes, with a daily maximum of $8 in the long-term lot and $12 for short-term.

International commercial service comes in only from Canada, and passengers are pre-cleared in Canada. Customs service is available 24 hours a day with a four-hour notice to clear international general aviation flights. The service is provided on a user-fee basis. Call Homeland Security at (760) 318-3880 for more information. The agency's hours of operation are Mon through Fri 8 a.m. to 5 p.m.

Other Area Airports

BERMUDA DUNES AIRPORT
79-880 Avenue 42, Bermuda Dunes
(760) 345-2558
www.bermudadunesairport.com
Bermuda Dunes (FAA designation UDD) is located just southerly of I–10 between Washington and Jefferson streets, in the eponymous unincorporated community, so it is a convenient spot to put in if heading to Palm Desert, Indian Wells, La Quinta, and Indio. The privately-owned, uncontrolled field has one runway measuring 5,002 feet and offers a full-service FBO with both Jet–A and 100LL fuel, catering services, and SUV and luxury/exotic car rental. Another perk: just next door you'll find one of the desert's not-so-secret-gem eateries, Murph's Gaslight, where it is ALL about the all-you-can-eat fried chicken and fixin's.

JACQUELINE COCHRAN REGIONAL AIRPORT
56-850 Higgins Dr., Thermal
(760) 399-1855
www.rcjcra.com
Thermal's Riverside County-owned Jacqueline Cochran Regional (FAA designation TRM) sits in the southeastern corner of the valley, right in the path of where a good bit of the area's growth pressure is being vented. The airport touts its uncongested airspace and proximity to the resorts and clubs of La Quinta and Indio's many yearly festivals, and it is home to the Jacqueline Cochran Air Show held every Nov. The uncontrolled field boasts a newly-lengthened runway measuring 8,500 feet, thereby supporting even the largest private jets, even during the heat of summer. Jet-A and 100LL fuels are available.

Private Plane Facilities and Services

ATLANTIC AVIATION
145 South Gene Autry Trail
(760) 320-7704
Unicom: 122.95
www.atlanticaviation.com
Atlantic Aviation, on the east side of Palm Springs International Airport, offers fuel, supplies, towing, maintenance services, and aircraft storage. Other features include a conference room with wireless Internet access, lounges, a pilots' lounge, flight planning room, game room, pool and spa, cafe, and concierge service. The facility is being expanded to offer 16 individual hangars for turbo props and midsize jets. It is open from 6 a.m. to 10 p.m. daily.

SIGNATURE FLIGHT SUPPORT
56-850 Higgins Dr., Thermal
(760) 399-1855
Unicom: 123.00
www.signatureflight.com
Signature is located at Jacqueline Cochran Regional Airport in Thermal, south of Indio, and offers fueling, ground handling, maintenance, storage, and car rental service. Signature is open from 7 a.m. to 7 p.m. daily, with call-out after hours.

ℹ Sun, swaying palms, soaring mountains, effervescent sky . . . warmth, if ever there was a place to take advantage of a convertible when renting, this is it. And if you have a jones for something a bit racier, trendier, or downright fit for Monaco, a number of the vendors listed in this book rent exotic sports cars, Hummers, Rollses, and other vehicles of such ilk. Don't forget the Wayfarers.

GROUND TRANSPORTATION

Rental Car Companies

ALAMO
530 S. Vella Rd.
(760) 778-6271, (800) 327-9633
www.alamo.com
Airport pickup and drop-off at no charge.

AVIS
(760) 778-6300, (800) 331-1212
www.avis.com
Located at the airport.

AZTEC RENT-A-CAR
477 South Palm Canyon Dr., #4
(760) 325-2294

74-527 Hwy. 111, Palm Desert
(760) 341-1995
www.aztecrentacar.apg.com

BUDGET RENT A CAR
(760) 778-1960, (800) 527-0700
www.budget.com
Located at the airport.

DOLLAR RENT A CAR
(760) 325-7334, (800) 800-4000
www.dollar.com
Located at the airport.

EAGLERIDER
(760) 251-5990, (877) 736-8243
www.eaglerider.com
Grab a Hog at the airport.

ENTERPRISE RENT-A-CAR
4041 Airport Center Dr.
(760) 778-0054, (800) 325–8007
www.enterprise.com
Airport pickup and drop-off at no charge.

FOXY WHEELS CAR RENTAL
68350 East Palm Canyon Dr., Cathedral City
(760) 837-1900
www.foxywheelsrentacar.com
Call for airport pickup and drop-off of a range of vehicles from standard to quite interesting (see if a Porsche convertible is in the house).

GO RENTALS
145 S. Gene Autry Trail
(760) 320-7704
www.gorentals.us
Located at Atlantic Aviation on the east side of the airport. Typically used by general aviationists, Go Rentals will pick up commercial flyers at PSP. The company offers a broad range of vehicles, from Audi TTs and the Mercedes 5 series to Minis and Toyota Tundras (call for specific availability).

HERTZ
(760) 778–5100, (800) 654-3131
www.hertz.com
Located at the airport.

NATIONAL
(760) 327–1438, (800) 227-7368
www.nationalcar.com
Located at the airport.

THRIFTY
(877) 283-0898
www.thrifty.com
Located at the airport.

Trains and Buses

Trains

AMTRAK

(800) 872-7245

www.amtrak.com

Train service into the valley has never been good, even back in the days when Indio had a regular depot. After much cajoling from the cities, Amtrak built a lone platform at Indian Avenue just south of I-10. Service is spotty, and there are no facilities other than a public phone. The area is isolated and trains may stop here in the middle of the night, so it is absolutely necessary to call for a schedule and reservations and to make pickup arrangements.

Amtrak also provides daily bus service to and from the Bakersfield station with stops in Indio at Jackson Street and the Southern Pacific tracks, in Palm Desert at Westfield Shoppingtown, and in Palm Springs at Palm Springs International Airport.

Buses

GREYHOUND BUS LINES

Palm Springs Train Station

No direct number, (800) 231-2222

45-525 Oasis St., Indio

(760) 347-5888

www.greyhound.com

Palm Springs' Greyhound service has been moved out to the unattended Amtrak platform beside I-10. Call Greyhound about service options.

Local Buses

SUNBUS

(760) 343-3451, (800) 347-8628

(866) 311-7433 for mobility-impaired service

www.sunline.org

SunBus has daily, regularly scheduled routes throughout the valley. Wheelchair lifts and bike racks are available. Fares are $1.00, $0.85, and $0.50 for adults, kids, and seniors/disabled, respectively, with $0.25 transfers. Exact fare is required. Schedules are available from bus operators, hotels, restaurants, and other tourist information centers.

Limousines, Shuttle Services, and Taxis

Limousines and shuttle services require advance reservations. Limo rates average approximately $100 per hour, with variations for type and size of vehicle, hours booked, and the like. Shuttle rates to Ontario International Airport, for instance, vary depending on if the service is scheduled or a custom pick up, but plan on about $115 per person for each leg of the trip. Limousines can be reserved for any time, but the shuttle services usually run on preset schedules.

Unless you are getting a taxi at the airport, plan on calling ahead for one. Despite the number of taxi companies listed here, you will have a very hard time just hailing a taxi anywhere in the valley. Also keep in mind that many of the taxi companies shut down during the summer season—June through mid-Sept—and thus the wait time for a cab ride might be as long as 45 minutes, depending on where you are and where the taxi is. All taxis are licensed under the auspices of SunLine Transit Agency and required to have standard insurance and pass annual inspections for safety. Some of the larger hotels offer airport pickup service, which can be a bargain, considering that you'll pay at least $35 for down-valley destinations. The drop fee is $2.50, and per-mile rates are $2.64.

Limousines

AAA LIMOUSINE SERVICES

(760) 322-4454

www.aaalimoinc.com

ALL OCCASIONS LIMOUSINE

(760) 773-5305

i If you're parking your car outside during daylight hours in the summer, do what the locals do and bring along gloves, a towel, or even oven mitts to handle the super-hot steering wheel until the air conditioning cools it off.

AMERICAN LIMOUSINE
(760) 340-1051
www.amrlimoservice.com

CARDIFF LIMOUSINE AND TRANSPORTATION
(760) 568-1403, (800) 669-0355
www.cardifflimo.com

CLASSIC TRANSPORTATION
(760) 322-3111

FIRST CLASS LIMOUSINE
(760) 578-7172, (866) 724-5466
www.desertlimos.com

GOOD LIFE TRANSPORTATION
(760) 341-2221

LIMO 4 U
(760) 322-1881, (888) 546-6148
www.limo-ps.com

LION TRANSPORTATION
(760) 771-0201
www.liontransportationsvcs.com

MY CHAUFFEUR LIMOUSINE SERVICE
(760) 321-4001
www.mychauffeurlimo.com

ROYAL LIMOUSINE
(760) 346-7333

Shuttle Services

AT YOUR SERVICE
(760) 343–0666, (888) 700-7888

ℹ️ The Palm Desert Shopper Hopper is a great way to get to all of that city's shopping areas. Just park near one of their stops and jump on—this open-sided, trolleylike bus runs all day.

DESERT VALLEY SHUTTLE
(760) 251-4020, (800) 413-3999
www.palmspringsshuttle.com
Provides scheduled service to and from major airports in Southern California and custom service to destinations from Orange County up through the San Fernando Valley.

R LIMO
(760) 416-8888
www.rlimosite.com, www.rlimoservice.com
Provides service between the desert cities, and Los Angeles and Orange counties.

Taxis

A few taxi companies do not accept credit cards. We have not listed them here.

A VALLEY CABOUSINE
(760) 340-5845

AIRPORT TAXI
(760) 862-9000

CITY CAB
(760) 416-2594

CLASSIC YELLOW CAB
(760) 321-8294

COUNTRY CLUB TAXI
(760) 779-5937

INDIAN WELLS CAB
(760) 641-0955

LA QUINTA CAB
(760) 347-4141

R&C EXPRESS CAB
(760) 567-2780

UNITED TAXI
(760) 601-6283

USA CAB
(760) 251-5803

YELLOW CAB
(760) 345-8398

Services for the Mobility-Impaired or Seniors

DISABLED MEDICAL TRANSPORT SERVICES
(760) 360-2068

SUNDIAL
(760) 341-6999
www.sunline.org
SunDial is a daily, curb-to-curb service operated by SunBus for the mobility-impaired. ADA certification is required. The cost is $1.50 within your city and $2.00 outside your city, and 10-ride passes are available (no unit cost-savings).

ℹ There isn't a single parking meter in the Palm Springs desert area, but keep your eye out for time-limited parking zones in downtown Palm Springs parking lots.

IMPORTANT PHONE NUMBERS

Emergency Assistance

For emergency police, fire, or medical assistance dial 9-1-1, free from any telephone.

Fire and medical aid for all cities in the Coachella Valley: (800) 472–5697

Police

Bermuda Dunes, Indian Wells, North Palm Springs, Rancho Mirage, and Thousand Palms: (800) 950-2444
Cathedral City: (760) 770-0300
Desert Hot Springs: (760) 329-2904
Indio: (760) 347-8522
La Quinta: (760) 836-3215
Palm Desert: (760) 836-1600
Palm Springs: (760) 323-8116

Emergency Roadside Assistance
AAA AUTOMOBILE CLUB OF SOUTHERN CALIFORNIA
(800) 400-4222
www.aaa-calif.com

Hospitals and Care Centers

DESERT REGIONAL MEDICAL CENTER EMERGENCY ROOM
1150 North Indian Canyon Dr.
(760) 323-6511
www.desertmedctr.com

EISENHOWER MEDICAL CENTER EMERGENCY ROOM
39-000 Bob Hope Dr., Rancho Mirage
(760) 340-3911
www.emc.org

EMC IMMEDIATE CARE CENTERS
78-822 Hwy. 111, La Quinta
(760) 564-7000

67-780 East Palm Canyon Dr., Cathedral City
(760) 328-1000
The centers are open from 8 a.m. to 8 p.m. Mon through Fri and from 8 a.m. to 4 p.m. Sat and Sun.

JOHN F. KENNEDY MEMORIAL HOSPITAL EMERGENCY ROOM
47-111 Monroe, Indio
(760) 347-6191
www.jfkmemorialhosp.com

General Information
Phone directory assistance: 4-1-1
Road conditions: (800) 427-7623
Weather: (760) 345-3711

ℹ If you're visiting Palm Springs from outside the country, change your foreign currency before you arrive, preferably at the airport where you clear customs. The desert has limited currency exchange facilities, mostly for euros, pounds, and Canadian dollars.

VISITOR CENTERS AND VISITOR INFORMATION

CITY OF PALM SPRINGS OFFICIAL VISITORS INFORMATION AND RESERVATION CENTER
2901 North Palm Canyon Dr.,
at the intersection of Highway 111 and
Tramway Road
(760) 778-8418, (800) 347-7746
www.palm-springs.org
Operated by the city of Palm Springs and its Bureau of Tourism, this center is a one-stop clearinghouse for all manner of things Palm Springs-ian. It's housed in a former gas station, of all things, designed by mid-century-modernist architect Albert Frey; the building itself is a desert icon. Visitors can learn about hotels, museums, restaurants, shops, and events in the city, plus valley attractions, and they can make reservations. The center's newest attraction is the "Modernism Kiosk," an interactive multi-media trip through the heyday of desert modernism design and the vibrancy of life here during the mid-part of the last century. The facility includes the de rigueur gift shop so folks can stock up on publications, gift items, and PS-branded souvenirs. Staffers are desert experts, so ask away. Bus and RV parking is provided, if you're cruising in a land yacht. Hours are 9 a.m. to 5 p.m. daily, closed Thanksgiving, Christmas, and New Year's Day.

INDIAN WELLS VISITORS INFORMATION
44-950 Eldorado Dr., Indian Wells
(760) 346-2489
www.indianwells.com
This is the address for city hall. It's a pretty sleepy place, city hall, and that's just the way city residents like their city hall and their port city. There's a bit of commercial here in town, some great eats, the best-trained palm trees you'll ever see—look at 'em, soldiers don't stand at as rapt attention—and several stellar resorts. We're not done. Chuck in a ton of golf history, an awesome public golf clubhouse that most any private club would covet, and the fact that it's home to one of the most prestigious tennis tournaments in the world, even if the Williams sisters boycott it.

And some swank residential development. Stress the swank. Now there was also a pretty cool sex scandal several years back involving hot tubs and some key folks from a very large and popular church in town. It really perked up the public discourse for a while, but now it's back to subtle luxury, checking the investment accounts online, driving the Bentley to fetch a dozen eggs and a sixer, and just generally keeping it sleepy. For some beta on what to see and do in town, check out the city's tourism Web site above. City hall has brochures and the like, and if you stop by do take a moment to absorb the Eisenhower Walk of Honor and Veterans Memorial on the corner of Eldorado and Highway 111.

JOSHUA TREE NATIONAL PARK VISITOR CENTERS
74485 National Park Dr., Twentynine Palms
(760) 367-5500
www.nps.gov/Jotr/index.htm
Located at the primary (north) entrance to the national park, this visitor center has a great little gift shop, featuring art from locals, photography of the park, books, pamphlets, and very specific-to-the-desert souvenirs, as well as good maps and postcards. Other information centers are located at the northwestern entrance in the town of Joshua Tree and at the southern entry point at Cottonwood 30 miles east of Indio. There is also a nature center at Black Rock in the park's northwest corner, accessed from Yucca Valley.

LA QUINTA VISITORS INFORMATION
78-495 Calle Tampico, La Quinta
(760) 777-7000
www.playinlaquinta.com
Now that's a slick URL for a public agency, in this case the city of La Quinta. The renaissance in "old" La Quinta, while still a work in progress, has been a beauty to watch unfold. You probably don't need to drive down to city hall just to get a brochure—and with SilverRock, La Quinta, and PGA West in town, you should be out on the course—so the Web site can suffice for the nuts and bolts of what to do, where and how. But if

the Embassy Suites or a libation at Hog's Breath is on your radar, nose around a bit.

PALM DESERT VISITORS INFORMATION CENTER

72-567 Hwy. 111, Palm Desert
(760) 568-1441, (800) 873-2428
www.palm-desert.org

This conveniently located center—right on Highway 111 as you drive into Palm Desert—stocks brochures and pamphlets on Palm Desert hotels, restaurants, and businesses, as well as for attractions and events throughout the valley. If you want to contribute to the local economy and help spread the PR word there is a good selection of Palm Desert logo merchandise, such as hats and polo shirts. The visitor center is open from 9 a.m. to 5 p.m. daily, closed on major holidays.

PALM SPRINGS DESERT RESORT COMMUNITIES CONVENTION AND VISITORS AUTHORITY

70-100 Hwy. 111, Rancho Mirage
(760) 770-9000, (800) 967-3767
www.giveintothedesert.com

As this is a consortium dedicated to promoting the entire desert region—and CVA members—to individual, group, incentive, and business travelers from around the world, don't expect a lot of warm and fuzzy turista stuff at the center. What you will find are nice people and some outstanding brochures and guides, both general and content-specific. If you'd like to do some research in advance check out the Web site and request to have one of the desert guides mailed to you. Hours are 8:30 a.m. to 5 p.m. Mon through Fri.

RANCHO MIRAGE VISITORS INFORMATION/ CHAMBER OF COMMERCE

42-520 Bob Hope Dr., Suite B, Rancho Mirage
(760) 568-9351
**www.ranchomirage.org, www.relaxrancho
mirage.com**

The Beverly Hills of the desert—relatively compact city notable for high-end housing, a select number of getaway resorts, per-capita-heavy financial-type services commercial sector, chic golf, and bring-the-401(k) shopping—Rancho Mirage tries to be subtle as it clubs you with oozy richness. It's fitting that the "visitor center" would be, therefore, housed in a masterpiece of architectural … er, it's in the Chamber of Commerce office. The chamber's Web site has a fair amount of material on eats, sheets, and the like. "Relax Rancho Mirage" is the city's effort in cyberspace, and it has more bells and whistles. The chamber is open 9 a.m. to 4 p.m. weekdays and from 10 a.m. to 2 p.m. on Sat.

SANTA ROSA AND SAN JACINTO MOUNTAINS NATIONAL MONUMENT VISITOR CENTER

51-500 Hwy. 74, Palm Desert
(760) 862-9984
**www.blm.gov/ca/st/en/fo/palmsprings/
santarosa.html**

The Santa Rosa Mountains form Palm Desert's southern boundary; the San Jacintos prop up Palm Springs' backside. The visitor center, located on Highway 74 at the north base of the Santa Rosa Mountains, provides information on the nature, culture, and history of the area. It also serves as a gateway to myriad hiking, biking, and horseback riding trails. In addition, the center is home to a Cahuilla garden of plants used by Native Americans. This is a good spot to pick up maps that concentrate on the area's natural features and to talk with the staff about the most scenic spots to photograph on the way up Highway 74 to Idyllwild. The center is open 8 a.m. to 3 p.m. Thurs through Mon during the summer, daily from 9 a.m. to 4 p.m. the remainder of the year, excluding Thanksgiving, Christmas, and New Year's Day.

HISTORY

It took Palm Springs little more than a hundred years to grow from a dusty dirt-street town of cowboys, pioneers, and Native Americans to a world-famous resort that, along with its brethren cities, attracts more than three million visitors a year. The stories of how those cowboys, pioneers, and Native peoples built their dreams out of sand and palm trees are in turn flamboyant, mundane, courageous, cowardly, inspiring, and dispiriting. It's a fascinating tale that explains a lot about the character of the Palm Springs area today.

INDIAN HERITAGE

When Spanish army captain Juan Bautista de Anza passed by the Indian Canyons in Palm Springs on his way to the Los Angeles Basin in 1774, the ancestors of the present-day Cahuilla people had been living there for perhaps 2,000 years. At the time, they were divided into around a dozen clans, each of which inhabited large areas of land—mountain areas where they summered and desert areas for the winters. A peaceful and complex society, the Cahuilla lived by hunting and gathering and had strong ties with other tribal groups as far away as the California coast and into Arizona.

The Agua Caliente Band of Cahuilla Indians spent much of the summer in the cool oases of the Indian Canyons, just a few minutes from downtown Palm Springs. In the winter, social and religious life centered around the Agua Caliente hot springs, site of today's Spa Resort Casino downtown. At the eastern end of the Coachella

Valley, other Cahuilla villages flourished in the palm oases along the San Andreas Fault.

As the Spanish began setting up missions, the Cahuilla strengthened their political control by confederating clans, and, as late as 1860, the Cahuilla outnumbered Europeans in the desert. But in 1862 a smallpox epidemic swept the desert, a wave of settlers from the East Coast began arriving, and the Cahuilla found themselves at the beginning of a 100-year struggle to regain control of their land.

In 1864 Congress gave huge areas of the desert to the Central Pacific and Union Pacific railroads as incentives to complete the lines to the coast. The presence of an Indian labor force was considered another enticement, and in 1872 Indio was selected as the division point for the new Southern Pacific Railroad.

The railroads received a checkerboard of land—10 alternating mile-square sections on each side of the right of way. In 1876 the first trains from Los Angeles pulled into Indio, and a year later the final link in the southern transcontinental route was completed to Yuma, Arizona. That same year the government set up almost a dozen reservations on the land not owned by the railroads—almost half of Palm Springs, a third of Cathedral City, and smaller areas in the eastern part of the valley. Although the Indians now owned 48 sections of land throughout the valley, the government held every square inch of it "in trust," making it impossible for the tribes

> **i** Street names in Palm Springs tend to honor influential members of the Agua Caliente Band of Cahuilla Indians as well as early pioneers: Andreas, Arenas, Amado, Belardo, Lugo, Patencio, Saturnino, and Chino are all Cahuilla surnames; Murray and McCallum were early pioneers. Farrell Drive is named for actor and Racquet Club founder Charlie Farrell.

to sell or set up long-term leases to earn money from their holdings.

With land as their only asset, the Agua Calientes in Palm Springs fought to have their 32,000 tribal acres divided among individual members. The Mission Indian Relief Act of 1891 gave the Secretary of the Interior authority to do just that, but he refused.

In the early part of the last century, when heat and sun were thought to be cures for tuberculosis, Palm Springs began attracting notice as a spot for health seekers. Many a pioneer family came for a visit with ailing children and then put down roots as the little community grew.

All this time, the Cahuilla stayed focused on their land. Finally, after tribal leader Lee Arenas took the battle all the way to the Supreme Court in 1944, most members were allotted 47 acres each. In Palm Springs the tribe retained ownership of the Indian Canyons and most of Section 14, which encompassed the hot springs, the tribal cemetery, and most of present-day downtown. That same year, the city bought the landing strip area from the tribe. It is now the site of Palm Springs International Airport.

Even after the allotments, the land division was unequal, with some individuals owning parcels on mountain land that held virtually no development potential and others owning the land under such revenue producers as the Canyon Country Club and major downtown hotels. At last, in 1959, President Eisenhower signed an equalization bill that gave each tribal member an allotment worth no less than $335,000.

By this time many of the Cahuilla's rituals and sacred songs had been lost, discarded by

i The tall palm with fanlike fronds that trail shining "threads" in the breeze—*Washingtonia filifera*—is the only palm, one of two species of palm native to North America and grows abundantly in the natural palm oases of the desert. For the Cahuilla Indians, it provided food, shelter, fuel, and material for beautiful baskets.

generations trying to rise out of enforced poverty and adapt to a different culture. But as the tribal members who were small children in the 1960s grew up, they began to look for ways to preserve the language and traditions for their own children. Using the income from admission fees and film location permits for the Indian Canyons, they slowly put aside money for a cultural center and museum.

Tahquitz Canyon, a beautiful wild area butting up to the western edge of Palm Springs just two blocks from downtown, had been scarred by graffiti and littered with trash for years, but the tribe lacked the funds to patrol and clean the area. Planning carefully, the tribe first fenced off the area and then enlisted the help of local volunteers to clean it and keep transients away.

In 1987 the legal system that had kept the Cahuilla in second-class status for so long suddenly opened the door to enormous riches. The U.S. Supreme Court ruled that California could not bar gambling on Indian land. Despite intense lobbying from Nevada gaming interests, the state eventually legalized Indian gaming, and in 1995 the Agua Caliente Cahuilla brought slot machines into the Spa Hotel in the very heart of downtown Palm Springs. Following the lead of the Agua Caliente, the Morongo, Augustine, Cabazon, and Twenty-Nine Palms Bands all have desert casinos.

The Agua Caliente now own and operate the $90 million Spa Resort Casino in downtown Palm Springs and the elaborate Agua Caliente Casino just off I–10 in Rancho Mirage. They have set up scholarships and provided health coverage for members, invested, and created their own bank. As a sovereign nation, they hold near absolute authority over zoning and building on tribal land, making their decisions of prime importance to the City of Palm Springs.

Today Tahquitz Canyon is home to a beautiful interpretive center where rangers lead hikes to the impressive waterfalls and give visitors an appreciation of the Cahuilla heritage. The tribe is one of the valley's most generous and consistent benefactors, donating hundreds of thousands of dollars to local charities each year. The Cahuilla language is being taught in special classes, and oral histories are being recorded.

AGUA CALIENTE BECOMES PALM SPRINGS

In 1884 this little oasis and stage stop was still known as Agua Caliente. That year John Guthrie McCallum became the first non-Indian to settle here permanently. A San Francisco lawyer looking for a warm, dry climate to help his son's tuberculosis, McCallum had big dreams for the desert. He bought more than 6,000 acres, set up the township that today makes up downtown Palm Springs, and founded the Palm Valley Land and Water Company, building ditches to bring water into the new Palm City.

Land sales boomed, and Dr. Welwood Murray moved in from Banning to build the Palm Springs Hotel across from the McCallum house, which now sits on the Village Green downtown and is headquarters for the Palm Springs Historical Society.

i Horseback riding and hiking were the original entertainments in the desert, decades before the first golf course was built. For trail maps and regulations, contact the Santa Rosa Mountains Visitor Center (760-862-9984) or the City of Rancho Mirage (760-324-4511).

In 1893 a record 21-day downpour washed out crops and irrigation ditches, only to be followed by an 11-year drought. Murray and his family were among the handful of residents to stay on, running the hotel until his death in 1914. By that time another generation of pioneers had sunk roots, building hotels and attracting writers and artists who first came for their health and later returned for the beauty and small-town camaraderie.

In 1901 *The Riverside Press* newspaper reported that amusements included "tennis, cro-

quet, baseball, mountain climbing, and tramps along desert." A warm, dry climate was prescribed by physicians for those with respiratory diseases, and Nelson's Health Camp, near the Southern Pacific railroad depot in Indio, was one facility that provided a place for invalids to recuperate.

HOLLYWOOD COMES TO THE DESERT

By 1925 more than 35,000 tourists were visiting each winter. And Hollywood discovered the desert. Former Palm Springs mayor Frank Bogert, who came to Palm Springs as an 18-year-old horse wrangler and soon became the city's most famous and successful public relations spokesperson, was on the spot to chronicle the stars at play through the 1950s. "In the early days," he writes, "Hollywood studios were used only for close-up scenes; Palm Springs served as a location site for Arabia, North Africa, Mexico, and other global areas. As many as ten movies were made each season and both guests and townsfolk turned out to watch the proceedings."

With its close proximity to Hollywood, the city became the favored playground for stars who wanted to escape the prying eyes of the press and let down their hair. El Mirador Hotel, now the site of Desert Regional Medical Center, was at the center of the action, and Bogert was their star, not only snapping photos of celebrities but also starring in a few of those photos himself with siren Clara Bow and other lovelies.

Before long, film stars Charlie Farrell and Ralph Bellamy built the Racquet Club on the north end of town, and it soon became a hot rival for El Mirador's famous guests. The Racquet Club's tennis, cocktails, and glamorous parties attracted some of Hollywood's most popular stars, as well as scores of hopeful would-be starlets. Legend has it that Marilyn Monroe was discovered by the Racquet Club pool. Rudolph Valentino, Shirley Temple, Theda Bara, and what seemed like the entire cast of every movie shown in town were familiar faces on the streets.

Hollywood's Love Affair with the Desert

Some of the films and television programs shot in the Palm Springs area:

The Hoax (2006)
Bone Dry (2005)
Mission: Impossible III (2005)
Alpha Dogs (2004)
Phat Girls (2004)
Alias (2003)
Curb Your Enthusiasm (HBO, 2003)
Santa Trap (2002)
Ocean's Eleven (2001)
The Opposite of Sex (2001)
The Princess and the Marine (2001)
Fugitive Nights (1997)

Beverly Hills 90210 (1994)
P.S. I Love You (1990)
After Dark, My Sweet (1990)
Funny About Love (1990)
General Hospital (1985)
Dressed to Kill (1979)
6 Million Dollar Man (1977)
Columbo (1972)
Kotch (1971)
Mission Impossible (1969)
Hanging by a Thread (1964)
Lost Horizon (1937)
Lone Star Rush (1915)

In the late 1930s and early '40s, big-time stars started investing in second homes in the desert. Cary Grant, Bob Hope, Frank Sinatra, William Powell, Daryl Zanuck, and dozens of others made the Las Palmas neighborhood their winter home.

In 1930 Indio incorporated, becoming a city right before the Depression era's largest local construction project kicked off. With Indio as their distribution base, mining crews built 92 miles of tunnel through the eastern mountains for the Metropolitan Water District of Southern California's Colorado Aqueduct to carry water from near Parker, Arizona to the Los Angeles basin.

The aqueduct transformed Los Angeles into a major city but had little impact on the sleepy desert, which remained a charming winter playground for Hollywood stars and those in their orbit.

In 1938 Palm Springs became a city, and the tourists just kept coming. With nine stables, the O'Donnell Golf Course, and several tennis courts, the city boasted that it had more swimming pools than any other place in the country. Neighboring Cathedral City was a mecca of nightclubs and gambling.

Hollywood had adopted Palm Springs as its permanent playground, and not even World War II could dim the desert's glamorous aura. El Mirador Hotel was commandeered to become a hospital, and the soldiers and their visiting families turned the village into a year-round resort. When the war ended, the tourists were back with a vengeance, and the real land boom was on.

Frank Bogert was a partner in the desert's first golf course country club, Thunderbird Ranch, in Rancho Mirage. Aviatrix Jacqueline Cochran built the next golf course in the Coachella Valley— what became today's Indian Palms in 1947 on her ranch just south of Indio. Not far off, a group of investors bought 1,600 acres for a hotel, country club, homes, and offices. Thirty years later this became the city of Palm Desert.

Desi Arnaz helped build the first resort hotel in Indian Wells—close to the site of the present-day Miramonte Resort on Highway 111. After his first visit to the desert in 1954, President Dwight D. Eisenhower returned to Washington to sign the Equalization Bill that finalized the Agua Caliente's land allotments. He made Indian Wells his winter residence and contributed his name and considerable fund-raising clout to the Eisenhower Medical Center in Rancho Mirage. Since Eisenhower, the valley has been a winter-time destination for most presidents.

BEYOND THE "VILLAGE" OF PALM SPRINGS

As the 1960s began, the valley's growth slowly shifted away from the city of Palm Springs and moved east, where vast stretches of vacant land and less restrictive development regulations held the promise of lucrative investment.

Cathedral City, which had long sought to become a part of Palm Springs, was a solid middle-class city of its own now. Indio was still the desert's largest city, and the communities in between—Rancho Mirage, Palm Desert, Indian Wells, and La Quinta—were on the way to becoming world-class cities with posh residential areas, exclusive country clubs, and, most importantly, prime retail areas. Desert Hot Springs, a little community in between the "high" and "low" desert areas, was being discovered as a place with abundant natural hot springs, sweeping views, and great land values.

The city government in Palm Springs, responding to the wishes of its residents, was extraordinarily strict in its building standards,

i The General George S. Patton Memorial Museum on the summit of Chiriaco Hill on I–10 east of Indio is a treasure house of World War II memorabilia. It sits on the site of Camp Young, the command post for the Desert Training Center, where Patton's troops prepared for combat in North Africa. In fact, across the desert there are places where tank tracks are still visible. Another interesting item at the museum is a relief map of the American West that was shown to Congress in an effort to win approval of the Colorado River Aqueduct Project. The museum is open 9:30 a.m. to 4:30 p.m. daily, except Thanksgiving and Christmas. Admission is $4.00 for ages 12 to 61, $3.50 for older visitors, and children are free. In-uniform members of the military are admitted free of charge. Call (760) 227-3483 for more information, www.generalpattonmuseum.com.

banning neon, high-rises, and drive-through restaurants, and regulating paint colors and virtually every aspect of a building's appearance. The so-called "cabaret" ordinances kept live music off the streets and dining off the sidewalks until the city council approved the Thurs night VillageFest in 1991.

With such tight control, it was no surprise that the desert's first big indoor mall was built in Palm Desert after being rejected by Palm Springs in the early 1980s. The mall would have completely changed the city's downtown. Without it, Palm Springs could no longer compete for the tourist dollar, and many of its high-end boutiques moved east to Palm Desert, relocating in the mall or on that city's burgeoning El Paseo Drive.

Palm Springs opened the now-vacant Desert Fashion Plaza in 1984, but the die had been cast. Following the trend eastward, new megaresorts and golf courses opened in virtually every other desert city in the early 1980s, leaving Palm Springs in the shadow of newer, more glamorous developments. What today is the Bob Hope Classic on the PGA Tour opened in 1960 on a rotation of courses outside the city, and today every major sports tournament in the valley has other than a Palm Springs home.

The exodus of money and fame had some unexpected good news for Palm Springs. Without name recognition of their own, many of the other desert cities relied on the name of Palm Springs in their marketing and promotion, efforts that indirectly paid off for a city strapped for cash.

The tight development and sign ordinances also were responsible for bringing back some of the vanished Hollywood cachet, in the form of Sonny Bono. Bono, who owned a second home in the city, was embarking on a second career as a restaurateur. Stymied in his efforts to build a flamboyant entrance for his new restaurant, he jumped into politics and was elected mayor in 1988.

Over the next four years, Palm Springs and Sonny Bono were constantly in the headlines. Trying to end a boisterous spring break tradition, Bono banned thong bikinis in public. He

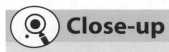

Close-up

Mid-century Architecture

Endless sunshine and clean, uncluttered vistas were a natural backdrop for postwar modern architecture, with its stripped-down lines and generous use of natural materials. In fact, what has come to be called "the modern idiom" was being practiced in Palm Springs well before the 1940s.

Rudolph M. Schindler, one of Frank Lloyd Wright's disciples, built the first truly modern house here in 1922, using concrete, wood, and canvas in an echo of the house he built for himself in Los Angeles the same year. In 1937 Richard J. Neutra built his first residential commission in the desert, the Miller House. It was considered his best small house of the 1930s and was included in the 1938 Museum of Modern Art traveling exhibition.

Other significant homes of the 1930s included the 1933 home designed by William Gray Purcell (a disciple of Louis Sullivan) and Evera Van Bailey; the grand 1936 Davidson House designed by Los Angeles architects Eric Webster and Adrian Wilson; and the 1934 Kocher-Sampson Building. The Kocher-Sampson Building was a collaboration between A. Lawrence Kocher, then managing editor of *Architectural Record,* and Albert Frey, the first of Le Corbusier's disciples to build in America. It was featured in the Museum of Modern Art's 1935 exhibition, "Modern Architecture in California."

A native of Switzerland, Frey moved to Palm Springs from New York to supervise the Kocher-Sampson construction. He stayed on, starting a partnership with architect John Porter Clark that lasted almost 20 years.

E. Stewart Williams and William E. Cody arrived in 1946 and 1945, respectively. With Frey and Clark, they created a substantial body of work, and much of their mid-century modern architecture remains today. Along with Neutra, John Lautner, William Burgess, A. Quincy Jones, Frederick E. Emmons, Craig Ellwood, Donald Wexler, and Ric Harrison, they were responsible for such elegant public buildings as Palm Springs High School, the Palm Springs

presided over the creation of VillageFest, which successfully attracted tourists and locals from all over the desert. Under his leadership the city launched its own promotion department, taking the story of the city to the rest of the country and overseas. Most significantly, Bono founded the Palm Springs International Film Festival in 1990. The festival now marks the beginning of "high season" in January and attracts thousands of stars, movie industry decision makers, and film buffs from all over the world.

i Frank Bogert, "the cowboy mayor," was an avid horseman and rode to the very end of his life. The bronze statue of a rider on a galloping horse in front of Palm Springs City Hall is none other than Frank, modeled from a photo of him taken in the 1930s.

Art Museum, and the downtown Bank of America and Washington Mutual Bank buildings, all superb examples of modernist architecture.

Albert Frey's legacy is especially important in Palm Springs. His Frey House 2 is now owned by the Palm Springs Art Museum and has been restored to its original simplicity and purity, wrapped around a mountain overlooking the city below. His designs for the Palm Springs City Hall, the Palm Springs Aerial Tramway Lower Station, and the Tramway Gas Station (now the Palm Springs Visitor Center) are just three of the most visible and public of his works. The Gas Station has become a recognizable emblem of the city, with its sweeping parabolic roofline and almost cartoonlike simplicity.

Adele Cygelman, writing in her book *Palm Springs Modern,* says, "The impact that these architects and homeowners had on the desert oasis between the 1940s and the 1960s is immeasurable. The town's current revival as a 'hot' hot spot and the worldwide acclaim being accorded its architecture [are] gratifying to those who thought their work had gone undiscovered or, worse, ignored. Now it has come full circle, for some in their own lifetime."

SUGGESTED READING

Ainsworth, Katherine. *The McCallum Saga: The Story of the Founding of Palm Springs.* Palm Springs: Palm Springs Public Library, 1996.

Bean, Lowell John, with Sylvia Brakke Vane and Jackson Young. *The Cahuilla Landscape.* Menlo Park, Calif.: Ballena Press, 1991.

Bogert, Mayor Frank M. *Palm Springs First Hundred Years: A Pictorial History.* Palm Springs: Palm Springs Associates Heritage Printers, 1987.

Cygelman, Adele. *Palm Springs Modern.* New York: Rizzoli International Publications, 1999.

Hubbard, Doni. *Favorite Trails of Desert Riders.* Redwood City, Calif.: Hoofprints, 1991.

Rosa, Joseph. *Albert Frey, Architect.* New York: Rizzoli International Publications, 1990.

All through the 1980s, as development fever raged in the east end of the valley, Palm Springs seemed caught in a time warp, desperately trying to re-create a past that had moved on. Then, as the century came to a close, "mid-century" architecture suddenly became hugely popular all over the country. Palm Springs discovered that it was blessed with dozens of extraordinary buildings that had been spared from demolition simply because the developers' attention was elsewhere.

Every major travel magazine and newspaper rediscovered the city as "hip, hot, and happening." Film people and investors from Los Angeles snapped up ranch-style homes that had been empty for years. A new group of hoteliers came to town, restoring old motels and buying homes themselves.

In the last 15 years, Palm Springs has taken on a new life as a charming reminder of a gentler, more carefree past. Hollywood stars and players are once again buying homes in the "village," and another land boom is on.

ACCOMMODATIONS

Apocryphal or not, with the generally accepted belief around here that the population doubles in high season, you can be sure things feel a lot more frenetic come the Ides of March than the dead of summer. Since a good number of seasonal "visitors" are second-home owners or arrive turtlelike with their own mechanized shell, you won't go lacking for a place to bunk down. Trust us. At last count there are nearly 20,000 hotel rooms in the valley.

How much you pay for that place will vary wildly, from rock-bottom rates at small motels in the middle of summer to sky-high prices at megaresorts in February. If you can plan your visit for November, December, April, or May—shoulder season—you'll have a good chance of getting good rates and good weather at the same time. If you don't mind 100-degree-plus days and want the best value, book June through October, though the edges of "low" season have been compressing inward for some time.

Palm Springs has been a vacation mecca for almost a century. And it could almost be argued that the Cahuilla wintering springs-side qualifies as a high-season respite. Virtually every national and international hotel company is represented here, from budget places like Super 8 and Howard Johnson's to super-luxurious hoteliers like KSL, Ritz-Carlton, JW Marriott, and Waldorf Astoria. Midsize, mid-priced hotels such as the Embassy Suites and Hilton are a good value for business travelers and others seeking solid amenities and a predictable level of quality.

The valley has its share of small inns and boutique hotels, as well as accommodations catering to specific niche markets such as gay men, lesbian women, and travelers looking for clothing-optional places.

Hotels number in the hundreds in the desert. We have not listed every single one but rather have chosen to highlight those that are outstanding in some way and are consistently recognized as clean, comfortable, and reputable, perhaps special, and often nicely unique. Instead of listing hotels by city, we are listing them by type of accommodation. Please note that if you are looking for familiar national chains, at whatever level of the hierarchy, such as Super 8, Motel 6, Howard

Johnson's, Courtyard by Marriott, and Embassy Suites, for instance, these are well represented in the desert.

"Boutique" hotels and inns include those that are small—almost all have fewer than 100 rooms—and offer a high level of individuality, personal service, and quality. These are "personality places" with lots of charm, good locations, and often an intriguing bit of history, if not the entire laundry list of amenities of a full-scale resort.

As a result of economic forces that first came into play in the 1980s, the overwhelming majority of boutique hotels and inns are in Palm Springs. During the 1980s megaresorts were the trend in hotel construction. A lack of empty land and a restrictive building code kept these huge resorts out of Palm Springs. For years the city was passed over in favor of cities to the east when it came to any new hotel development.

Then, when Palm Springs was "rediscovered" as a hip and charming little village in the 1990s, little mom-and-pop inns found that they were suddenly very attractive, to both visitors and developers. A renewed interest in mid-century architecture and a tourism trend that saw more travelers looking for a personal touch all came together to lift the little hotels out of obscurity and into the level of "caliente, caliente, caliente." Today many little places that were first opened in the 1930s, '40s, and '50s have been restored, revamped and recharged so as to appeal to a new generation of traveler.

The Hotels category includes hotels that are in the 100 or so rooms range and larger, and offer a level of service and amenities above that which would be found in a basic motel. They have restaurants and room service, and often such extras as concierge service, gift shops, and valet parking.

Resorts are destination spots, places where you could spend your entire vacation without ever stepping outside the property. They have full concierge service, gift shops, restaurants and room service, spas, and fitness centers. They either have full business centers or offer basic business services such as faxing and copying. They also often feature tennis courts and golf courses. The desert resorts are like cruise ships: If you want to take a "shore visit" to see the rest of the area, fine; if you want to leave your car in the parking lot and call the hotel home, you will want for nothing.

Finally, the desert has a good number of accommodations that fall into the Specialty Lodging category. These include hotels that cater specifically to the GLBT crowd, places that are clothing optional, and RV resorts. Condo and home rental companies and portals—like www.vrbo.com— will offer a variety of varied-term (from a few days to several months) options, from celebrity homes to simple studios on a golf course.

Because the desert is such a seasonal destination, hotels are highly competitive with rates and packages, and they spend a lot of time checking rate structures and offerings at comparable places. This means that you may not find a great deal of variation in rates if you're comparing hotels of roughly the same size and level of quality. Still, it pays to shop around, particularly at the larger resorts that do a lot of convention business. Cancellations or group confirmation numbers that are smaller than expected will open up space for leisure travelers and give you some bargaining power. If golf, spa, or some other resort amenity or offering figures to be part of your desert experience, check out package pricing. With so many third-party providers picking up blocks of rooms and offering them at discounts, hotels and resorts have in recent years gone to great lengths to re-capture that business, so inquire about rate-match guarantees; the Internet revolution, indeed. And don't forget all the usual suspects when it comes to discounts, from your credit union affiliation to AARP, AAA, and government/military.

As for the when of it all, you take your chances by waiting until the last minute, and we wouldn't advise doing that in high season, but you may get a great 11th-hour bargain.

Despite the fact that California's public areas are nonsmoking zones, some hotels still offer rooms for smokers, and truth be told, some smokers smoke in nonsmoking rooms. If smoking or its immediate aftermath are a problem for you consider a totally smoke-free property.

Another quirk that Palm Springs shares with many resort destinations is the ebb and flow of visitors during the week. Weekends are almost always busy, even in summer, when travelers from Southern California leave the urban areas to spend a few bargain days in the desert. If you're staying just a few days, try to make those days Monday through Thursday—you'll get a better rate. Finally, if you're visiting during high season, you may find that hotels require a minimum stay of two or even three days.

The hotel tax—or Transient Occupancy Tax (TOT)—is not included in the quoted rates when you book a room, so be sure to factor that in. TOT typically runs about 10 or 11 percent, though Palm Springs levies at a rate of 13.5 percent on "Group Meeting" or business hotels; it's 11.5 percent on other hotels. TOT is one of those rare taxes in California that is both left to the local prerogative and relatively easy to enact since no super-majority vote is required, hence the variation city-to-city. If you feel like you're being singled out as a visitor, remember every vacation destination in the land levies hotel taxes, so some of your back-home services are being funded by others. TOT is applied on all vacation rentals of fewer than 29 days. If you're staying in any rental accommodation for more than 29 days, you've just saved yourself a nice piece of coin.

Another levy that's not likely to be openly advertised at some properties is the so-called "resort charge" or "amenity fee," that little exaction for the paper, parking, morning nosh if offered, the gym you don't plan to use, or some other goodie that logic would dictate is just part and parcel of a stay at that particular hotel. If your Web search or phone chat with a reservation clerk doesn't include an overt mention of such a charge, be proactive and ask the question.

Price Code

The price codes represent rates for two adults for one night in a standard room during high season, which is generally considered to begin in mid-Jan and end some time in Apr or May. Many hotels typically have three published rate structures: one for low season, in the summer; one for "shoulder season," from the fall through early Jan and often again in the late-spring through early-summer; and one for the winter months. Hotels in the desert have a history of experimenting with extra amenities, such as allowing pets, but this service is spotty and may be nonexistent in high season. If you are planning to travel with a pet, always double-check the hotel's policy and extra charges, if any. Most hotels offer rooms for smokers. If you are a nonsmoker, be sure to specify a nonsmoking room when you make your reservations. Unless otherwise noted, all hotels take major credit cards.

The following symbols indicate the price range for each accommodation listed. Price ranges do not include the Transient Occupancy Tax, resort charges, or other extra surcharges that might pop up from time to time. Inquire about any add-ons when you make your reservations.

$.................	Less than $100
$$	$100 to $200
$$$	$201 to $300
$$$$	More than $300

BOUTIQUE HOTELS AND INNS

ANDREAS HOTEL & SPA $$–$$$
227 North Indian Canyon Dr.
(760) 327-5701, (888) 327-5701
www.andreashotel.com
Built in 1935 and gorgeously renovated to the Spanish Revival and Craftsman styles of that era, the Andreas, formerly known as the Springs, has a great location right in the heart of downtown. Like many resurrected older-era properties, the inn is oriented around a courtyard, and in this rendition it is one of the best with its ample shading, places to kick it and outdoor fireplaces. Rooms have graceful iron beds, elegant custom cabinetry and furniture, fireplaces, and coffeemakers. The Andreas has 25 rooms, including a clutch of one- and two-bedroom suites, a pool, fitness center, and full-service spa.

CALIENTE TROPICS RESORT $–$$
411 East Palm Canyon Dr.
(760) 327-1391, (888) 277-0999
www.calientetropics.com
The Caliente Tropics Resort, a prime, kitschy example of the Polynesian-themed motels from the 1960s, was closed for a number of years. It reopened in 2001 after a $2 million restoration that added tiki decor and furnishings and revamped the large private pool area. The site attracts tiki fans from all over country, particularly for the annual festivities that usually feature tiki carving, revelry around the pool, and a showing of an appropriate period movie or TV show such as *Hawaii 5-0*. The hotel has 90 rooms and suites, which are quite large and have coffeemakers and minifridges. It's located on East Palm Canyon, a fair drive from downtown but conveniently located near the Sunrise shopping center, with a grocery store, post office, and small shops. Pets are allowed.

CALLA LILY INN $$–$$$
350 South Belardo Rd.
(760) 323-3654, (888) 888-5787
www.callalilypalmsprings.com
A 1950s-era motel converted into a charming tropical-themed inn, Calla Lily has three queen/ king rooms, three studios, one junior suite, and two one-bedroom suites arrayed around a pool and the property is surrounded by a wall for privacy. The owners are always on-site and delight in offering the kind of personal service rarely found in any large hotel, including complimentary cordials in the evening. Rooms have coffeemakers and refrigerators, and studios feature a kitchen. The inn is located in the old Tennis Club area, along with many other small boutique places. Adults are preferred, no pets allowed.

CASA CODY $$/$$$$ (ADOBE)
175 South Cahuilla Rd.
(760) 320-9346
www.casacodypalmsprings.com
Built around a collection of 1930s adobe-style bungalows that have been nicely restored with a Santa Fe–style decor, wood-burning fireplaces, and full kitchens, Casa Cody is one of the original Palm Springs hotels; think La Quinta Resort on a cozy scale. It's just a block or two from downtown and is set against the foothills. The two pools and private patios make this a comfortable spot to spend more than a few days. There is great variety among the 23 rooms/suites so it's a good idea to ask for visuals before you book and to check out the room when you arrive. There is a two-bedroom 1910-built adobe available to visitors. A four-bedroom house is still in the making.

THE CHASE HOTEL $$
200 West Arenas Rd.
(760) 320-8866, (877) 532-4273
www.chasehotelpalmsprings.com
Located one block off Palm Canyon in the heart of downtown, the Chase is another of the many mid-century-style hotels that make this area so unique. It was built in the late 1940s and has the clean, simple lines of that period. All rooms face the saltwater pool and many have full kitchens. A continental breakfast is provided. Relax and play a few games of shuffleboard, then grill some steaks and pour a martini—you've just traveled back to the golden years of the old Palm Springs. Pets are allowed.

COYOTE INN $$
234 South Patencio Rd.
(760) 327-0304, (888) 334-0633
www.coyoteinn.net
A newly renovated, Spanish Mission-style inn done up in festive hues and a mantel of vibrant foliage, the Coyote is walled and gated for lots of privacy. The seven suites, which face the pool and a beautiful mountain view, all have full kitchens, raised fireplaces, a hardback library, charming iron beds, and slick tile floors. It's another of the many small hotels in the Tennis Club neighborhood.

i Every hotel in the desert has at least one pool, and many have two or four or 41 like La Quinta. Don't worry—they're all heated in the winter months and ready for a dip.

DEL MARCOS HOTEL $$
225 West Baristo Rd.
(760) 325-6902, (800) 676-1214
www.delmarcoshotel.com
The Palm Springs Modern Committee gave the Del Marcos its 2005 Design Preservation Award. Designed by famous desert architect William F. Cody, this hip little spot features the classic motel-with-pool design where rooms surround a courtyard and pool. Its 16 spacious rooms are decorated in clean mid-century style, and the Tennis Club neighborhood is the perfect spot to take a spin on one of the hotel's vintage bikes. Check for special Internet pricing that has been as low as $49 in recent summers.

THE HORIZON HOTEL $$-$$$
1050 East Palm Canyon Dr.
(760) 323-1858, (800) 377-7855
www.thehorizonhotel.com

One of the most gracious of the old Palm Springs hotels, the 22-room Horizon fronts busy East Palm Canyon Drive and looks for all the world like a tiny little inn from the street. Inside, you'll find a two-plus-acre oasis of landscaped lawn and flowers; a low building housing spacious rooms and suites and a separate two-bedroom, two-bath house with a pool; a sunken fire pit; and a martini bar that was a favorite of the Rat Pack years ago. Decor is classic mid-century Modern, with cool white brick walls, plantation shutters, and clean-lined furniture. The staff is exceptionally warm and helpful. The main office/lobby also offers a library, classic table games, and bikes for roaming around town.

INGLESIDE INN $$-$$$
200 West Ramon Rd.
(760) 325-0046, (800) 772-6655
www.inglesideinn.com

Once the home of the heirs to the Pierce-Arrow automobile fortune, the 1925-era Ingleside is a local landmark, a favorite place to have Sunday brunch at Melvyn's restaurant, and a magnet for Hollywood types—or wannabes—who want a nostalgic hideaway. It's just off Palm Canyon Drive, a few blocks from the center of town in a quiet location across the road from Tahquitz Canyon. Rooms are all different, furnished with an eclectic mix of 1940s to 1960s antiques and bric-a-brac. The service is wonderful and personal—they will never forget a name here. Melvyn's is the site of an old-time piano bar and hosts a regular Sun evening jam session that attracts local blues and jazz artists. Suites have private terraces, fireplaces, and minifridges stocked with complimentary snacks, fruit, and cold drinks. The inn has 30 suites and villas, as well as a pool.

KORAKIA PENSIONE $$-$$$
257 South Patencio Rd.
(760) 864-6411
www.korakia.com

Owner/architect Doug Smith spent a lot of time operating a restaurant in the Greek islands, where he made a lot of connections with the rich, famous, and very hip, who frequent this Moroccan-style oasis just a few blocks from downtown. The main building was built in the 1920s by Scottish painter Gordon Coutts to remind him of his life in Tangiers. After Coutts died, it languished as an apartment house for many years. Then Doug got his hands on it and proceeded to work magic, cleaning and buffing and adding authentic bits and bobs from Greece and Morocco. The 20 spacious rooms are a TV-free zone, and the guests often gather in the main courtyard for a freshly cooked, full American breakfast or impromptu cocktail party. Doug has also restored the little adobe-style villa across the street and added guest bungalows to create a uniquely simple and luxurious compound that is consistently full. Rooms have minifridges and coffeemakers, and there are two pools. Deposits are required when you book. There is a two-night minimum on weekends and a strict cancellation policy—give at least two weeks' notice (45 days on holidays) or lose the deposit.

LAKE LA QUINTA INN $$$-$$$$
78-120 Caleo Bay, La Quinta
(760) 564-7332, (888) 226-4546
www.lakelaquintainn.com

This sprawling, award-winning, 13-room bed-and-breakfast overlooking private Lake La Quinta proves a stunning visual sensation with its European-chateau-plunked-down-at-the-foot-of-the-seer-Santa-Rosa-Mountains effect. Popular as a honeymoon spot, the inn serves up enormous cushy beds, tasteful country-estate decor, lots of elbow room, a fresh to-order breakfast every day, and private patios that encourage idling and daydreaming; romantic, indeed. It also has a pool. Some guests report a lack of soundproofing, which might make for some TMI moments involving eager honeymooners.

ORBIT IN/OASIS & HIDEAWAY $$–$$$
562 West Arenas Rd.
(760) 323-3585, (877) 996-7248
www.orbitin.com

When the mid-century craze hit Palm Springs, a Portland, Oregon, couple bought two older bungalow motels a few doors apart and created a totally hip, charming little spot with lovely 1950s decor (furnishings by Eames, Noguchi, and Paulin), a day spa, saltwater pools, a convivial atmosphere at breakfast and happy hour, and an attitude of laid-back luxury. Orbit has nine studios and Hideaway has 10. The cruiser bikes are a good excuse to leave your car in the parking lot and explore the town in the open air. It's located in the Tennis Club neighborhood, where most of the this-ain't-a-motel-chain little inns have popped up in the past 10 years.

PARKER PALM SPRINGS $$$$
4200 East Palm Canyon Dr.
(760) 770-5000, (800) 543-4300
www.theparkerpalmsprings.com

The Parker has had a lot of incarnations over the years. As the Gene Autry, it spent many years as a local landmark, where locals came to have a belt at the bar and admire the Singing Cowboy's silver-trimmed saddle in the lobby. It was later purchased by Givenchy and revamped with a huge rose garden and faux-French decor, but it never caught the imagination and struggled with low vacancy rates. Today's Parker is the result of a $27-million renovation in 2004 and a more recent re-renovation of a smaller scale. The rose garden is gone, replaced with a central area that's become a social hub, drawing the Hollywood "in" crowd and featuring pétanque and croquet, fire pits, oversized outdoor furniture, and paths that wind through the desert-style landscaping and a huge tropical palm garden. The 13-acre, 131-room property is done up in high "Rat Pack" style, with decor and ceramics specially designed by Joseph Adler and a high level of service where virtually every staff person knows your name within minutes of check-in. The large rooms feature feather beds, sheepskin throw rugs, and photos of such '60s icons as Warren Beatty and Julie Christie. Twelve villas and Gene Autry's original residence are now available for rent, as well. The Palm Springs Yacht Club spa and fitness center has been recently upgraded and offers a full range of skin and body treatments.

The Parker attracts a younger crowd than the Desert Springses of the valley, and their getaway orientation is much less given over to maximizing the daylight hours. The resort itself has a far different feel and air than the mega-shops, which is exactly why it is here in boutique land despite the number of rooms it provides. Children and conventions are welcome, but they are not the main scene, and they don't take over the landscape. The hotel offers two sex-segregated indoor pools at the spa and two outdoor pools (one saltwater), tennis, two restaurants, and a poolside cafe. There's an adjoining 18-hole executive golf course and arrangements can be made for golf across the valley, including some of the private playpens. The property is affiliated with Starwood.

PEPPER TREE INN $$–$$$
622 North Palm Canyon Dr.
(760) 318-9850, (866) 887-8733
www.peppertreepalmsprings.com

A nothing-short-of-miraculous renovation has transformed a drab little motel into a charming Spanish colonial-style retreat of red tile and wrought iron and the shock of bougainvillea. The inn features 32 guest accommodations surrounded by high walls and gates for a nice sense of privacy. The location is in the up-and-coming Uptown Art District, with interesting shops, galleries, and restaurants a stroll away. Rooms are arranged in clusters. One is poolside—another saltwater pool, by the way—and are known as the "Poolside Rooms"; very novel thinkers here. The "San Jacinto Rooms" look out at the … you got it. Rooms have refrigerators and coffeemakers. Some have fireplaces, terraces, and Jacuzzis.

RENDEZVOUS $$–$$$
1420 North Indian Canyon Dr.
(760) 320-1178, (800) 485-2808
www.palmspringsrendezvous.com

One of the first small hotels to get in on the mid-century Modern revival, Rendezvous is cool kitsch, with each of its 10 rooms done in a different '50s theme: "Rebel Without A Cause," "Route 66," "Crooners" … well, you get the picture. Built in the late '30s and tagged Mira Loma, some famous faces used to congregate here, including Joe DiMaggio's wife, who is rumored to have preferred the room dubbed "Pretty In Pink." That's the ticket if you want to snooze away 'neath the visage of Marilyn Monroe. A gourmet breakfast and afternoon appetizers and martinis are included. Rooms feature fridges, microwaves, and coffeemakers, sitting areas and so the A/V presentation is a bit better than in the era of "TV Shows," flat screens, and DVD players. This cool B&B is oriented around a courtyard with a small pool.

SMOKE TREE RANCH $$$$
1850 Smoke Tree Lane
(760) 327-1221, (800) 787-3922
www.smoketreeranch.com

Once a private resort where the cottages were all owned individually, Smoke Tree has modernized and opened to the traveling public. It's a western-style property with native desert landscaping that's a stark contrast to the overwatered, brilliant green lawns and flower beds of most Coachella Valley hotels and resorts. All accommodations are in 53 little cottages with refrigerators and modern essentials such as Internet access, DVD player, fridge, and coffeemaker. Many cottages have fireplaces and carports. In the "Ranch House," meals are served daily, and guests gather to swap tales of a rough day on the golf course. Breakfast and full American plan add-ons are offered at $9 and $39, respectively, for kids 5–11 and $15 and $78 for "oldsters." Amenities include use of the adjacent Smoke Tree Stables, a kids' playground, and old-fashioned fun such as croquet, lawn bowling, and horseshoes. The property also has a pool, fitness center, guest laundry, clubhouse, basketball, tennis, and putting green. Smoke Tree is closed summer through mid-fall.

SUNDANCE VILLAS $$$$
303 Cabrillo Rd.
(760) 325-3888, (800) 455-3888
www.sundancevillas.com

Located in the city's north end, in a quiet residential area, Sundance was originally built as time-shares and private homes. It's a sprawling gated compound of 19 spacious two- and three-bedroom villas with enclosed courtyards, private pools and spa, and such homelike amenities as gas barbecues, two-car garages, washers, and dryers. Sundance also offers tennis and a large community pool. For a family or group of friends who want to stay a while and have all the comforts of home—or homes if taking down a block of accommodations—this is an excellent value. The only drawback is that the homes are about two miles from downtown so a car is a must.

i Although wireless Internet is gaining popularity in the desert, it still has some kinks. Some hotels offer it only in the lobby, and some of the providers offer software that works with PCs, but not with Macs. Indeed, some of the hotel wired Internet connections work only with PCs. If all else fails, visit a local Kinko's, Starbucks, or other known quantity.

VICEROY PALM SPRINGS $$$$
415 South Belardo Rd.
(760) 320-4117, (800) 670-6184
www.viceroypalmsprings.com

Formerly the Spanish Mission-styled Estrella Inn, the 66-room Viceroy is a collection of bungalows, suites, and rooms built around a beautifully landscaped, sprawling property with three courtyards and pools. The bungalows date from the 1930s and have been redone in a glamorous, rather over-the-top "Hollywood Regency" style heavy on mirrors and a color scheme of black, white, and yellow. The small spa and fitness center are sparkling and modern, and the Citron bar/restaurant is a local favorite for evening drinks or desserts. It's located in the Tennis Club area, just a block from downtown.

VILLA ROYALE INN $$$
1620 South Indian Trail
(760) 327-2314, (800) 245-2314
www.villaroyale.com

This Mediterranean-style compound once was the estate of a Palm Springs old-timer. Re-imagined and rebuilt by a Palm Springs City Council member who had been a Hollywood set designer, it's an unexpected bit of whimsy in the desert. The 30 rooms and suites are each decorated in the style of a different European city or region, and no two have the same theme. Several courtyards, fountains, and garden areas, plus a charming poolside bar and the award-winning Europa Restaurant have made this a favorite for romantic getaways. Rates include full American breakfast.

THE WILLOWS $$$$
412 West Tahquitz Canyon Way
(760) 320-0771, (800) 966-9597
www.willowspalmsprings.com

The Willows is the only AAA Four-Diamond property in Palm Springs (2009 ratings), and it's a beauty. With just eight rooms, this could be the most luxurious and personable small hotel in the entire desert. Gloriously restored from the days when it was a private home hosting such luminaries as Carole Lombard, Clark Gable, Marion Davies, and Albert Einstein, the Mediterranean-style villa has won a pile of awards, including *Condé Nast*'s "Most Outstanding Inn in North America" and *USA Today*'s "Top Ten Romantic Inns." Each room is different and lovingly furnished with antiques, fine linens, fireplaces, hardwood floors, handmade tiles, and luxurious baths, as well as up-to-the-minute electronics. A hillside garden and waterfall, small pool, cozy parlor, and outdoor dining area complete the

hideaway. Catered meals from neighboring restaurant Le Vallauris are always available. The hotel is open only to registered guests, so the privacy is complete. It's right next door to the Palm Springs Art Museum, yet nestled up against the foothills away from the bustle of downtown.

HOTELS

AGUA CALIENTE CASINO RESORT SPA $$$
32-250 Bob Hope Dr., Rancho Mirage
(888) 999-1995
www.hotwatercasino.com

It is becoming standard practice to build a hotel and call it a resort. And while this sister property to Spa Resort Casino in downtown Palm Springs isn't exactly the JW Marriott in terms of size or sizzle, there's enough in the way of amenities and cachet to let this place slide with the naming convention. The newest new-construction luxo-property in the desert, Agua Caliente serves up 300+ very large guest rooms (and 26 suites) featuring 42" plasmas, deep soaking tubs, walk-in rain-head showers, safes, coffeemakers, and two things every decent property should have: in-room irons/ironing boards and Wi-Fi. The hotel sits out near I-10, so while it's not necessarily near anything else, getting anywhere in the valley is a relative snap. And because it really is a resort, guests won't go lacking for eats and treats—six restaurants, full-service spa and gym, pool, lounge, and a little something called a casino.

BEST WESTERN LAS BRISAS $-$$
222 South Indian Canyon Dr.
(760) 325-4372, (800) 346-5714
www.bestwesterncalifornia.com

On busy Indian Canyon Drive near downtown, this property renovated in 2008 is an affordable step above a basic motel all set down in a downtown-convenient spot. Rooms are sparkling clean and roomy, with light desert colors. Refrigerators, flat screens, and coffeemakers in every room, free American breakfasts, and a well-priced lunch make it a good choice for budget-minded travelers and families who want a little something extra. The Las Brisas also offers a pool, lounge, and restaurant. You won't find many value chain national brands sporting such a cool Mediterranean look, either.

DESERT HOT SPRINGS SPA HOTEL $$
10805 Palm Dr., Desert Hot Springs
(760) 329-6000, (800) 808-7727
www.dhsspa.com

One of the oldest spa hotels in Desert Hot Springs, this one is a favorite for fans of natural hot mineral springs. Everything—including the 50 rooms, lounge/bar, and restaurant—is centered around the pool area. An Olympic-sized main pool and seven smaller soaking pools, all natural mineral water, plus a large Jacuzzi offer a lot of soaking and sunning. The hotel also has a fitness center. Rooms are basic and serviceable, with decor and soft goods that date back several years.

EMBASSY SUITES LA QUINTA $$
50-777 Santa Rosa Plaza, La Quinta
(760) 777-1711, (800) 445-8667
www.embassysuites1.hilton.com

Part of a multi-phase project to reinvigorate Old Town La Quinta—yes, there is a downtown La Quinta—this several-year-old property brings another option to an area rich in resort history— the archetypal La Quinta Resort & Club—if not hotel density. Embassy has the formula wired: well-outfitted, big accommodations, made-to-order breakfast, daily cocktail reception. And in La Quinta there's a twist or three, foremost of which is the on-site spa. Ready access to golf, tennis, shopping, and some notable local eats—Arnold Palmer's, Hog's Breath Inn, local seafood standout Fisherman's Market & Grill—makes it a win-win all the way around. It's also refreshing being down in "the Cove," away from the bustle of Highway 111. (There is an Embassy Suites in Palm Desert, as well.)

FANTASY SPRINGS RESORT CASINO $$
84-245 Indio Springs Parkway, Indio
(800) 827-2946
www.fantasyspringsresort.com

Fantasy Springs Casino has been building and improving from day one. And when the Cabazon Band of Mission Indians added this 12-story, 250-room hotel topped by a happening lounge, the transformation from slot palace to getaway spot was nearly complete. Nearly, with the only thing remaining being golf, which was accomplished in 2008 with the opening of Eagle Falls Golf Course, designed by one-time Ryder Cupper Clive Clark. No one will ever presume they've put into Vegas. Yet with the buzz of the casino, multiple restaurants spread across the property— pizza, Starbucks, chophouse, cafe, buffet, and a notable bistro—gym, gorgeous pool, beach volleyball, and an entertainment center bringing in an endless string of second-tier acts, the resemblance ain't too bad. Rooms have flat-screen TVs, minifridges, and coffeemakers, and crisp new furniture and soft goods; they aren't overly large but they're stylish, and the beds are great. Request a northward view and you'll think you can touch the nearly-at-hand Indio Hills and Little San Bernardinos. It should be noted that smoking is not verboten in the casino, and for all the modern technology the smoke and aroma are palpable. Luckily, for the smoke-intolerant, the hotel is smoke-free.

HILTON PALM SPRINGS RESORT $$$
400 East Tahquitz Canyon Way
(760) 320-6868, (800) 522-6900
www.hiltonpalmsprings.com

Following a renovation several years ago of the public space, all guest rooms, and its main dining room, this property remains a mainstay of downtown digs. The pool is one of the most convivial in town, with a well-run pool bar and a good central location. The hotel has 266 rooms and 71 suites as well as a concierge, restaurant, lounge, business center, fitness center, massage salon, and gift shop. Rooms are oversize and offer all the amenities you'd expect in a midlevel city hotel, from good TVs to high-speed Internet to balconies or patios. As in real estate, it's all about location, location, location.

HYATT REGENCY SUITES
PALM SPRINGS $–$$
285 North Palm Canyon Dr.
(760) 322-9000, (800) 554-9288
www.palmsprings.hyatt.com

This place caused quite a commotion when it opened in the early 1980s as a venture of Pierre Cardin. It was the first structure in town that was more than three stories, and it was part and parcel of the Desert Fashion Plaza, an indoor shopping mall that was shuttered in 2001 and has become the city's biggest white elephant. The Hyatt is an all-suite hotel, with 600-plus-square-foot suites opening onto a central atrium lobby/dining room; true suites, not the sleight-of-hand, bigger-than-standard-room-type "suite" that hoteliers increasingly are trying to pass off as suites. The dining room and adjacent bar are great places for people-watching, as the hotel is right on Palm Canyon Drive and is a regular stop for locals and celebs looking for a cool drink or a generous happy hour. The pool is a tiny slice of water on the back of the hotel, but it commands a spectacular view of the San Jacinto Mountains foothills that tower over the nearby Palm Springs Art Museum and O'Donnell Golf Course. A top-to-bottom rehab—Hyatt Grand Bed, dueling 42" LCDs, iHome docking stations, clean, modern look—of the resort's 194 suites was recently completed. The hotel offers a business center, concierge, putting green, gym, and day-spa services.

MARRIOTT'S SHADOW RIDGE $$–$$$
9003 Shadow Ridge Dr.
(760) 674-2600, (888) 236-2427
www.marriott.com

OK, it's not a boutique and despite resortlike amenities it's not a resort. Shadow Ridge is part of the Marriott Vacation Club network of fractional-ownership properties. Before turning in horror at the prospect of a KGB-grade time-share interrogation, give this place some thought. The mid-valley location is great. It's intertwined with one of the best little-known golf courses in the

desert. The pool complex sports a waterslide, and guests can play tennis or volleyball. There're on-site eats, a small market, and a fitness club. The rooms and one- and two-bedroom accommodations are airy and spacious, the latter two have full kitchens and en suite laundry facilities, and all serve up nice open views of mountain or desert, whether in natural or coifed form. And Costco is right down the road. Shadow Ridge is a vacation getaway with the conveniences of home.

PALM COURT INN $
1983 North Palm Canyon Dr.
(760) 416-2333, (800) 667-7918
www.palmcourt-inn.com

A good spot for families and budget travelers, the 107-room Palm Court is, at one mile away, a bit far from the center of town, but it offers a wonderful mountain view, good basic rooms, and one of the best rates around, period. Rooms include microwaves and refrigerators, and the hotel has a large pool with a Jacuzzi and a children's wading pool, wireless coin-op laundry, and an exercise room, and there's a diner-style restaurant next door with a few Cuban items on the menu.

RESIDENCE INN PALM DESERT $$–$$$
38-305 Cook St., Palm Desert
(760) 776-0050, (888) 236-2427
www.marriott.com

Located close enough to the Interstate to be easily accessible and far enough away so traffic is not a bother, this is a great property for business or leisure travelers. The hotel has 130, 600-square-foot studios and 800-square-foot suites, each with full kitchen. Beds and linens are home-grade and you even get a choice of foam or feather/down pillows. Being a Residence, buffet breakfast is included, as is complimentary beer and wine later in the day. There's a beautifully landscaped pool on-site. The University of California/California State University complex is kitty-corner from the hotel and that's the back nine of Desert Willow's stellar Firecliff Course just over the fence. A gym, tennis courts, and putting green round out the deep offerings.

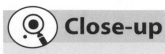

Close-up

Smoke Tree Ranch

Perhaps the desert's most exclusive and hidden getaway since the 1930s, Smoke Tree Ranch had its beginning in 1887, when a group of land speculators bought hundreds of acres on the north side of Smoke Tree Mountain. Their elaborate plans called for a new city—to be called Palmdale—with parks, homes, a narrow-gauge railroad to connect with the Southern Pacific, and acres of citrus orchards, grapes, and melons. A stone irrigation ditch was built, the narrow-gauge tracks were laid, and the project was set for prosperity when an extended drought set in, turning the growing fields to dust and scattering the dreamers.

Adobe ruins on the Ranch grounds today are all that remain of the spot's early history. Forty years went by before Fred and Maziebelle Markham bought the property and quietly began building a desert legend. A woman who prided herself on being a gracious and welcoming hostess in homes the couple had in Altadena and Balboa Island, Maziebelle thought of the Ranch as another version of a well-run home with extended-stay houseguests. She and her husband created the many cottages as a place where their friends and like-minded acquaintances could count on family-style holidays in exclusive surroundings.

For these highly successful and well-connected businesspeople, the Ranch must have been a bracing change from their lives on the "outside." Ranch life was simple and spare. The roads were dirt, kept in check by a roving sprinkler and scraper team. Barbed wire separated the property from the surrounding desert, and the landscaping was pure nature. The cowboys from Smoke Tree Stables, also owned by the family, led horseback rides and sang songs around the bonfires at night.

In 1945 the Markhams sold the entire property—400 acres—to the Colony, as the steady visitors had named themselves, and new Colonists could come in only with the approval of the entire group. Walt Disney was one of the newcomers. He bought a cottage in 1948 and used it

---

SPA RESORT CASINO　　　　　　$$
100 North Indian Canyon Dr.
(760) 778-1772, (888) 999-1995
www.hotwatercasino.com

Originally built in the 1960s as the first development on Indian-owned land, the Spa has undergone a series of needed and effective transformations over the years, morphing from a basic hotel into a stylish, bustling hub for locals and visitors. Part of the draw is the world-famous spa, built around the city's original hot mineral springs, and fitness center. The pool is one of the largest and most social in town, and the neighboring casino brings a touch of Vegas to downtown Palm Springs; visitors who remember the tentlike casino of not long ago will be amazed at how the new casino is reminiscent of Sin City's Green Valley Ranch or Red Rock Resort. A half-dozen eateries—

buffet, deli, cantina, noodle and sushi bar, cafe, and steakhouse—round out the offerings.

RESORTS

**DESERT SPRINGS,
A JW MARRIOTT RESORT & SPA**　　$$$$
74-855 Country Club Dr., Palm Desert
(760) 341-2211, (888) 236-2427
www.desertspringsresort.com

If the desert were to offer a Disney World–like experience—in the positive sense of such an experience—Desert Springs is it. Situated on 450 acres of lavishly landscaped grounds and lagoons, this sprawling oasis-style resort opened with an over-the-top splash in 1987. Not nearly the southwestern region monolith it was at opening—Marriott itself has far larger properties in several as a place to relax and plan his new Southern California dream park. While he was imagining, he had his designers create six cottages that still exist on the site today. Walt loved this place so much that he snuck a little reminder of the Ranch into Disneyland. The statue of Disney that stands outside Sleeping Beauty's Castle has the brand insignia of Smoke Tree Ranch.

Life at the Colony was a several-months affair for many of the owners, who settled in from October through May. Children spent the mornings at the Ranch's school, whose three buildings and playground stood along the western border, not far from today's gate. Afternoons were free for sports or studies, then an early dinner with the teachers. At 6:30 p.m. on the dot, adults came together for a family-style dinner on the long wooden tables in the Ranch House. Each diner had a special branded clothespin hanging on the dining hall wall to use as a place card, napkin holder, and emblem of prior visits—each visit earned a hash mark, and the more marks your pin had, the greater your status.

A rodeo field hosted professional rodeos and gymkhanas, and cowboy crooners were called on to lead songs in the evenings. In many ways it was a make-believe western world, created in the minds of men and women raised with the images of Roy Rogers and Gene Autry, and it was the polar opposite of the Palm Springs lifestyle sought by most other affluent visitors.

Today, though the Ranch is open to the traveling public, more than 300 acres are reserved for the Colony's 85 homes, many of which are enjoyed by the children and grandchildren of the original Colonists. The Markhams' descendants continue to be involved in the Ranch, which still retains its simple, western dude-ranch aura.

Walt Disney's cottages and 51 other bungalows are available to visitors, who can also opt for a full meal plan or just enjoy the surroundings. Cowboy singers still entertain at night around a bonfire, and the days hold long, lazy hours for swimming, playing tennis, wandering the nature trails, and dreaming the Hollywood western dream.

locales—what we have here remains the New York City of Coachella Valley resort and convention complexes. Nearly 900 rooms, 36 holes of golf, and boats that transport the wide-eyed to remote parts of the property will do that for you. Guests are greeted by flamingos as they transit the entry drive, which effectively is an advertisement for the riot of colors and plants that revel in this desert when enough water is at hand. The main lobby and reception area is an eight-story atrium backed by lake-to-ceiling windows. The spa has undergone several renovations in recent years, and while the modernization brought it fully forward, what remains are superlative spa offerings and that comely spa-patron/adult-only lake-side pool area. One bit of irony is that with the resort's just-completed makeover, as the tropical was taken out of the atrium and public spaces—envision stacked stone and wood—more color was put into the accommodations. The resort has two very active pools just past the lobby, a new Taylor Made Performance Lab at the Ted Robinson-designed golf club, 18-hole putting green, 20 tennis courts (hard, clay, and grass), fitness center, hair salon, basketball courts, croquet, bikes, business center, Kids' Klub for children 4 to 12, retail arcade, and a dozen or so restaurants and lounges covering every possible taste. Desert Springs is not for everyone and that is not for a lack of quality, service, or ambience. For this market it is a huge property, popular with families and Gen X sun worshipers and business groups. Yet if you are shy, there are any number of places to find a quiet corner.

i Most of the large resort hotels have multilingual staff and can provide a basic translation service for visitors who are not fluent in English. If you know you or your traveling companions will need this, call ahead to see if your particular needs can be accommodated (then again, if you are reading this you don't need help).

DORAL DESERT PRINCESS RESORT $$

67-967 Vista Chino, Cathedral City
(760) 322-7000, (888) 386-4677
www.doralpalmsprings.com

The 285-room Doral is located on the north edge of Cathedral City not far from Palm Springs. The hotel partners with the adjoining 27-hole Desert Princess Country Club, which is a primary draw of this property as the club serves up good desert-style palm-and-water golf at a more reasonable spot on the pricing scale. Rooms have coffeemakers and fridges, and good-sized patios or balconies where guests can take in the verdant grounds, golf course, and mountains. With its pool and hot tubs, fitness center and spa, racquet club, and restaurant, the property is a good mid-market option for visitors looking for a quiet, sunny getaway that won't break the bank. (Condo rentals are available at Desert Princess, as well.)

HYATT GRAND CHAMPIONS
RESORT AND SPA $$$-$$$$

44-600 Indian Wells Lane, Indian Wells
(760) 341-1000, (800) 554-9288
www.grandchampions.hyatt.com

Another property that's treated to a continuing cycle of big-buck renovation and improvement, the 530-room Grand Champions remains a strong contender for the title of "best megaresort" in the valley. The once-famous tennis stadium is gone, replaced by Aqua Serena Spa & Salon, which is uniquely paired with the Medical and Skin Spa. Here, guests can get a host of noninvasive cosmetic procedures done—Botox, skin peels, laser treatments, and fillers such as Restylane. Golf takes place at the adjoining Indian Wells Golf Resort,

where Clive Clark and John Fought stopped by in 2006 and 2007 to completely explode the pedestrian Ted Robinson courses of old.

Rooms are spacious—550 square feet—and some of the best standard accommodations anywhere in the valley. While not suites, the sleeping and living areas are separated by a step down and a low wall, and the marble bathrooms are flush. The fourth and fifth floors are taken over by Hyatt's Regency Club accommodations, with private access, room-amenity upgrades, concierge, and food and beverage service through the day. The property also offers a number of one- and two-bedroom villas that are detached from the main complex and come with butlers to handle those special needs and requests (as in one guest from overseas, who didn't like the quality of American newsprint, asked that his morning paper be ironed—no joke). "Pool Garden" features seven cement ponds, from a kids' pool with water slide to lap pools to the adults-only Oasis Pool with requisite bar. Grand Champions isn't as deep in eats as Desert Springs, but gourmands won't suffer. There's also an outlet of the hoteliers signature kids' program, Camp Hyatt.

LA QUINTA RESORT & CLUB $$$-$$$$

49-499 Eisenhower Dr., La Quinta
(760) 564-4111, (800) 598-3829
www.laquintaresort.com

The desert's first resort, La Quinta was built in 1926. At the time, it was a true hideaway—surrounded by miles of empty desert and a very long way, indeed, from Palm Springs. Today it's in the heart of fast-growing La Quinta and has itself grown to encompass hundreds of acres and 90 holes of some of the country's best golf both on- and off-site, with courses by Dye, Nicklaus, and Norman, and including the infamous Stadium Course at PGA West and the picturesque Mountain Course at La Quinta Resort itself. This is a true destination resort—one where you can hand over the car keys at check-in and pick them up days (or weeks) later when you tear yourself away. The spa is a brilliant combination of indoor and outdoor treatment spaces, a huge fitness center, and Yamaguchi Salon, one of the desert's best full-service beauty salons. Also located adjacent to the spa is the WellMax Center for Preventive Medicine, a facility that features a wide array of tests and medical evaluation procedures, supervised and performed by doctors on staff at local hospitals. This is aimed at those who want to seriously evaluate and adjust their lifestyles and has become increasingly popular with high-stress executives.

Accommodations are in guest rooms, casitas, suites, or villas. The 796 accommodations are decorated in California Mission-style, with rugged wrought-iron and wood furniture and warm earth tones. All rooms have coffeemakers and minifridges; some have fireplaces. The casitas and villas have private patios and a lot of room. Some come with private pools and kitchens, and over the decades they've been favorites for writers (Frank Capra, for one), actors and actresses, and more mundane business types needing a beautiful secluded spot to work. On-site eats encompass Twenty6, an American bistro, and long-running Adobe Grill. The new Ernie's Bar & Grill at PGA West is a kicked up sports bar, and there is clubhouse dining at both the Mountain and Greg Norman courses. The central Plaza is a lovely spot landscaped like a hacienda courtyard with flowers, fountains, and handmade tiles. Surrounded by an assortment of shops and two of the resort's restaurants, it feels like the center of a small town. Other amenities include a massive tennis complex, fitness center, a business center, and the requisite concierge. Toss in 41 pools and 53 hot tubs—that is no typo—and you get the feeling that La Quinta just must put the grande

i Families with small children should ask if the hotel is set up for children or if it is more appropriate for adults. Of course, kiddie pools and children's menus signal that a hotel welcomes small ones. But a lot of businesses don't want to turn away business, even if that business isn't the best business for its business.

in mega-resort, yet the vibe is much more that of a rancho, from a simpler time.

MIRAMONTE RESORT & SPA $$$–$$$$
45-000 Indian Wells Lane, Indian Wells
(760) 341-2200, (800) 237-2926
www.miramonteresort.com

Remember the Erawan? The Adventureland-looking edifice that long sat along Highway 111 in Indian Wells, and for some period of its late life in some type of arrested decay. Yes, the Erawan has been gone for at least 10 years, but the constant reminders of how cool the site is today as the Miramonte can't help but ignite flashbacks to Burma-Gone-Wrong (OK, it was probably chic in the day). Now it is Tuscany in the Desert, a haven of crafted stone, fountains, exploding bougainvillea, and meandering walks. The resort's 215 accommodations are arrayed in villa-style buildings scattered across 11 acres of citrus and garden. There are two pools and cabanas and day beds, a dedicated golf concierge—there is no golf on-site but the Indian Wells Golf Resort is just across the road—and for tennis players an affiliation with the Indian Wells Tennis Garden, home to the BNP Paribas Open. The Well Spa checks in with a regimen of water and earth. Watsu brings the pressure-point and facilitated stretching of shiatsu to a salt water, body temperature pool—very East-meets-West—and the River Bench Grotto is a secluded pool with an easy cascade of 103-degree water similarly lacking in chlorine. Couples or groups can opt for the Pittura Festa ("painting festivity," strictly translated) in which participants paint, smear, or splatter one another from a palette of therapeutic muds, with a menu of apropos add-ons that would make a domestic car purchase seem an option-light exercise. Miramonte really has created its own category—that of the small luxury resort knowing exactly what it is, and thankfully what it is not.

RANCHO LAS PALMAS RESORT & SPA $$$
41-000 Bob Hope Dr., Rancho Mirage
(760) 568-2727, (866) 423-1195
www.rancholaspalmas.com

Often overshadowed by the glitzy resorts at the eastern end of the valley, Rancho Las Palmas actually has one of the best locations. Almost dead center between Palm Springs and La Quinta, it's right across the street from The River, the huge "retailtainment complex" that packs in the tourists and locals all year. If you're staying here, you can stroll across the street and back, casting a smug glance at the dozens of cars circling the lot looking for prime—any, in-season—parking spots. A 27-hole Ted Robinson-designed resort-y golf course, 25-court multi-surface tennis complex, a surprisingly serene spa with fitness center and multiple pools, and eateries are big draws. If looking for a bigger draw—and this is one of the reasons why this property is so popular with families—take a gander at Splashtopia, two acres of water slides, sandy beach, lazy river, fountains and erupting sprinklers, "mountain"-side Jacuzzi, and another swimming pool. The resort's 466 rooms and suites are scattered about the massive property in a couple dozen buildings, all sharing the Spanish Revival look that's long been Las Palmas' hallmark. Rooms are done in tasteful light "desert" tones and they are very large, another plus for the family travelers out there, along with the relative price advantage over other like-situated properties here. Las Palmas recently emerged from extensive renovations, a series of which have kept this place relevant through time and multiple owners. It's also popular with business travelers.

RENAISSANCE ESMERALDA RESORT AND SPA $$$$
44-400 Indian Wells Lane, Indian Wells
(760) 773-4444, (866) 236-2427
www.renaissanceesmeralda.com
The Esmeralda is elegant. That might resonate like a "doh!" revelation here in the glam desert. But for all the historic glitter of Palm Springs, the wow of Desert Springs, the easy chic of La Quinta; for all the business travelers who pour through, the golf guys taking holiday, the happily delirious kids, this place oozes style. It's a big resort, not something

boutique-y, with a massive atrium and nearly 600 rooms. Yet it feels Bond. Why fight it? No one seems to mind if you descend either of the broad, double stairs of marble and wood in flip-flops and an aloha shirt. Perhaps that has something to do with the pools "out back," one of which is edged in sand beach. This resort shares a massive hunk of Indian Wells with the Hyatt Grand Champions and the city's two revamped golf courses. For all the look, the comfy rooms and the justly famous food—signature Italian eatery Sirocco is a Zagat notable—what perhaps stands out most is Spa Esmeralda, a long-after-the-resort-opened addition that ranks with the best spas in the region, not just this desert. The spa ranks at the bottom on the intimidation scale and the couples suites, garden relaxation area, and outdoor treatment alcoves will take even the most spa-bumbling to their happy place.

THE RITZ-CARLTON $$$$
68-900 Frank Sinatra Dr., Rancho Mirage
(760) 321-8282, (800) 542-8680
www.ritzcarlton.com
They're back. After opening under the auspices of Ritz-Carlton, then going to Rock Resorts and being treated to a partial do-over, this most intimate and secluded of desert resorts came back online with a whole new look and Ritz at the helm. Ritz Uno was somewhat of an anomaly for the desert, being all dredged up in oriental carpets and formal 19th-century Boston decor. Under Rock's tutelage a significant amount of work was done on the property, but there remained a disconnect in style and finish. While the paint has not yet dried, expectations are high. The resort is perched on 24 acres, 650 feet above the valley floor in the Santa Rosa Mountains foothills, so the view is nothing short of spectacular. This is desert bighorn sheep country, and while interaction with humans and human activities aren't the best things for these endangered and noble critters, it's nonetheless been a thrill when over the years guests have been treated to the site of several sheep noshing on the resort's lawn. The Ritz has

260 rooms and suites, and the requisite Ritz Club Level, plus the 24,000 square-foot La Prairie. The resort has partnered with noted LA chef/restaurateur Joachim Splichal on its signature restaurant, Pinot Mirage, and outdoor "cliffside" casual dining can be taken at The Edge. The tennis facility is a classic and the resort will continue its golf partnership with the area's best courses, which in the past meant access to Mission Hills Country Club, home of the Kraft Nabisco Championship.

THE RIVIERA RESORT & SPA $$$$
1600 North Indian Canyon Dr.
(760) 327-8311, (866) 588-8311
www.psriviera.com

The Palm Springs Riviera Resort and Racquet Club was closed in 2008 for some much needed renovations. A fixture in Palm Springs since the 1960s, the "Riv," as its known locally, was fashioned after Vegas icons the Sands, Flamingo, and Dunes, and it was that era's most famous celebrity hangout in a town thick with celebrity. Those freewheeling days are long gone, and the most frequent guests leading into the closure period were business travelers and participants in the yearly White Party, a gay men's circuit event. The Riv is back, now dubbed Resort & Spa, with $70 million having put sparkle back in the grande dame. SpaTerre specializes in southeast Asian therapeutic rituals. Fire pits blaze poolside. Circa 59 brings the classic martini-era chophouse modern with Kobe flat iron steak and lobster pot pie. And 400+ rooms and 45 one-, two- and three-bedroom suites given over to mid-century modern design and furnishings produces a place just large enough to buzz, and cool enough to purr.

i **Many larger hotels and a surprising number of small ones are pet-friendly. They have designated rooms set aside for pets and somewhat higher rates to cover the extra work and potential cleaning. If you're traveling with a pet, be sure to check on this and ask about any limitations, such as the size or type of pet allowed.**

THE WESTIN MISSION HILLS
RESORT AND SPA $$$$
71-333 Dinah Shore Dr., Rancho Mirage
(760) 328-5955, (800) 228-3000
www.westin.com/missionhills

The Moorish-styled Westin was one of the first "mega"-resorts in the desert, and despite its tenure always has seemed to struggle with its place on the accommodations map. Is it a golf property? Most certainly There's a sporty Pete Dye 18 right out back and a mile or so away a very good, very underrated Gary Player course. Business and incentive travel? Loads of it. Is it a vacation destination? Four eateries, seven-court tennis complex with teaching academy, 500+ rooms and suites, the most basic of which start at right about 600 square feet, spa, gym, and even a running concierge cover the "getaway" stuff. And what about the kids? Well, there are multiple pools, the mandatory water slide, playground, and a Westin Kids Club. So what is the Westin? A bit of everything. If this sounds like a bummer blanket, that's not the intent. Service is good, the grounds are gorgeous, for all the bustle the property exudes a sense of warmth, and there's a ton of "there" there even if the individual components might be exceeded, individually, by Resorts A and B, Y and Z. Count on driving while you're here as the valley's action—shopping, movies, other golf courses, theater, dining, and even the relatively nearby Agua Caliente Casino—is down the road.

SPECIALTY LODGING

GLBT Hotels

Palm Springs has been a GLBT-friendly destination for decades, and you won't find any hotel that discourages GLBT visitors or treats them with anything but respect and warmth. In addition, more than 35 hotels and inns in Palm Springs and Cathedral City cater specifically to gay and lesbian travelers. These are all small and mostly gay-owned and/or -managed. Most of them are in Palm Springs and are located in three neighborhoods, none of which are more than a mile or so apart.

Warms Sands, just a few blocks east of Palm Canyon Drive, is the most established gay residential neighborhood, with a number of gay men's properties. A few blocks to the south in the Deep Well community and on San Lorenzo Road are several more groups of gay and lesbian hotels. Just north of downtown near the old Movie Colony neighborhood is a third scattering of hotels and spas for the gay traveler.

Many of these small hotels are still finding their particular niches in the gay tourism business—wild and rowdy or quiet and more subtle. On occasion, a previously gay-oriented hotel will change hands and do an about-face, marketing to the general tourism industry. And, every year, a small inn or two changes its emphasis from general travelers to gay travelers.

The city of Palm Springs and the Desert Gay Tourism Guild have worked together for years to promote gay tourism to the valley. They publish an excellent and informative Gay Tourism Guide that lists gay- and lesbian-oriented hotels, and they also have up-to-date information on the guild's Web site, www.palmspringsgayinfo.com. For reservation information on gay hotels, contact the Palm Springs Visitor Information Center at (800) 347-7746, (760) 778-8418 locally, or visit www.palm-springs.org. The valley's larger tourism organization—Palm Springs Desert Resort Communities CVA—is also a rich source for GLBT accommodations information, on both its Web site and in its free publications (www.givein tothedesert.com).

Since 1989 the White Party in Palm Springs has been promoted all over the world as the premier event on the gay party circuit. It's the biggest annual tourism-revenue-generating event for the city, stretching over nine days and attracting as many as 25,000 revelers. Festivities are typically held Easter Week—2010 is a notable exception—with the actual White Party held on Sat night at the Palm Springs Convention Center.

With so many partygoers in town, several of the city's large hotels have capitalized on the crowd by offering up their entire hotel for the duration, hosting afternoon pool parties that are the daytime highlights of the week. Downtown hotels such as the Hilton, Wyndham, Hyatt, and Spa get in on the action, as does the Riviera at the north end. The White Party is generally confined to downtown Palm Springs, with more mainstream spring vacationers booking into the hotels in other cities. For complete information about each year's White Party, visit promoter Jeffrey Sanker's Web site, www.jeffreysanker.com.

A few of the city's notable GLBT hotels are listed below. For directional purposes all are in Palm Springs.

CASITAS LAQUITA $$
450 East Palm Canyon Dr.
(760) 416-9999, (877) 203-3410
www.casitaslaquita.com
This lesbian-friendly inn is a one-acre-plus compound done in Mission style, with charming small bungalows built around a courtyard and pool area. All rooms have full kitchens, and many have large southwestern-style fireplaces. The hotel is close to downtown and has great mountain views. A pool, barbecue areas, catering, and spa services are available.

DESERT PARADISE RESORT HOTEL $$
615 Warm Sands Dr.
(760) 320-5650, (800) 342-7635
www.desertparadiseresorthotel.com
The 14 suites are named after famous diva/actresses like Cher, Barbra Streisand, Elizabeth Taylor, and more. Furnishings are simple and clean, and the suites all include wide-screen TVs and full kitchens. All rooms are built around the central area, which contains a pool, fire pit, gazebo, and breakfast patio. Guests can enjoy the Jacuzzi. A complimentary expansive, more-than-continental breakfast is provided. Clothing is optional.

EL MIRASOL VILLAS $$
525 Warm Sands Dr.
(760) 327-5913, (800) 327-2985
www.elmirasol.com
One of the desert's most venerable gay hotels, El

Mirasol has been around since 1975 and is said to have been built by Howard Hughes in the 1940s. The grounds are walled and gated like all the gay hotels and feature winding paths, lush landscaping around the two pools, and an outdoor steam room/shower. The lanai and fireplace are the central gathering spot for breakfast, lunch, and evening get-togethers. The rooms, located in newly remodeled bungalows, are spare and clean. Wet bars, kitchens, and private patios are available. Complimentary breakfast and daylong refreshments are provided, and clothing is optional.

THE HACIENDA AT WARM SANDS $$$–$$$$
586 Warm Sands Dr.
(760) 327-8111, (800) 359-2007
www.thehacienda.com

Out & About magazine included this on their first list of "Top 10 North American Gay Guesthouses." It's small, like all of the gay hotels, with 10 spacious guest suites opening onto two pools and a Jacuzzi. Rooms include full gourmet kitchens, two-man showers, teak and bamboo furniture, and well-chosen antiques. The larger suites have fireplaces. An extensive continental breakfast and full lunch are included in the price. There's a concierge, a large library of movies and books, beautifully kept grounds, the option of in-room massage by local therapists and a "Pillow Menu" from which to choose. The hotel is clothing-optional.

INNDULGE PALM SPRINGS $$
601 Grenfall Rd.
(760) 327-1408, (800) 833-5675
www.inndulge.com

A consistent winner of the *Out & About* Editor's Choice award, INNdulge is party central for many gay visitors to Palm Springs. There are 24 rooms and suites done up with custom-built southwestern wrought iron and pine furnishings. Arrayed around the 24-hour pool and what is billed as a "12-man Jacuzzi." A full gym is open at all hours. A complimentary breakfast is included, and clothing is optional.

INN EXILE $$
545 Warm Sands Dr.
(760) 327-5413, (800) 962-0186
www.innexile.com

One of the desert's more "happening" spots for gay men, this is a two-and-a-half acre walled compound with four pools, two hot tubs, full gym, billiard room, outdoor fireplace, outdoor misting system to temper the summer just a bit, and the "Gang Way" social room. Rooms are basic, with generic furnishings and decor. Complimentary breakfast and lunch are provided. Clothing is optional.

LA DOLCE VITA RESORT $$
1491 South Via Soledad
(760) 325-2686, (877) 644-4111
www.ladolcevitaresort.com

The gated and walled inn features 20 rooms and suites that open onto one of two pools or garden areas. Guests have access to private patios and cabanas around the grounds, an outdoor gym, steam room, and video and book library. French-doored rooms come with refrigerators and microwaves—some suites have full kitchens—upscale bath amenities from Aveda, and hardwood floors. Guests enjoy complimentary breakfast and evening cocktail hours. Clothing is optional.

TERRAZZO PALM SPRINGS $$
1600 East Palm Canyon Dr.
(760) 778-5883, (866) 837-7996
www.terrazzo-ps.com

In the Deepwell area near grocery and retail shopping, and restaurants not far from downtown Palm Springs, Terrazzo has received several awards from *Out & About* magazine. Its 12 rooms are nicely furnished in bamboo-tropical style, and all face the pool. Most have microwaves and refrigerators. Continental breakfast is included, as is water, snack, fruit, and sports drink service through the day; there's even an espresso bar. As is standard, clothing is optional.

Clothing-Optional Hotels

With 350 or so days of sunshine each year and a dry, warm-to-hot climate, the desert is the best place in California to run around naked. Even Albert Frey, the famous Swiss-born architect who lived and designed here until his death in his 90s, was a confirmed "naturist."

And it's fitting that one of Frey's designs is now a popular clothing-optional hotel, the Terra Cotta Inn. Located in the quiet north end of town, the Terra Cotta has been the recipient of numerous awards for its service and standards. There are at least five clothing-optional hotels in the desert, and all are extremely popular.

These places are quiet, private, and cater primarily to couples. For the voyeurs in the room, they're also on the up-and-up.

DESERT SUN RESORT $$$–$$$$
1533 Chaparral Rd.
(760) 322-5800, (800) 960-4786
www.desertshadows.com

This place is the site of the famous "nude bridge" that spans Indian Canyon Drive to connect the hotel's two sites. Building of the bridge caused quite a flap a few years ago, mostly because the city gave it a nice subsidy. Prurient drivers hoping to get a glimpse of bare suntans scampering across the bridge were soon disappointed as the high sides provide complete privacy. This is a Mediterranean decorated modern Southern California hideout with resort amenities aplenty: salt-water pool, whirlpools, tennis and basketball courts, fire pit for star-lit evenings, barbecues for guest use, on-site libations and eats, and a full-service spa. Nearly 100 rooms, villas, and fireplaced one- and two-bedroom suites are offered, with the larger units and some rooms having kitchens

LIVING WATERS SPA $$
13340 Mountain View Rd., Desert Hot Springs
(760) 329-9988, (866) 329-9988
www.livingwatersspa.com

Despite the fame achieved by Palm Springs for its springs, for hot water perking up through the desert floor, the north side of the valley has the big spigot, so it's logical several clothing-optional retreats would follow the water to Desert Hot Springs. The resort features nine poolside rooms, most with kitchens and a half-dozen two-bedroom condos. The story here is sun, relaxation, the natural spring waters and, well, more sun, relaxation and natural spring waters, so au naturel beach volleyballers and racket-wielders should look elsewhere. Spa services are offered and day-use access is available.

MORNINGSIDE INN $$
888 North Indian Canyon Ave.
(760) 325-2668, (800) 916-2668
www.morningsideinn.com

With just 10 rooms, the Morningside Inn caters to couples and has a convivial, homey atmosphere that is very different than the large, resort tone of Desert Sun. The rooms are just a few steps up from a basic motel, with refrigerators, microwaves, and VCRs. Some have full kitchens. The inn has a pool and massage services. The service is personable and warm, and the location is not too far from the middle of downtown.

SEA MOUNTAIN RESORT & SPA $$$$
Desert Hot Springs
(877) 928-2827
www.seamountaininn.com

An interesting mix of nightclub, spa, boutique inn, and nudism come together at this secret retreat in Desert Hot Springs, so secret in fact that the resort's physical address is not disclosed until visitors book a reservation. Sea Mountain has 15 recently revamped rooms, each with designer linens, LCD and DVD, and mineral water showers. Breakfast is included and in-room dining is provided by select vendors in the area. "Evening Spa" is held nightly, a "lingerie or less" chill party of dance, pool, and spa. It should be noted that access is limited to adult couples and women, be they overnight or day guests.

TERRA COTTA INN $$
2388 East Racquet Club Rd.
(760) 322-6059, (800) 786-6938
www.sunnyfun.com

The 17 oversize rooms have sitting areas, mini-fridges, microwaves, and coffeemakers. Suites offer full kitchens, private patios, sunken tubs, and big-screen TVs. On-site spa services are available in the rooms or in the poolside gazebo and include massage, waxing, facials, and nail services. The central pool is the site of a daily complimentary breakfast. Guests can use the barbecue or call for catered meals.

Vacation Rentals

Why not go "home" for the holidays or vacation? More and more travelers do. While hotels and resorts have their obvious upsides, sometimes individual, family, and even group vacationers want more options, more elbow room, and more privacy. Enter the private home or condo.

The Coachella Valley is particularly rich in limited-term rental homes. Be it for a week or a month or an entire season, from a simple studio in town to a five-bedroom, five-bath manse with infinity-edge pool overlooking a golf course, there's an overflowing cornucopia of housing out there. One way to match need to market is to contact someone who specializes in condo and home rentals. There are any number of such providers in the desert, and some are quite notable; we mention two below. The good ones provide turnkey service, providing the perfect residence for you and seeing that the fridge is pre-stocked with essentials and knowing where to find the best sushi, a good doctor, or the nearest shop to replace the 3-iron that somehow found a lake. (A large number of country clubs also operate rental services for on-site homes put into the rental pool by less-than-full-time owner-residents.)

Of the many revolutions unleashed by the Internet, one of the most beneficial is the ease with which travelers can find vacation rentals while lounging in jammies with a cup of joe in hand. As in all such transactions, caveat emptor

Here are a few of the many resources at your disposal:

CRAIGSLIST.ORG

Did someone say newfangled classified ads? At any time the online clearinghouse of clearinghouses will have hundreds of vacation rental listings covering the entire valley.

DESERT CONDO RENTALS, INC.
4741 East Palm Canyon Dr., Suite D
(760) 320-6007, (800) 248-2529
www.desertcondorentals.com

This company has a diverse portfolio of predominantly west-central valley properties. The staff is friendly, reliable, and resourceful and will help you make a selection based on your budget, preferred location, and length of stay.

MCLEAN COMPANY RENTALS
4777 South Palm Canyon Dr.
(760) 322-2500, (800) 777-4606
www.ps4rent.com

If you want to spend the week in the home of a now-deceased and once-famous Hollywood star, this is the place to go. Condos in virtually every country club in the desert are on the rental rolls, and the staff will do everything from stocking the fridge with goodies before you arrive to arranging theater tickets and dinner reservations. McLean has more than a quarter-century of experience in the desert.

VACATION RENTALS BY OWNER
www.vrbo.com

This could be the ultimate arm's-length short-term rental site. The cataloging is fantastic, with the desert broken down by individual city or unincorporated community and from their by specific development (even phases of a development), with an "others" category. Searches can be sorted high-low/low-high by number of beds, how many people the unit will sleep, or even the number of photos posted with each listing. There are quick-look icons as to whether the rental takes pets or accepts credit cards or is accessible, usually tons of photos, in-depth description, availability calendar, rate schedule, a link to contact the owner, and a "vacation rental features" chart with loads of boilerplate (that at times isn't as perfectly clear as you'd like). The site has something like 125,000+ listings worldwide.

Time-shares

The desert has a number of time-share properties that offer rentals to the public. Almost all time-share units have at least minimal "homelike" attributes, and the newest properties are as decked out as the most posh resorts, save perhaps on the food front. Time-shares might also be more readily accessible for truly short-term use—weekend/week—than fee-owned rentals. Beware the sales hawks and the promise of free show tickets or a balloon ride that end up costing $15,000 when the thumbscrews and "short 90-minute presentation" break you down. These rentals are typically handled by the parent time-share company or a contracted vendor.

MARQUIS VILLAS RESORT $$$
140 South Calle Encilia
(760) 322-2263, (877) 288-5463
www.marquisvillas.com
This property has 63 extremely spacious (900 square feet minimum) one- and two-bedroom villas just a block from the heart of downtown Palm Springs. Now operated by Diamond Resorts International, the rooms and public areas have received a much-needed sprucing up and are both comfortable and elegant, with full kitchens, fireplaces, wet bars, and private balconies. The resort also has a small fitness center and tennis courts.

MARRIOTT'S SHADOW RIDGE RESORT $$–$$$
Please see the listing for this warm, comfy time-share property in the "Hotels" section above.

MARRIOTT'S DESERT SPRINGS VILLAS $$$–$$$$
1091 Pinehurst Lane, Palm Desert
(760) 779-1200, (888) 236-2427
www.marriott.com
Like it's newer sister property, Shadow Ridge, this time-share resort offers spacious guest rooms and one- and two-bedroom condo-type accommodations, with the latter two having complete kitchens. The nearly 500 units are nestled in multiple two-story buildings scattered about the southeastern portion of the massive JW Marriott property of the same name, with many fronting portions of the resort's two golf courses. The villas have a large pool complex, game room, and barbecue and picnic areas, and guests get access to the facilities of the JW Marriott. The environment here is a bit more active and frenzied that at Shadow Ridge.

WESTIN MISSION HILLS VILLAS $$$–$$$$
71-777 Dinah Shore Dr., Rancho Mirage
(760) 328-5955, (800) 472-3713
www.starwoodvacationownership.com
A community of large two-bedroom, one-bedroom, and guest room villas. All feature full kitchens—no oven in the guest room—private patios or balconies, Bose Wave radios and DVD players, washer and dryer, and sofa bed. The larger units add twin fireplaces, whirlpool tubs and more elbow room. Guests have access to the many facilities of the adjoining Westin Mission Hills Resort.

RV Resorts

Despite a wee spot of an economic hiccup recently, RVing retains a strong hold on the American public. While any wide spot with a hole in the ground and a rickety picnic bench could be considered a "site," RVing in the desert is done on a scale that is more reminiscent of a Four Seasons stay than anything the Joads experienced. Mom-and-pop RV "parks" remain, here are two cut from a different cloth.

EMERALD DESERT GOLF & RV RESORT $
76-000 Frank Sinatra Dr., Palm Desert
(760) 345-4770, (877) 624-4140
www.emeralddesert.com
At one time this was quite possibly the ritziest RV resort in Southern California, and as it is it still stands pretty near the top. The park is deep in goodies with pools and whirlpools, a putting green (there was previously a short golf course), clubhouse, lighted tennis courts, fitness center, minimarket, complete laundry facilities, Internet access, sparkling bathrooms and showers, fax and copy service, and even indoor, climate-controlled storage for folks who want to leave their super-luxury RVs on-site all year. They even have rental condos. There's a full calendar of activities through the week, from bridge and watercolor painting to line dancing, water aerobics, yoga, and golf lessons. Barbecues, horseshoe pits, billiards, bocce ball, and croquet courts are part of the amenity-crammed site. The full amenities are only available Oct through May, however, and the resort has a strict policy about children under 18—with few exceptions, they are not allowed. This is not a family-oriented place but rather is geared toward older adults. The property has 251 spaces, way down from its early-this-millennium peak owing to development pressures.

SHADOW HILLS RV RESORT $
40-655 Jefferson St., Indio
(760) 360-4040
www.shadowhillsrvresort.com
Near at hand to Sun City Shadow Hills, golf, and much needed commercial, this RV mecca has all the amenities that vacationers in 45-foot (park maximum) RVs have come to expect when they put down roots for the season. There's a huge clubhouse and fitness center, a pool and spa, a full kitchen, bathrooms and showers, and an Internet and small business center. The resort has 100 sites.

RESTAURANTS

There are hundreds, likely thousands of places to eat in the Coachella Valley, from ramshackle taquerias to chic foie gras palaces.

As it's impossible to list every restaurant in the desert, we've chosen those that work well for both locals and visitors because of their food, service, price, (good) quirkiness, atmosphere, or some combination thereof.

To help you find your way to a great meal, we've organized the restaurant listings by cuisine. That's not exactly rocket science, we realize. Then within those categories you'll find the all-important coin component, and some discussion as to why the place is listed in the first place. As we're of the persuasion that most places are suitable for kids who don't mind eating past the mac-n-cheese, you won't find broad chunks of No-Kid Zone here, and that includes some places that might have a large array of tap handles. If we think junior should sit one out, we'll tell you. With a few exceptions, we do not list dining spots inside casinos or hotels, as these tend to go through frequent changes. We also do not list fast-food places or huge national chains but instead concentrate on those restaurants that are unique to the desert or not widely represented outside the region. Rest assured, you will be able to find all the insipid fast-food places here: McDonald's, Pizza Hut, Domino's, Jack in the Box, Wendy's, Taco Bell, Dairy Queen, Arby's, Burger King, and so on. The moderately priced chain restaurants, such as Denny's, Ruby's Diner, Tony Roma's, Hamburger Hamlet, IHOP, California Pizza Kitchen, and Marie Callender's, all reside in the desert if not this book. On the high end, the chain prohibition means you'll have to find the likes of a Ruth's Chris or a Morton's of your own volition; psssst, they're here.

A word about geography: Wherever you are in the desert, you're never far from a good selection of dining spots. The layout of the valley, with Palm Canyon Drive-become-Highway 111 running right through the middle of each city, means that most large shopping, dining, and entertainment clusters are right there, taking advantage of the constant flow of traffic. So, in Palm Springs, you'll find most restaurants along Palm Canyon Drive downtown and in the half mile or so around the downtown core.

Restaurants in Cathedral City follow this rule as well, with a collection of fast-food places on the western city limits and more upscale places to the east. In Rancho Mirage the stretch of highway known as Restaurant Row stretches from Shame on the Moon on the western city limits to Wally's Desert Turtle on the east. In between these two elegant signposts is The River, one of the desert's most popular eating/retail/entertainment complexes. A number of regional chains, such as P. F. Chang's and the Cheesecake Factory, are here, as well as a fine selection of dining and drinking places, from the ubiquitous Starbucks to Baja Fresh, the Yard House, Piero's Acqua Pazza, and Fleming's Steakhouse.

i Some say that the Early Bird is the official bird of the Palm Springs area. With the exception of fast-food places and the most upscale dining spots, most every restaurant features "early-bird specials" at some time during the year. Choices are limited and you'll have to eat early, often before 6:30 p.m., but the value is great.

In Palm Desert, restaurants are concentrated both on Highway 111 and along El Paseo Drive, which parallels Highway 111 for a number of blocks. Here you'll find eating choices that range from fast-food outlets and high-quality chains such as California Pizza Kitchen, to quirky locals spots and haute cuisine. As Palm Desert fades into Indian Wells on the east, the restaurant tally drops precipitously while the gems-per-capita quotient rises, perhaps peaking at the Renaissance Esmeralda's Sirocco, an Italian restaurant of legitimate note.

La Quinta also has its share of fine dining, with restaurants scattered all over the city, from the old-become-new downtown to small shopping malls and La Quinta Resort.

Restaurants in Indio are more down-to-earth, with the full complement of fast-food eateries as well as a number of moderately priced Mexican, Italian, and American places.

Choosing where to eat in the Coachella Valley is often a matter of deciding how far you want to drive and where you want to be at the end of the evening. And if you're suddenly starving at the end of the day, just head to most any stretch of Highway 111/Palm Canyon Drive as good food is always just a few minutes away. Restaurants come and go, and one that's been a mainstay for 20 years may have moved, closed, or been renamed by the time you are using this guide. Also, hours change with the seasons. A place that requires reservations in February may be happy to take walk-ins during the summer. Always call ahead to avoid disappointment. The same holds true for days of operation. During high season, most restaurants are open seven days a week. There is no consistent day of closing for six-day restaurants, though Monday and Tuesday are most common. Again, call ahead.

Price Code

Peoples' respective price sensitivities might be more volatile than the discussion that ensues when the annual newspaper readers' poll again selects Olive Garden as the best Italian restaurant in town. While our moderate might be your cheap, we need something for comparative purposes, so the following categories embrace the expected cost of a typical meal for an adult, less tax, tip, and alcohol; see, no value-loaded words get in the way when symbols are used. What's typical? Let's go with an entree—burger, omelet, whatever if it's more of a breakfast/lunch place—and a requisite starter and side if it's one of those run-up-the-tab a la carte shops. It might not be the most expensive entree on the menu, it won't be the least expensive. Dessert? We didn't save room. But please free free to indulge.

$................. Less than $10
$$ .... $10 to $20
$$$ .... $21 to $35
$$$$ .... More than $35

Readers should assume that all the establishments listed accept major credit cards unless otherwise noted. While alcohol service is rather standard, if that is not the case that too will be noted. All restaurants in California have a no-smoking policy, even in the bar areas. Some restaurants have outside patios where smoking may be allowed.

AMERICAN

ARNOLD PALMER'S
RESTAURANT $$$–$$$$
78-164 Avenue 52, La Quinta
(760) 771-4653
www.arnoldpalmers.net

It's the desert and it's Arnie, so of course there's a putting green outside this La Quinta eatery. A hearty man with a hearty appetite for life, it's only fitting that the King's eponymous restaurant tees off with craftily spun comfort food, prime rib, and other cow cuts from the grill, a good sampling of fish, and a changing chef's menu. There's also a pub with a lower-priced broad-ranging menu of its own. The house is replete with Arnie memorabilia and the dining areas are named for the four majors. There's outdoor dining by the putting green and an inner courtyard with fireplace. The pub opens at 3 p.m. and dinner service in the "restaurant" begins at 5 p.m.

BILLY REED'S RESTAURANT $–$$
1800 North Palm Canyon Dr.
(760) 325-1946
www.billyreedspalmsprings.com
This is a Palm Springs institution, as popular for breakfast and lunch as it is for dinner. It's a bustling spot with several dining areas, including cozy tables, booths, a counter, and a separate bar/lounge area. You'll find all ages and income levels here, all coming for the yummy pot roast, meat loaf, fried chicken, enormous salads, and fresh, multilayered chocolate cake. It's all home-style cooking, with generous portions and very reasonable prices. The wait staff has been here for at least a thousand years, and they know how to make everyone feel at home.

i All indoor (and many outdoor) public spaces in California are no-smoking zones, although some establishments do offer small outside areas where you can light up, and the "cigar zone" seems to come and go in different places. The glaring exceptions are in the Indian-owned casinos. Although these places have wisely made their dining rooms nonsmoking, smoke does not confine itself to the casino areas.

CITRON AT VICEROY PALM SPRINGS $$$$
415 South Belardo Rd.
(760) 320-4117
With its sunny yellow and white decor, white marble floors, and abundance of mirrors, this place evokes a '50s-meets-the-new-millennium charm. Citron is an apt place to enjoy a traditional or "spa cuisine" breakfast, stop in for a cool-down at lunch, or linger for a romantic dinner. A covered patio and tables poolside are good choices when the weather is mild. The food is what the chefs call "California modern," featuring grilled lamb rack, steak frites, fresh halibut, and monkfish filet.

DAILY GRILL $$–$$$
73-061 Hwy. 111, Palm Desert
(760) 779-9911
This is a city grill, as in the type of all-encompassing, cook-everything, cook-it-all-well, bustling eatery you'd find in a big city. "Grill" in the title has less to do with grilled eats and meats, though that does happen here, and more with a style of approachable yet sophisticated restaurant where deals get hammered out over steak and gin while the tables on either side are filled with a swooning couple and a group of eight friends fueling up for a night on the town. Big city stuff. Daily Grill serves breakfast, lunch, brunch, and dinner.

HAMBURGER MARY'S $–$$
415 North Palm Canyon Dr.
(760) 778-6279
www.hamburgermarysps.com
There are a dozen or so of these joints spread about the Great Republic, and if you don't have one near you, get near this one, very near, like inside, ordering. Palm Springs' variant heads long toward sandwiches and burgers, big fat luscious half-pound wonders done many ways. There's a full bar and "Little Lambs" selections for the … we don't need to spell it out, do we? It's a fun frenetic place. And it's Palm Springs so all are welcome.

IN-N-OUT BURGER $
72-265 Varner Rd., Thousand Palms
82-043 Hwy. 111, Indio
www.in-n-out.com
THE quintessential California burger joint and in fact fast-food joint. Indeed, it is fast-food and In-N-Outs can be found in four western states, but trust us, this is a destination stop. The menu is formulaic—burgers, fries, sodas, shakes—and it's all fresh and cooked to order the moment you place your order. That's why it works. Always has. Always will. Buy one of the iconic t-shirts.

HOG'S BREATH INN LA QUINTA $$
78-065 Main St., La Quinta
(760) 564-5556
www.restaurantsofpalmsprings.com

An offshoot of Clint Eastwood's popular Carmel bar and restaurant, the La Quinta version features a drop-dead view from its second-story perch in up-and-coming Old Town La Quinta, murals inspired by Eastwood movies, lots of fireplaces, stacked stone and wood, and indoor and outdoor seating. A big-screen TV, piano bar, and wide array of tequilas and margaritas add to the atmosphere. The food is familiar—burgers, seafood, beef, pasta, and homemade desserts—but handled deftly and with a spot of imagination. Keep an eye out for rotating seasonal specials. Open for lunch (summer excluded) and dinner only.

KAISER GRILLE PALM SPRINGS $$$
205 South Palm Canyon Dr.
(760) 323-1003
www.restaurantsofpalmsprings.com

About as evergreen as an eatery can be, Kaiser is a long-time standby favorite with locals and visitors. Kaiser is known for its substantial happy-hour appetizers and drinks; a broad menu featuring prime rib, sandwiches, pizza, salads, and fresh seafood; and its generous house-made desserts. It's a busy, loud place with a full bar and patio seating right on Palm Canyon Drive in the middle of downtown. Open for lunch and dinner only.

KEEDY'S FOUNTAIN GRILL $
73-633 Hwy. 111, Palm Desert
(760) 346-6492

In the case of Keedy's, grill isn't some nuevo culinary catchword. It stands for the device that's churned out for so many years a never-ending stream of fantastic hashbrowns and huevos rancheros and thick juicy double-bacon burgers. With tables packed like rush hour in Beijing, and an old-style counter, dining at Keedy's is as much about bonding with your neighbor as savoring lox and a bagel on Sunday morning. Get here early and do not miss out on the opportunity to have the best milkshake in the desert. Breakfast and lunch only, no alcohol.

MATCHBOX VINTAGE PIZZA BISTRO $$
155 South Palm Canyon Dr.
(760) 778-6000
www.matchboxpalmsprings.com

Visitors who remember Louise's Pantry, once a staple on Palm Canyon Drive famous for its pies and long lines, will find that times have changed indeed. Louise's is long gone, replaced by this cute little bistro-style spot serving wood-fired pizzas, creative salads, appetizers, and innovative entrees from snapper to New York strip steak. The lines are just as long as ever, so get there early if you want a bite to eat before catching a performance at the Fabulous Palm Springs Follies next door. Open for lunch and dinner only.

MORE THAN A MOUTHFUL CAFE $
134 East Tahquitz Canyon Way
(760) 322-3776

Culinary Institute graduates run this high-quality breakfast and lunch spot in the heart of downtown Palm Springs. Everything is fresh, and made on the spot. The menu changes constantly, and the chefs-in-training use a lot of imagination in the preparation and presentation. Service can be a little rough, and the more inventive creations may not always be successful—but it's a lively place and a nice change from the more predictable sandwich and soup spot. Plus, you may be one of the first to sample fare from Southern California's next big celebrity chef. No alcohol.

MURPH'S GASLIGHT $$
79-860 Avenue 42, Bermuda Dunes
(760) 345-6242

73-155 Hwy. 111, Palm Desert
(760) 340-2012
www.murphsgaslight.com

Murph's opened in the mid-'70s at the Bermuda Dunes Airport. In recent years a second outpost was established, likely because for the bazillions of pounds of chicken the original moved, it just wasn't enough. And despite a full dinner menu, lunch service, and breakfast at the whippersnapper location in Palm Desert, Murph's is about the deep-fried chicken with all the usual suspects on the side, served family style. It's all you can eat, and when you've eaten all you can eat a last plate often shows up, just to have something to take home. The throwback lounge pours a stiff drink, by the way.

SHAME ON THE MOON $$$
69-950 Hwy. 111, Rancho Mirage
(760) 324-5515
www.shameonthemoon.com

This popular restaurant began life as a humble cafe on Palm Canyon Drive in Cathedral City. In the new, elegant setting, the food is so good—stylish yet approachable New American—and the service so warm and accommodating, that it's become wildly popular with locals. Reservations are required, and it's often booked weeks in advance during season. Open for dinner only.

i If you're having trouble getting into the newest, hottest restaurant, try asking the concierge at your hotel. These men and women have connections and can make the right call to get a reservation. Remember to provide a little "thank you"—verbal and green—for all services and assistance rendered.

SIMBA'S RIB HOUSE $
190 North Sunrise Way
(760) 778-7630

This is the place to abandon all thought of healthy, calorie-conscious eating and just dig in to amazing soul food—collard greens, hush puppies, jambalaya, fried chicken, barbecued ribs. Buffet was the way back in the day but that has given way to menu-only ordering, but all those old faves are on the carte.

SPENCER'S RESTAURANT $$-$$$$
701 West Baristo Rd.
(760) 327-3446

Located in the historic Tennis Club area right up against the foothills west of downtown Palm Springs, Spencer's is a favorite for long lunches, Sunday brunch, and romantic dinners where the tastes run to a French–Pacific Rim twist on American classics. Not many restaurants fit all of these specs, and Spencer's has the right combination of service, location, know-how, and chutzpah to make it work.

TYLER'S BURGERS $
149 South Indian Canyon Dr.
(760) 325-2990

Get there early, because the lines can be formidable at noon, when what seems like all of downtown Palm Springs shows up for juicy burgers, crispy fries, and plates of little "sliders," baby-sized burgers or cheeseburgers. It's in the former home of an A&W drive-in, and there's only room for the kitchen, a small counter, and a couple of seats inside. Outside, you can find a bit of room under a canopy and watch the tourists shop in La Plaza, the original shopping area in Palm Springs. But the burgers are what will bring you back and keep you waiting in line. Open for lunch only, closes in Aug. No alcohol.

i Valet parking may be your only option at a hotel restaurant or on a busy street. These services have excellent reputations, and damage or theft is extremely rare. For peace of mind, though, use everyday caution when you're out, leaving valuables behind or storing them out of sight in the trunk.

ASIAN

BANGKOK FIVE $$$
70-026 Hwy. 111, Rancho Mirage
(760) 770-9508
www.bangkok5.com

A sophisticated place for authentic Thai cuisine, this spot features fresh, original creations as well as perfectly replicated traditional dishes: curries, satay, the ubiquitous Pad Thai, crisp whole catfish with chile sauce, duck, the works. Dishes are prepared to order on a heat scale of 1 to 10, and if you think you're brave for having downed that chile relleno over at El Torito, you might want to think again how Thai can bring the heat, gringo. The space—a spare, elegant area with rice paper and wood lanterns, softly colored walls, and simple flower arrangements—can be broken into one or several private dining areas. There's a full bar with a good selection of the kind of specialty consumables that go down way too easy. Dinner only.

i Happy hour can be as good a value as the early-bird special, particularly if you like adult beverages with your food. What's offered where varies, and you're most likely to find smaller versions of standard dinner offerings, bar-only entrees and sandwiches, and of course appetizers, which in some places are like mains. Happy "hour" is usually clustered around the prime dinner times, so late afternoon into early evening and again après 9 or 10 p.m., and more often it's midweek.

CITY WOK $$
74-970 Country Club Dr., Palm Desert
(760) 341-1511
www.citywok.com

A popular place that does a phenomenal takeaway trade, everything is fresh and imaginative at City Wok and you won't find American-style chop suey here. Always good bets are lettuce wraps with savory bits of pine nuts and chicken, steamed potstickers, and Buddha's Feast, a huge vegetarian dish that mixes several different vegetables and spices in a most delicious way. And they deliver. Open for lunch and dinner only.

KOBE JAPANESE STEAK HOUSE $$-$$$
69-838 Hwy. 111, Rancho Mirage
(760) 324-1717
www.koberanchomirage.com

Kobe has been in the desert for three decades, packed every one of those thousands of nights,

and dining here is equal parts fun and food; it's teppan, after all. Beef, chicken, prawns, vegetables, and tofu—you know the routine, and it's a pretty good bargain 'cause you've had your entertainment so don't have to buy movie tickets later in the evening. There's a special kids menu and sushi is available, too. Open for dinner only.

MIDORI JAPANESE RESTAURANT $$-$$$
36-101 Bob Hope Dr., E-1, Rancho Mirage
(760) 202-8186
www.midori-japanese.com

This desert old-timer finally found a much needed new home a couple years back, a fresh contemporary space with a spiffy granite-topped sushi and martini bar and a spacious dining room. Authentic Japanese foods also include noodle specialties, steamed dishes, tempuras, and boat dinners—samplers for two or more. Open for lunch and dinner only.

MIKADO AT THE JW MARRIOTT
DESERT SPRINGS $$$$
74-855 Country Club Dr., Palm Desert
(760) 341-2211
www.desertspringsresort.com

Desert Springs is the granddaddy of the modern desert megaresort, and for all the good eats in the house over its two-plus decades of life, chow has been a moveable feast at times; Mikado is an original. Teppan, sushi, sashimi, the restaurant tags all the bases of a Japanese "steakhouse." What's unique here is that you take a boat to dinner. Dinner only, and while the little ninjas don't exactly eat for free here, they enjoy a big cut in price … and they get ice cream.

BRAZILIAN

PICANHA CHURRASCARIA $$$
68-510 Hwy. 111, Cathedral City
(760) 328-1818
www.picanharestaurant.com

This Brazilian "steakhouse" is a vegan's worst nightmare. Eating here is all about one thing: MEAT. Cow meat, chicken meat, lamb meat, pork meat, and whatever meat goes into Brazilian sausage; huge skewers of grilled meat carried about the eatery and carved tableside right at your plate. Of course there are sissy sides like vegetables and rice, and something called a salad bar. It's a bit of a rowdy place so bring the gang— and kids under 10 eat for half price—and, well, have some meat for dinner.

> **i** If you're stuck at the hotel and don't have the option of room service, call the front desk and ask for menus from the local restaurant delivery service. This is becoming more popular in the desert, with a good variety of restaurants participating. If all else fails, there's always Domino's.

BREAKFAST

BIT OF COUNTRY $
418 South Indian Canyon Dr.
(760) 325-5154
A local favorite for old-fashioned (forget the "heart-healthy" dishes—you won't find them here) trucker-style breakfasts and burgers. Try the scrambled eggs mixed with bits of ham and order it with the hot biscuits and country-style gravy. It's a tiny place, with a handful of tables outside on busy Indian Canyon Drive, and no more than a dozen booths inside. The wait is worth it. Open for breakfast and lunch only. No alcohol.

> **i** "Jackets not required"—that's the time-honored dress code in the desert, where the weather and the laid-back atmosphere give everyone the chance to relax. But, guys, please engage the gray matter. Don't wear jeans or shorts or a wife-beater to a top-end French joint, and remove your headware—you, too, cowboy—indoors. OK, you can keep the horns if the Vikings are on the tube in a sports bar. Nice golf attire, for both men and women, works higher up the food chain here than other places, as well.

CHOP HOUSE $$$$
262 South Palm Canyon Dr.
(760) 320-4500

74-040 Hwy. 111, Palm Desert
(760) 779-9888
www.restaurantsofpalmsprings.com
A venture of the outfit that also operates the Hog's Breath Inn, Jackalope Ranch, and Kaiser Grille, these spots specialize in top-quality steaks, chops, and seafood. Befitting a steak place occupying such a high rung on the ladder, all the beef is aged and cut on premises, the service is spot-on, and the atmosphere is sophisticated but not stuffy. Add a classic iceberg lettuce wedge with blue cheese dressing and some French-cut green beans, plus a scoop of homemade ice cream and an after-dinner port, and you've got the best of American cooking (with a drink assist from Iberia, of course). Dinner only.

CLIFFHOUSE RESTAURANT $$$
78-250 Hwy. 111, La Quinta
(760) 360-5991
www.laquintacliffhouse.com
Wedged, literally, into the side of Point Happy, a mountain-ette of rock that sits right about where Indian Wells becomes La Quinta, or vice versa if heading westbound, the Cliffhouse is almost about it's dramatic setting and gorgeous upscale ranch decor as what's on the menu. And what's on the menu is quite good indeed, thank you very much, a bounty of steak and fish that qualifies the restaurant to be considered a chophouse even if the New American/California touches render it just a bit more unique. Nightly happy hour in the Cactus Grill is a happening time as the bar menu is one of the best in town—have the cowboy skirt steak or the grilled salmon salad—and it's all nicely discounted, as are drinks, and each night of the week features some unique food/drink special, as well. The views around sunset are gorgeous, and the outdoor seating pinched in between the rock and the whitewashed building, accented with water and fire features, is sublime. The point is to be happy, after all. Open for lunch and dinner.

DON & SWEET SUE'S CAFÉ $
68-955 Ramon Rd., Cathedral City
(760) 770-2760
www.donandsweetsues.com

The cafe has delicious burgers, sandwiches, and salads, but breakfast is the all-star production here—massive waffles and pancakes, plates overflowing with ham and eggs and bacon and biscuits and gravy, oh my! You can find some reasonably healthy fare with fruit on the side, but why bother? This is a very popular breakfast spot, so expect a line on weekends. So simply chat up your neighbors in between bouts of anticipation for the Paul Bunyanlike portions. The restaurant serves breakfast (until 2 p.m.), lunch, and dinner, which runs long toward American–United Nations comfort food: goulash, dumplings, chicken cordon bleu, parmigiana, etc. No alcohol.

ELMER'S $ (BREAKFAST)
1030 East Palm Canyon Dr.
(760) 327-8419
www.elmers-restaurants.com

A bustling pancake house that's been serving big Benedicts and delicate crepes and be-sure-not-to-miss-it Dutch babies for decades, Elmer's is a diner close to the heart of many a local and even more visiting Pacific Northwesterners who grew up on this fine stuff. Home-style pot roast, fried chicken, and roast turkey dinners are the best bet for dinner. Open for breakfast, lunch, and dinner. No alcohol.

THE FALLS $$$$
155 South Palm Canyon Dr.
(760) 416-8664
www.thefallsprimesteakhouse.com

This is another of those "prime steakhouse and martini bar" joints, a trendy young spot that hawks great cuts o' cow and martinis, nearly two dozen of 'em. Now that latter bit is nothing short of a miracle since a martini is gin and vermouth, shaken over ice and served up in one of those cool stemmed glasses. If we want to allow that "martini" extends to vodka and vermouth, who are we to argue with James Bond? And of course he had the wherewithal to call it a vodka martini. They have an entire "Martini Menu" here, with names like "Agave Tini"—that would be tequila—and "Bikini Tini" that easily could pour from a tiki-etched vessel. Hey, if you got 'em, shake 'em, I guess. And the food? Rock solid. They have all the usual cuts and fish of a chophouse, raw bar, and the wedge and Caesar. Yet the wedge is "new school," with avo, sweet corn, and raspberry port vinaigrette along with the bacon, blue, and tomato. The appetizers are very novel, be they date poppers, ahi Napoleon or a shrimp-stuffed poblano. And jerk chicken? The Falls has imaginative wired. It also burns a mean steak. Dinner only.

LG'S PRIME STEAKHOUSE $$$$
74-225 Hwy. 111, Palm Desert
(760) 779-9799

255 South Palm Canyon Dr.
(760) 416-1779

78-525 Hwy. 111, La Quinta
(760) 771-9911
www.lgsprimesteakhouse.com

LG's is a desert institution. Or maybe culinary Rock of Gibraltar. This is a traditional-style steakhouse specializing in enormous portions of USDA Prime beef and its usual chophouse partners in crime, lamb, lobster, daily fish, and a real honest-to-goodness tableside-made Caesar for two. The wine list is exhaustive. Some have noted over the years that service can be harried, and servers push the upsell, and around here adding a spud and another side adds about the cost of dinner elsewhere in town. We've never found that a real problem. But staff does rightly cast a bit of the stink-eye if you order much past medium, medium-rare; come on people, it's USDA Prime, it's artwork, leave some life in it. Open for dinner only.

VICKY'S OF SANTA FE $$$–$$$$
45-100 Club Dr., Indian Wells
(760) 345-9770
www.vickysofsantafe.com

Vicky's gets our vote for least chatted up top-end restaurant in the valley. A warm inviting home of an eatery that would fit in perfectly you-know-where—it's the look and the hospitality, not Hatch chiles or posole, that makes Vicky's of Santa Fe. The menu is simplicity perfected, one single page, chops here, seafood there, a spot for comforting, and very well priced, "House Favorites," and the requisite starters, salads, and sides. Add in great wine offerings and an embracing lounge, and it's easy to see why Vicky's wears class as easily as old money wears Sperry's and a fave blazer.

DELI

MANHATTAN IN THE DESERT $
2665 East Palm Canyon Dr.
(760) 322-3354
This spot has gone through a lot of different incarnations, and it seems as if the current one may stick. It's a consistently good place for breakfast, lunch, and casual dinner, with affordable prices and a menu that offers more than 100 different sandwiches, salads, and entrees. There's a full bakery and deli here, as well as a limited selection of wines and beers.

SHERMAN'S DELI & BAKERY $$
401 East Tahquitz Canyon Way
(760) 325-1199

73-161 Country Club Dr., Palm Desert
(760) 568-1350
www.shermansdeli.com
A real-deal deli with house-baked breads and desserts, lox and bagels, scratch matzo-ball soup, and corned beef never to be subjected to an idiot trying to mate it with Wonder, Miracle Whip, and a slice o' Velveeta. Sherman's is the place where old-time residents meet to catch up on local gossip. The Palm Springs Sherman's is also a good place to spot Hollywood movers and shakers during the annual Palm Springs International Film Festival each January. Breakfast and dinner book-end the immense array of lunch sandwich (and other) offerings. No alcohol.

ECLECTIC

CHARLOTTE'S $$$
6 La Plaza
(760) 327-9066
www.charlottespalmsprings.com
The same-named chef-proprietor brings an international flair to her cooking, serving up such dishes as Cuban-style roast pork rack, veal piccata, New Zealand lamb, French onion soup, and poached fresh salmon. Dining is in several little cottages just off the historic plaza in downtown Palm Springs. The decor is charming, with tiny fireplaces, soft hues on the plastered walls, and fresh flowers everywhere. Afternoon tea, by reservation, is a special treat for those so inclined, with delicate sandwiches and pastries. Open for lunch and dinner, seasonally.

DESERT SAGE $$$$
78-085 Avenida La Fonda, La Quinta
(760) 564-8744
This is an absolutely stunning restaurant, with a lively bar and several separate dining rooms. The food is an imaginative blend of fresh ingredients and classical preparation—seafood, game, lamb, and beef along with fresh seasonal fruits and vegetables, elegant sauces, and fresh baked goods. The wine list traded off length for length's sake in favor of perfect representation. Sunday brunch and dinner, seasonally.

EUROPA RESTAURANT
AT VILLA ROYALE INN $$$
1620 Indian Trail
(760) 327-2314, (800) 245-2314
www.villaroyale.com
Two decades ago, a Palm Springs city councilman who had been a pretty good Hollywood set decorator before moving to Palm Springs bought this historic compound and turned it into one of the most eclectic and charming inns in the valley. A big part of the charm is the cozy, wildly romantic Europa and its award-winning cuisine. Like the inn, which decorates each room in the style of a different European country, the menu may

feature German schnitzel one night, Parisian duck the next, and Italian veal on another. Reservations are a premium, so call early. Open for lunch and dinner only.

JILLIAN'S $$$$
74-155 El Paseo Dr., Palm Desert
(760) 776-8247

This romantic, unpretentious spot—filled with antiques, old-world paintings, fresh flowers and all set behind a dove-white wall of stucco—features four dining rooms connecting to a garden courtyard. Jillian's has been in the desert since 1986, and most of the staff has been here since the beginning. Winner of many awards, including perennial recognition from *Wine Spectator,* this is a local favorite, and reservations are at a premium. The eclectic cuisine features fresh fish, lamb, USDA Prime beef, a bevy of pastas, and housemade breads and desserts. Open for dinner only.

JOHANNES RESTAURANT $$$–$$$$
196 South Indian Canyon Dr.
(760) 778-0017

Austrian + Pan-Pacific = Cosmopolitan? Perusing the menu at Johannes, the range of the menu is stunning. Not in sheer number of items, rather in inspiration. And then there is the sense of awed admiration for whomever it is who sources salmon from Scotland, scallops from Maine, beef from Australia, and lamb from New Zealand. Johannes Bacher is at the helm of this ship of the world, and for coming up with Thai shrimp curry and schnitzel on the same night you just gotta wonder what they put in the water in Austria. Is this guy Puck's little brother? Johannes is perhaps the most persnickety of the valley's high-end eats, with every item a complex and imaginative blend of ingredients and a visual treat that screams both forethought and execution. At times it might get just too-too refined for some, and portions don't necessarily run to Golden Corral dimension. But it is bright and lively and provocative, and it all comes together in one of the loveliest spots in town. Dinner only and they work right through the summer.

LORD FLETCHER'S INN $$–$$$
70-385 Hwy. 111, Rancho Mirage
(760) 328-1161
www.lordfletcher.com

Since the mid-'70s this chophouse mated to an English manor has been churning out prime rib, lamb shanks and racks, various swimmers, and just enough British Isles-reminiscent pot roast and rice pudding to warrant those twin banners of "Jolly Olde" and "steak place." It's all rather Windsorian in look, and while that might seem more kitschy today than in years past, it works. The lord serves commendable chow at very good prices—entrees include soup/salad, bread, and sides—and there are nightly specials that lower the price bar even farther. After almost 40 years, this is still a desert favorite, with affordable prices and generous portions of such comfort food as roast chicken and meat loaf, as well as lamb, ribs, and fresh fish. English rice pudding is a staple dessert, made fresh daily and served with whipped cream. The pub, main dining room, and Shakespeare Room are stuffed with interesting bits and pieces of British bric-a-brac, and the service is always warm and unpretentious. Open for dinner only. Closed in the summer.

PIERO'S ACQUA PAZZA $$
71-800 Hwy. 111, Rancho Mirage (The River)
(760) 862-9800

A "California-style bistro" with an Italianate name that gives a nod toward Mediterranean cuisine in that all-American creation the "retailtainment" center that's named The River even though it's in the middle of the desert…what a mix. And it continues on the menu, which has a certain Cheesecake Factory we-are-the-world diversity to it if not done up in a bit higher culinary fashion. There are burgers and panini, entree salads of every ilk, pizzas and a raw bar, and surf, turf, pasta and rotisserie. Piero's is a happening place and when the weather is right, sitting outside "river" side is the way to go.

FRENCH

CAFÉ DES BEAUX-ARTS $$
73-640 El Paseo Dr., Palm Desert
(760) 346-0669
www.cafedesbeauxarts.com

Right in the heart of the El Paseo Drive shopping district, this is a great place to people-watch while refueling from a hard day of browsing art galleries, jewelry stores, and gift boutiques. Sidewalk seating is at a premium, and changing exhibits of fine art from neighboring galleries provide color. The menu features sandwiches and soups with a Mediterranean–French flair, classics such as coq au vin, and a great children's menu with a twist—ham-and-cheese crepes instead of a standard grilled cheese. There's a standard prix fixe, three-course dinner, with a good selection of French and Californian wines. Open for breakfast Fri through Mon and for lunch and dinner daily.

CUISTOT $$$$
72-595 El Paseo Dr., Palm Desert
(760) 340-1000
www.cuistotrestaurant.com

Designed with a contemporary interpretation of a grand French farmhouse, this spot features a huge stove island surrounding the open kitchen so diners can see the chefs at work. There's also a spacious patio with an outdoor fireplace and waterfall, as well as a wine room for private parties. French-born Chef Bernard Dervieux has been at the helm since 1987 and has won numerous awards for his creative, consistently high-quality cuisine that marries "modern light" to classic Gallic. Open for lunch and dinner only.

LA QUINTA BAKING COMPANY $$
78-395 Hwy. 111, La Quinta
(760) 777-1699
www.laquintabaking.com

This combo bistro-bakery is a winner breakfast, lunch, and dinner. Plopped down in the middle of one of those oh-so-La Quinta-looking shopping centers of faux abode and red tile, it's a little touch of Paris in the California desert. Pastry, crepes savory or sweet, croque-monsieur, quiche,

rack of lamb or sole meunière, this place moves through every taste of the day from its waiting-at-the-door 8 a.m. opening to lights out 13 hours later. Put LQBC on your short list and bring a newspaper because you'll be far from the only ones doing so. Dinner reservations are taken, however. Et pommes frites? Mais oui. (By the way, they were invented by Belgians.)

LE ST. GERMAIN $$$$
74-985 Hwy. 111, Indian Wells
(760) 773-6511
www.lestgermain.com

It's east valley high-brow at this Indian Wells dinner establishment, where France meets a bit of Italy. While "French" in the desert often strays far from the reservation, Le St. Germain keeps it close in, as in filet crusted in Roquefort with a reduction, lamb rack with a coat of pistachio and mint jus, or duck breast and leg confit brought nicely local with a date relish. There are private rooms for 20–100, and a lot of politicking and deal-making has been done in 'em over the years. If crust has an upper this is where it hits the top of the wood-fired brick oven, so to say, and Timmy and Little Lisa might prefer pizza at home with the sitter.

LE VALLAURIS $$$$
385 West Tahquitz Canyon Way
(760) 325-5059
www.levallauris.com

For seemingly eons, Le Vallauris has been the place to go to impress your date, your boss, or even just yourself. This is old Palm Springs money combined with old Palm Springs warmth. When the Gabor sisters—for the young 'uns in the audience think mid-range players on a Pleistocene TV set—were all alive, this was their favorite luncheon spot, and it is still the favored place for wealthy, stylish ladies who lunch. The walled, tree-shaded patio is misted or heated depending on what the Weather Channel is saying. Inside, the bar and several dining rooms ooze casual elegance. The food is classic French, always fresh, and surprisingly reasonable in the sense there is immense quality and value for the coin outlay. The service is impeccable, and as with Le St. above perhaps just beyond where the kids are really gonna get it. Open for lunch and dinner only, seasonally.

POMME FRITE $$
256 South Palm Canyon Dr.
(760) 778-3727
www.pomme-frite.com

Set off busy Palm Canyon Drive, this is a real find, a cozy European-style bistro with French–Belgian specialties such as steamed black mussels, beef stew, bouillabaisse, and lots of Belgian beers. The tables are close enough to hear your neighbors' conversations, so don't book this if you're hoping for a romantic, private meal. Hey, that sounds so European. Open for dinner only, closed Tuesdays.

WALLY'S DESERT TURTLE $$$$
71775 Hwy. 111, Rancho Mirage
(760) 568-9321
www.wallys-desert-turtle.com

Long before the influx of restaurants featuring California/New American/Nuevo Continental/WhateverFusion cuisine, Wally's set the standard for opulent dining. With its fine French-whisper of Italian food and showy elegance, it still resonates for both foodies and "occasion" dinners. With flickering candles reflected in mirrored walls and polished silver, fresh flowers everywhere, and extremely attentive service, there's a venerable rich and famous ambience of another era to the place. Dinner served seasonally.

ITALIAN

AL DENTE PASTA $$
491 North Palm Canyon Dr.
(760) 325-1160
www.aldente-palmsprings.com

The menu includes homemade pasta, grilled chicken, steaks, veal, and fresh seafood. The scaloppini marsala and the four-cheese pasta are notable, as is the fresh bread that is always warm from the oven. It's a small, intimate spot perfectly placed for the first or last stop on a stroll around Palm Canyon Drive. The restaurant features an extensive wine list and is open for lunch and dinner only.

CAPRI ITALIAN RESTAURANT $$–$$$
12260 Palm Dr., Desert Hot Springs
(760) 329-6833
www.capri-italianrestaurant.com

One of the best restaurants in the desert and certainly the best in Desert Hot Springs, this busy, casually elegant place is famous for its thick, juicy steaks—either USDA Prime or Choice—as much as its more traditional Italian fare, be that shrimp fra diavolo or tortellini. The atmosphere is warm and noisy. You'll leave feeling like a very well-fed member of a large Italian family. Open for dinner only, closed Mondays.

CASTELLI'S RISTORANTE $$$$
73-098 Hwy. 111, Palm Desert
(760) 773-3365
www.castellis.cc

With 20-plus years in the desert, this spot has a well-established reputation for personal service and classic Italian cuisine, be that something as simple and rustic as fettuccine Alfredo or something more layered like osso buco. Castelli's is also a good reminder that Italian cuisine is far more than pasta and pomodoro, and that spit-roasting (spiedini) is a cornerstone of the cucina, so consider some carne. It's a cozy, intimate space, perfect for that someone special. Open for dinner only, closed July and Aug.

CIRO'S $$
81-963 Hwy. 111, Indio
(760) 347-6503
www.cirospasta.com

A lot of "up-valley" folks think food ends not far from the noon-time shadow of Mt. San Jacinto. While we know great eats scatter about the valley, if pizza is the gig, Ciro's is the place. The menu is rounded out by all the usual suspects, done the Joisey Italian way.

MAGIE RISTORANTE ITALIANO $$
333 North Palm Canyon Dr.
(760) 322–1234

Set in a sunken patio on North Palm Canyon Drive, Magie is a great place for people-watching while you savor a garlicky pasta, chicken, or veal dish. Everything's fresh, and the service is gracious. It's neither avant-garde nor contemporary—just good American-traditional Italian. Open for lunch and dinner only.

THE NAKED NOODLE $$
81-944 Hwy. 111, Indio
(760) 347-9999
www.nakednoodle.net
No, it just sounds like Little Italy, what with Ciro's and this joint right across the highway from each other. Anyway, which Little Italy would it be, the Jersey-Sicilian variant or Naked's more ecumenical approach to Boot Country Cuisine? As the name implies, pasta is big here. Ironically it is dressed more ways than Cher in a three-hour performance.

PAPA DAN'S $$
73-131 Country Club Dr., Palm Desert
(760) 568-3267

38-180 Del Webb Blvd., Building A,
Palm Desert
(760) 360-3456
www.papadanspizzaandpasta.com
If you insist on acting out the pizza equivalent of the Hatfields and McCoys, Dan tosses 'em neither New York nor Chicago. So there. They're thicker-not-thick-yet-not-readily-foldable crust pies with the ingredients assembled in the "correct" order, and the edges get the necessary bubbling. Extremists can call it a eunuch's compromise. We call it delicious. Then there is the array of baked and twirl-able pastas, seafood, cutlets of various species, and subs. This is a popular place, more so at dinner than lunch, and at times the front of the house does NOT handle the pressure well. Thankfully the kitchen is immune.

RISTORANTE MAMMA GINA $$$–$$$$
73-705 El Paseo, Palm Desert
(760) 568-9898
www.mammagina.com
Mamma does Italian. Every course. With nearly an encyclopedic array within each. From zuppe to dolce, she is all about how dining is done in

the old country—which is fitting as there is a ristorante in the famiglia back in Firenze. The design is clean, modern, almost clublike, in a toned-down sense, and there's not a checkerboard cloth or a Chianti candle in sight, and a wine bar has been added. Add in the professional staff and this gal could hold her own in any food-mad town.

SIROCCO AT RENAISSANCE
ESMERALDA RESORT AND SPA $$$$
44-400 Indian Wells Lane, Indian Wells
(760) 773-4666, (800) 552-4386
Far too often the most notable thing about high-end restaurants at high-end resorts is the number of times a patron has to hit the ATM while trying to pay off the tab. That's not to say there aren't all-star eats that weld value to quality and cost; there are a good number in the valley. But if looking for the all-world performer, certainly in Italian and perhaps of any ilk, follow the wind to Sirocco. Elegant, straightforward, impeccable, Sirocco does Italian as art. Bring a lot of money and if you are a son or daughter of Uncle Sam remember that not all the world eats by the stopwatch—have many courses and savor. Dinner only.

MEXICAN AND SOUTHWESTERN

ADOBE GRILL $$–$$$
49-999 Eisenhower Dr., La Quinta
La Quinta Resort & Club
(760) 564-411
www.laquintaresort.com
Befitting the original "Palm Springs" resort, Adobe Grill serves up the tastes and look of old Mexico, from the Saltillo paver flooring to the white-washed walls and horno fireplace to the several score tequilas, homemade tortillas, and zippy guacamole. The menu is as diverse as our southern neighbor and morphs with the changing seasons. Dine outside and take in the Santa Rosa Mountains and the comely resort's plaza.

BLUE COYOTE $$
445 North Palm Canyon Dr.
(760) 327-1196
www.bluecoyote-grill.com

This started out as a tiny cafe-cum-patio on North Palm Canyon Drive in the years before that area became known as the gallery and antiques section of town. It's been hugely successful, at least in Palm Springs, as several expansion attempts out into the valley over the eons have gone awry. Plenty of familiar plates dot the menu, but what sets the coyote apart is the heavy influence of southern Mexico and the Yucatan, so lots of citrus, achiote paste, a variety of meats, black beans. The signature margarita is, in a word, BUENO—likely the best we've found anywhere, and not just in the desert. And they are strong. Just ask a certain someone who will go nameless who had two and then rode out the post-dinner evening of shopping at the outlets sitting alone on a bench while everyone else shopped. It's a popular spot during happy hour, as you can imagine. The decor is vibrant and whimsical, whether dining outdoors or in one of several open-air indoor spaces. Open for lunch—not midweek during the summer—and dinner.

EL GALLITO RESTAURANT $
68-820 Grove St., Cathedral City
(760) 328-7794
This is the famous "hole-in-the-wall" Mexican restaurant you always want to find but hear about only after you've left town. If you yearn for fresh, simple, homemade Mexican food with salsa that sears every corner of your mouth, this is the place. Service is warm and friendly, prices are dirt-cheap, and portions are huge. Open for lunch and dinner only.

JACKALOPE RANCH $$$–$$$$
80-400 Hwy. 111, Indio
(760) 342-1999
www.restaurantsofpalmsprings.com
This could be the triple crown of cuisine—southwestern, barbecue, grill. The problem is, the first couple times by we kept on going 'cause the stone entry treatment, desert-as-a-nursery landscaping and exposed beam and tile building all added up to something—a boutique inn, an estate for someone with a lot of bucks and a cool sense of humor, a professional complex for the top-tier of star-serving clinicians, not a new and vibrant restaurant. Luckily the caricature of the mysterious and elusive, seldom-seen-in-the-wild jackalope finally penetrated thick skulls. The ranch is playful in design, atmosphere, and menu. Lunch runs toward rock shrimp or cochinita pibil tacos, big salads, and barbecue done as platters or sandwiches. Grilled meats and seafood and full-on barbecue move front-center at night, and the smoky good stuff comes with choice of traditional (depending on whence you hail) vinegar-based, prickly pear, or guava barbecue sauces. Included and added sides run from steakhouse-standard to more befitting the ranch, be that agave roasted sweet potato puree or southwest mac-n-cheese. Lope on over, preferably with dinner reservations in paw.

LAS CASUELAS—THE ORIGINAL $$
366 North Palm Canyon Dr.
(760) 325-3213

LAS CASUELAS CAFÉ $$
73-703 Hwy. 111, Palm Desert
(760) 568-0011

LAS CASUELAS NUEVAS $$
70-050 Hwy. 111, Rancho Mirage
(760) 328-8844
www.lascasuelasnuevas.com

LAS CASUELAS QUINTA $$
78-480 Hwy. 111, La Quinta
(760) 777-7715
www.lascasuelasquinta.com

LAS CASUELAS TERRAZA $$
222 South Palm Canyon Dr.
(760) 325-2794
The Casuelas restaurants are a desert legend and wildly popular with locals and visitors. All feature excellent, well-priced Mexican food, and each has its own specialties. Las Casuelas, the original family cafe, offers an unchanging menu of well-loved Mexican dishes, such as enormous burritos and enchiladas. Terraza builds on that base with heart-healthy items and a substantial children's

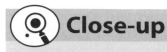 **Close-up**

Las Casuelas

In 1958 Maria Hernandez de Delgado and her husband, Florencio Delgado, opened the first Las Casuelas on Palm Canyon Drive in downtown Palm Springs. The two had met and married in Jerome, Arizona, where they operated the town's favorite Mexican restaurant, Armida's. Las Casuelas instantly became a hangout for everyone from Hollywood stars to local laborers.

All of the Delgado children grew up working in Las Casuelas—busing tables, serving, working the cash register, and learning in the kitchen. As the family grew, so did their restaurant business. Son Joaquin and his wife Sharon now operate the original Las Casuelas, known locally as "little Casuelas."

Some years later the Delgados opened Las Casuelas Terraza a few blocks south of the original on Palm Canyon Drive; it is now operated by daughter Patty, who is the eldest of the third generation. *Hispanic Magazine* has ranked Terraza among the "Top 50 Best Hispanic Restaurants in America" two years in a row. Numerous other awards and long lines waiting for tables year-round are testaments to the restaurant's popularity. Most locals refer to Terraza as "Las Cas," and no visit to Palm Springs is complete without a meal and a margarita here.

Named "Businessperson of the Year" and "Small Business Owner of the Year," Patty carries on the family tradition of community involvement, serving on the boards of the Desert Regional Medical Center, Agua Caliente Cultural Museum, Shelter from the Storm, and United Way of the Desert. As Patty says, "Part of what we've done at Terraza is to create a learning experience for those unacquainted with Mexican culture. The image of the comic-book Mexican lying under a cactus is so prevalent that we delight in dispelling it."

In 1973 daughter Florence and her husband Rick went on to open Las Casuelas Nuevas on Rancho Mirage's Restaurant Row. Patterned after a colonial hacienda in Mexico, this is the most elaborate of all the Casuelas establishments, and its central location draws diners from all points of the valley.

Designed by local architect David Christian, Nuevas fills the two requirements Maria and Florencio had: "Make it beautiful, and make it Mexican." The design takes the hole-in-the-wall stereotype of a Mexican restaurant and runs it out of town. Huge mahogany doors imported from Mexico, handmade saltillo and Talavera tiles, and wrought-iron chandeliers, lanterns, and arches lend an air of old-world elegance and style. Like its cousin Terraza, the restaurant rambles from patio to dining room to bar to more dining rooms, making a very large building seem intimate and cozy.

Kitchen design and efficient service are two Casuelas hallmarks, and the restaurants have set the standard for both in the desert. Every meal feels relaxed and intimate, even though each restaurant often serves as many as 1,000 a day. Newer additions to the restaurant family include Las Casuelas Quinta and Las Casuelas Café, both of which continue the Delgado tradition of presenting traditional Mexican fare in beautiful surroundings.

After more than 50 years in the desert, Las Casuelas is an intimate part of the community, and a good place to get a true feeling for the personality of Palm Springs—an ambitious and hardworking heart beneath a beautiful, relaxed face.

menu. Nuevas brings more salads into the mix; Quinta spotlights pasta, rotisserie, and barbecue; and cafe features breakfast fare along with the core of family favorites. All have a soft spot in their hearts for children and lots of seating options. All of the restaurants serve lunch and dinner.

LOS PEPES MEXICAN GRILL $$
73-091 Country Club Dr., Palm Desert
(760) 779-8977

The desert has mom-and-pop Mexican joints like cholla have spines. What's interesting about this well-appointed shop in a Palm Desert strip center is that for not much more than you'll spend at the corner taqueria, there's a noticeable step up in the care shown in assembling chile verde or tamale and no tell-tale trace of a bit too much grease left behind on the plate. There's a full bar where they shake a nice margarita that is assembled by someone who knows fresh lime is part of that equation and the proprietors truly appreciate your patronage. The fare is largely Sonoran but chef is not afraid to amble about the huge plate that is Mexico.

MACARIOS GRILL $$
80-783 Indio Blvd., Indio
(760) 342-5649
www.macariosgrill.com

The first time heading to Macarios you might be inclined to keep on driving, and maybe even more so during daylight hours than night. Please let the FULL parking lot be your beacon. Macarios is an institution in every positive aspect of that concept. The building seems to date from pre-war days—and that would be the Mexican–American War—and paint is likely the strongest element keeping it together. Patrons have been coming in so long they have personal rump patterns incised in multiple chairs, and the staff treats you as if it's Cheers, with pickled jalapeños and Modelo, of course. Feel free to venture across the menu, but do have a soup course and a queso fundido starter. Breakfast is served from 8 a.m. to 11 a.m. and there's a special dinner menu for the little ones. As for that URL, when Macarios morphed from a killer Mexican restaurant to a "grill" was lost on us.

SEAFOOD

FISHERMAN'S MARKET & GRILL $–$$
235 South Indian Canyon Dr.
(760) 327-1766

44-250 Town Center Way, Palm Desert
(760) 776-6533

72-840 Hwy. 111, Palm Desert
Inside the Westfield Mall
(760) 327-5880

78-575 Hwy. 111, La Quinta
(760) 777-1601
www.fishermans.com

With outstanding connections on the docks of San Pedro, they can guarantee fresh deliveries every day. The prices are very affordable, the atmosphere strictly paper napkins and Formica tables, the fish righteous; feel free to explore beyond the signature fish tacos, even if Anthony Bourdain and Rachel Ray did not. You order from the counter, and your food is cooked to order and delivered directly from the kitchen. The Palm Springs location has a funky little cocktail/oyster bar (Shanghai Reds) offering appetizers, beer, and wine from early evening. In Palm Desert and La Quinta, the restaurants are located in small shopping centers with plenty of parking, the Palm Desert mall location is a typical walk-up affair. All locations are open for lunch and dinner only, and if you're driving in to the desert from the west, there's another outlet in Banning.

OCEANS $$–$$$
67555 East Palm Canyon Dr.
Cathedral City
(760) 324-_54

Don't let the unprepossessing location fool you—Oceans is one of the best places in the desert for fresh seafood and fish done simply and served with panache. The specials change according to the market, the bread is fresh, and the setting is quiet and warm. A local favorite. Open for lunch and dinner only.

PACIFICA SEAFOOD
RESTAURANT $$$–$$$$
73-505 El Paseo, Palm Desert
(The Gardens at El Paseo)
(760) 674-8666
www.pacificaseafoodrestaurant.com

Upscale and vibrant, with great outdoor seating, as the name says, finfish and shellfish are the main attractions at Pacifica. Specials change daily in response to what's coming out of the water. Steaks, pasta, and salads are also available. This is a locals' favorite for happy hour and late-night cocktails. The children's bill of fare isn't cheap, but it's imaginative, with recognizable comfort fare on the "Beginning Diners" menu while "Future Fine Diners" might have shrimp, filet, or salmon from which to choose. Open for lunch and dinner.

SPORTS BAR

THE BEER HUNTER $–$$
78-483 Hwy. 111, La Quinta
(760) 564-7442
www.laquintabeerhunter.com
It's all about the numbers: 46+ TVs, 25 or so draft beers, close to 200 bottled beers, now that's some math that adds up. On the surface the food looks rather pub-standard—burgers, sandwiches, nachos. But at the Beer Hunter, the best sports bar in the desert, those are exceptional burgers, sandwiches made with real roasted turkey, and seriously wicked-good nachos. With dozens of bar spaces, big group tables and bleacherlike banquettes, there are many ways to plant your seat and take it all in, from the every-event-being-broadcast-right-now coverage to the, um, colorful fans of every-team-being-broadcast-right-now. Just keep the kids away from the Raiders contingent—they eat children, you know—and they'll love this joint. There's even free food for the little linebackers (two only, please, per paid adult) on Sun evenings.

YARD HOUSE $$
71-800 Hwy. 111, Rancho Mirage (The River)
(760) 779-1415
www.yardhouse.com
Don't bust our chips. Yard House is somewhat of a "chain," particularly across the Golden State. Other than the ability to replicate itself from spot to spot, it exhibits none of the symptoms that befall lesser replicants. The specialty of the house is beer, whether sold by the yard or the pint or the goblet. A lot of beer. As in, typically, 135 different kinds on tap as there is here in Rancho Mirage. (That's nothing, Long Beach's branch pushes pretty close to 300.) It's a "liquid bread" lovers dream of craft beers. The food is recognizable but imaginative, heavy on burgers, sandwiches, pizza, and pastas, but not to the exclusion of applewood smoked bacon mac-n-cheese, entree salads, fresh fish, and chops, with an emphasis on fusion, if not of "California Cuisine" proportions. The appetizer menu is stacked, and do have the deconstructed spicy tuna roll. In fact, you can make a meal of appetizers weekdays from 3 to 6 p.m. when most of them are half off, as are the pizzas. And of course the houses matches that with wine, beer, and martini deals. For sports fans there are flat-screens everywhere and they pump good old fashioned rock-and-roll through the sound system. Now if only the house would put its spin on breakfast.

VEGETARIAN

NATIVE FOODS $–$$
1775 East Palm Canyon Dr.
(760) 416-0070

73-890 El Paseo Dr., Palm Desert
(760) 836-9396
www.nativefoods.com
This is a consistently good "health food" spot, and make sure to check the menu because the daily specials change with regularity. One that might stick around owing to popular demand is the Palm Springs location's Saturday "chicken-fried steak" dinner featuring seitan as the star attraction. Tofu, tempeh, beans, and veggies are the mainstays, and the cuisine leans to Mexican and South American tastes. Open for lunch and dinner. No alcohol.

NIGHTLIFE

As recently as 20 years ago, the concept of "nightlife" in Palm Springs was limited to a handful of lounges with DJs or the occasional live group, playing tunes for two different crowds—the early 20-somethings or the late 60-somethings. Antiquated "cabaret" ordinances in the city of Palm Springs, which has the valley's only real downtown, banned outdoor dining and made it mandatory that neighborhoods around the downtown area were quiet after 9 p.m. This put a severe crimp on any high-stepping, hip-shaking, hollering fun. When the sun went down in the desert, people had dinner and went to bed early, all the better to get up for a dawn tee time or a few laps around the pool.

As Palm Springs began dying on the economic vine, the market forced a change, and in the late 1980s the city created Thursday night VillageFest to attract locals to the downtown area and encourage visitors to come early for the weekend.

VillageFest turned the sleepy downtown into a vibrant, crowded party where shops, restaurants, and bars stayed open late to entice business from the street fair. At about the same time, The Fabulous Palm Springs Follies opened downtown, followed by several new nightclubs and restaurants with live music. Cafes put tables and chairs out on the sidewalks. People started going to bed a little later and playing golf a little later the next morning.

In the large resort hotels, nightclubs, and dance spots opened to entertain guests and became favorite local hangouts. Then the casinos came along and stepped up the pace once again.

Desert nights have changed considerably in the past 20 years, but the variety and quality of entertainment is still nowhere near what you will find in Los Angeles, San Diego, or the beach communities in Southern California.

Sometimes there are too many fun things happening to get to all of them in one visit. The next time you come, you may find nothing but a few bars with recorded music. If that happens, do what the locals do—go to bed early and pop up the next morning for another day of brilliant sunshine.

One benefit of the desert's laid-back attitude is the rarity of cover charges. Only a few nightclubs routinely charge at the door, and those that do will rarely have a cover charge on Sunday through Thursday nights. We have noted those establishments with a cover charge policy. It is always a good idea to call ahead to verify this, particularly on weekend nights in season. One thing to keep in mind is the age requirement for entering casinos—it's 21, though families can bring their children to eat in the casino restaurants.

CASINOS

AGUA CALIENTE CASINO
32-250 Bob Hope Dr., Rancho Mirage
(760) 321-2000, (888) 999-1995
www.hotwatercasino.com
A beautifully designed facility that might come closest in the desert to capturing the look and style of Vegas—if you are a Sin City fan envision, say Green Valley Ranch—this is the second venture of the Agua Caliente, who were responsible for starting the high-end gaming business in Southern California. There are all the most popular table games, from Pai Gow Poker and Mini-Bac to Blackjack and Let-It-Ride, an 11-table nonsmoking poker room, a high-limit room, and

video poker and all the latest slots. Six eating spots include The Steakhouse, a deli, and coffee shop. The showroom and lounge feature live entertainment from the Vegas circuit and dancing to live local and regional groups.

AUGUSTINE CASINO
84-001 Avenue 54, Coachella
(760) 391-9500
www.augustinecasino.com
More casual and low-key than the big desert casinos, Augustine is the latecomer to the valley lineup. Its location, at the far eastern edge of things, past Indio, may keep it less popular and make it harder to attract the big crowds, but it's still a casino, and gamblers play there every day. Two restaurants offer moderately priced fare and the joint books some heard-of third-tier acts.

FANTASY SPRINGS RESORT CASINO
84-245 Indio Springs Parkway, Indio
(760) 342-5000, (800) 827-2946
www.fantasyspringsresort.com
This is the valley's most complete casino resort and it has the biggest permanent entertainment venue. Regular special events include top concerts, rodeos, and sporting events. In the 80,000 square feet of gambling space, there are almost 2,000 slots, 40 tables, poker, bingo, and off-track satellite horse wagering. The Springs cocktail bar also has 44 bar-top machines and loads of flat-screens. The adjoining hotel is surprisingly luxurious and well-appointed. The resort has a gym, a great pool complex, golf course, and bowling center.

For entertainment, Special Events Center books far more nearer-top-end talent than the competition, with the Fantasy Lounge taking smaller acts. Rock Yard happens every weekend, with a succession of tribute acts, and Velvet Palm Night Club atop the hotel is a hot place to chill and slurp a martini. Food runs the gamut with all the casino standards—steak, cafe, quick eats—and The Bistro is a notable addition to the east valley dining scene, with outdoor and inside-by-the-fire seating, an eclectic mix of California–

Italian fare, and sushi; does everyone sell sushi in this day and age? The Bistro also gives a nice break from the smoke of the casino.

MORONGO CASINO, RESORT & SPA
I–10 at Seminole Dr., Cabazon
(800) 252-4499
www.morongocasinoresort.com
Over many years and some number of lives, Morongo Casino has morphed from a bingo hall to a wannabe casino to a full-on destination resort. The casino offers nearly 150,000 square feet of gaming—one of the largest gaming floors on the West Coast. Numbers always vary, but count on somewhere in the neighborhood of 2,000 slots and 100 table games, a high-limit room, poker and bingo. With its location right on I–10 to the west of Palm Springs, Morongo attracts a lot of business from inland Southern California, as well as the desert and a sizeable lot of long-haul truckers taking a break from CB static and white line fever.

Multiple entertainment venues, including a 26th-floor, hotel-topping aerie of a bar that has a fabulous 360-degree view of the desert, with dramatic floor-to-ceiling windows. Mystique Lounge features live entertainment on the weekends, plus Sunday- and Monday-night football. There's also a full-service spa and a major hotel attached to the casino, should you feel in need of a nap and a facial before hitting the club. The entire complex is adjacent to the Desert Hills Premium Outlets and Cabazon Outlets shopping area.

SPA RESORT CASINO
401 East Amado Rd.
(760) 321-2000, (888) 999-1995
www.hotwatercasino.com
The desert's first casino and the only one in downtown Palm Springs, Spa Resort Casino offers 1,000 slots, 32 table games, a high-roller room, and continual promotions. Just across the street from the Spa Hotel, the casino takes up an entire city block and is within easy walking distance from almost all of the city's major hotels.

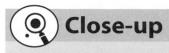 **Close-up**

Casinos

When the U.S. Indian Gaming Regulatory Act passed in 1988, it set in motion a cascading series of political maneuvers that have created the biggest change in the Palm Springs area since the arrival of air-conditioning. The act's intention was to make it legal for Indian tribes to offer the same types of gaming that were already legal in each state. That sounds simple on its face, but given the scale of gaming revenues and the fact that neither the states nor the federal government can tax these revenues (each Indian tribe is a sovereign nation), the game gets much more complex. In California it took years of lobbying and a series of referendums before the tribes could actually move on this new initiative.

In Palm Springs the Agua Caliente Band of Cahuilla Indians, owners of the Spa Hotel, had gone through all the required hoops to open a casino in that hotel. All, that is, with the exception of one odd regulation that made it illegal to transport slot machines within the state. They had purchased hundreds of the slots and were ready to install them for a planned grand opening. What to do? In a masterful move akin to cutting the Gordian knot, the tribe simply moved the machines in overnight, avoiding the watchful eyes of the regulatory commission staff, and the next morning they were open for business.

Because tribes do not report their revenues to local, state, or federal governments, the exact amount of their gaming revenue is a closely held secret. By any standards, though, the amount is stunning. Since opening the Spa Resort Casino in Palm Springs, the Agua Calientes have set up health and education funds for all their tribal members, donated impressive sums to local charities, built an elaborate new casino—the Agua Caliente—just off I-10 in Rancho Mirage, purchased their own bank, funded their Cultural Museum, and embarked on many other successful ventures.

The state of California, which fought so hard (with urging from Las Vegas lobbyists) to prevent Indian gaming, is now working just as hard to get a share of the gaming money. The state's power to negotiate compacts with tribes and approve additional slots, tables, and locations is their ace in the hole. Southern California is the fastest-growing gaming market in the country right now. Since the state can't tax the tribes, the governor is working on deals that would have the tribes pay "fees" for the gaming franchise, adding an additional "fee" for each machine they add.

In the Palm Springs area, the casinos have done much to change the sleepy, somewhat elitist feeling of the valley, drawing thousands of day-trippers from all over Southern California. They are also the main draw for big-name entertainers, many of whom spend their lives on the road traveling from casino to casino across the country. You'll find many of the same stars that headline Vegas here, as well as a constantly changing lineup of midlevel performers. The casinos' restaurants are among the best in the valley, and the prices are extremely good. After all, the dollars you leave at the table or slot machine on your way out the door after dinner will more than compensate for the pennies the kitchen gave up to serve prime rib at the best price within a hundred miles.

With their newfound financial success, the desert tribes have been excellent neighbors, contributing to valley charities and making sure that all their tribal members share in the bounty. Many desert old-timers feel that if the casino explosion has a downside for the valley, it has to do with the slight but growing loss of the small-town atmosphere and the influx of day visitors who come just for the gaming.

The Cascade Lounge draws a lot of locals to dance and drink and is one of the most popular downtown spots for visitors as well. Restaurants include steak, Asian, Mexican, and a buffet.

SPOTLIGHT 29 CASINO
46-200 Harrison Place, Coachella
(866) 377-6829
www.spotlight29.com
Owned by the small Twenty-Nine Palms Band of Mission Indians, the casino was formerly known as Trump 29, as the Donald's management company had the contract to run the place. Spotlight 29 is one I–10 exit east of Fantasy Springs, making it the last stop to put a handle in your hand before reaching Arizona. On the gaming floor there are 2,000 slots, 30 table games, and a poker room with hold 'em, Omaha and 7-Card Stud High-Low, and the casino sponsors a raft of daily tournaments. Spotlight is known for having a huge inventory of penny slots, to go along with the other denominations.

Blue Bar features Monday Night Football in season and DJ music on the weekend. Spotlight Showroom seats 2,200 and rotates a variety of live dance music on the weekends, plus country DJ music on Wed, salsa on Thurs, and Sunday-afternoon and Monday-night football. The jewel in the dining crown is JEM Steakhouse and Bar.

GAY NIGHTLIFE

Palm Springs is known around the country as having one of the hottest nightlife scenes for GLBT locals and visitors, and gay men in particular. In addition to the annual White Party (see Annual Festivals and Events), there are a number of bars, dance spots, and lounges catering to gay men.

BARRACKS
67-625 East Palm Canyon Dr., Cathedral City
(760) 321-9688
www.thebarracksbarps.com
This is just about as wild as it gets in the gay nightclub scene. Barracks is a leather/fetish place, so be prepared for just about anything on busy weekend nights.

BLAME IT ON MIDNIGHT
777 East Tahquitz Canyon Way
(760) 323-1200
www.blameitonmidnight.com
Set in the lower level of the building that houses one of the city's movie complexes, this has become a very dressy, ultra-chic spot to have dinner and check out the competition. The food is excellent, the drinks are strong, and the staff is engaging.

Gay bars and restaurants change names, locations, and owners frequently. For the most up-to-date information, pick up a copy of the local gay newspaper, *The Bottom Line* (www.psbottomline.com).

CONFESSION
611 South Palm Canyon Dr.
(760) 416-0950
This place, formerly Headhunters Dance Haus, is almost all dance floor, with a wild light system and a pounding selection of techno and disco. It seems to attract every gay man in Southern California at one time or another and is especially busy during White Party and Pride Weekend.

EL DESTINO NIGHTCLUB
83-085 Indio Blvd., Indio
(760) 864-6574
www.eldestinonightclub.com
Reputedly the first gay Latino nightclub in the valley, El Destino moves at least some of the nightlife scene away from the west valley.

HUNTER'S VIDEO BAR
302 East Arenas Rd.
(760) 323-0700
www.huntersnightclubs.com
One of the city's oldest gay spots, Hunter's is in the middle of the predominantly gay section of Arenas Road just off Indian Canyon.

TOOL SHED
600 Sunny Dunes Rd.
(760) 320-3299
www.toolshed-ps.com

Billing itself as "Palm Springs' only leather and Levis cruise bar," this is a no-frills corner bar known as a popular place to meet the burly, bearded guys who refer to themselves as "bears." Pounding recorded music and typical bar food set the stage for crowds every weekend.

i Gay men's clubs and bars in the desert offer a Sunday-night "beer bash," where inexpensive pitchers and an open-house atmosphere welcome men to move from club to club and catch up with friends.

TOUCANS TIKI LOUNGE
2100 North Palm Canyon Dr.
(760) 416-7584
www.toucanstikilounge.com
The decor is faux rain forest, with tropical touches, festive drinks, and "optional sarongs." This is one of the campiest spots on the gay scene, always a lot of fun and never serious.

NIGHTLIFE

What's nightlife? Is it a disco ball? A Deano-esque crooner trying to keep alive a bygone era? Two pitchers of Bud and tracking three games simultaneously at Chili's? Shaken drinks and cool conversation (or cool up until the point you wake up the next morn and marvel at what tumbles out of your mouth)? Loading up the Suburban and taking the brood to the multiplex. As with all cities and particularly vacation destination spots, you can find all of these across the valley. Following are a few thing to do. Think of them as representative, not exhaustive.

ARNOLD PALMER'S RESTAURANT
78-164 Avenue 52, La Quinta
(760) 771-4653
www.arnoldpalmers.net
Live entertainment nightly except Monday in the bar featuring desert favorite Kevin Henry and a tasty bar menu. The crowd is mostly middle-aged and country-clubby—men who spent the day on the golf course and women who took a lot

of time with their nails and hair before slipping in for a drink.

BLUE GUITAR
120 South Palm Canyon Dr.
(760) 327-1549
www.blueguitar.com
An anomaly in the desert, this little upstairs spot pumps out blistering soul, blues, and jazz with front man Kal David, singer Laurie Bono, and the Real Deal band. The cover is light and the space is quite tight, but the outdoor balcony gives a great view of the street action below on Palm Canyon, and the music is a shot of energy every time.

i Like everything else in the desert, nightlife runs hot and cold with the seasons. Check with your preferred spot to make sure it's open and live, especially in the summer. Many of the entertainers are on the Southern California circuit and are booked into beach spots in summer.

CANYONS LOUNGE, AGUA CALIENTE CASINO
32-250 Bob Hope Dr., Rancho Mirage
(888) 999-1995
www.hotwatercasino.com
All Indian casinos in the valley have some type of entertainment, and some nightly. This could be still-relevant giants of music or that comedy duo you remember from college, a DJ spinning classics or hip-hop, a live MMA event or Florida–Alabama on the big screens for all the SEC marbles. Canyons Lounge alternates mostly locally-hued entertainment and sports, so give a call over here to find out what's going on. And while it is a few miles out to Ramon and Bob Hope, it's nice that Agua Caliente sits mid-valley.

CASABLANCA ROOM
Melvyn's at the Ingleside Inn
200 West Ramon Rd.
(760) 325-2323
www.inglesideinn.com
Bits of Palm Springs cling to the past like gramps

lamenting the advent of divisional play in base-ball, so this is the place to go for real '50s-style piano bar music and sing-alongs in a tight little bar that clings to the aura of days gone by. Go early in the evening for a cocktail and some gossip. Late nights here tend to attract an older crowd looking for the old Rat Pack atmosphere.

COSTAS AT JW MARRIOTT DESERT SPRINGS
74-855 Country Club Dr., Palm Desert
(760) 341-1795
www.desertspringsresort.com
This is a high-energy nightclub with DJs and dance bands, and a frenetic atmosphere that harks back to the bad-hair days of the 1980s even as it steps across into a new century. Costas almost always charges a cover, and it's stuffed with tat-brat 20-somethings mixing with older couples or singles staying at the hotel on vacation or convention business.

HOG'S BREATH INN LA QUINTA
78-065 Main St., Second Floor, La Quinta
(760) 564-5556
www.restaurantsofpalmsprings.com
A cousin to Clint Eastwood's famous Carmel bar, this is a rowdy but cleaner version of an old-time saloon, with Hollywood memorabilia, a wide selection of tequilas and bottled beers, and a good bar menu. A piano bar provides entertainment on weekends.

JILLIAN'S
74-155 El Paseo Dr., Palm Desert
(760) 776-8242
www.jilliansfinedining.com
Piano entertainment Mon through Sat is a good accompaniment to drinks after dinner. Jillian's is a romantic little spot and very low-key, and the idea is to be a charming and witty conversationalist while cooly tapping your foot to a tune you don't realize was quite the rage at one point—no dancing or beer-bongs … sorry.

MCCORMICK'S NIGHTCLUB
74–360 Hwy. 111, Palm Desert
(760) 340-0553

Good, bad or otherwise, this may be the desert's best offering for dancers between 30 and 60, though that upper limit should be seen as more of a guideline than anything cast in concrete. Live rock 'n' roll brings out the hopefuls some nights, DJ tunes on others. There is usually a cover charge on weekend nights.

THE NEST
75-188 Hwy. 111, Indian Wells
(760) 346-2314
www.thenestindianwells.com
The Nest was a notorious spot back in the day, a pickup joint of repute for those who did such things before we all tried the John Travolta-in-*Saturday Night Fever* approach, and the tales of the exploits of pro golfers are legend. Well, the Nest is kinda in again and celebrities have been known to drop into the piano bar from time to time, so have a look-see for yourself. The dance floor is small so it can pack up as the hour gets later.

SULLIVAN'S STEAKHOUSE (THE GARDENS ON EL PASEO)
73-505 El Paseo Dr., Palm Desert
(760) 341-3560
www.sullivansteakhouse.com
This is a jumping spot for live jump blues, swing, and jazz. Martinis, wines, and cigars are the specialties from the bar. There can be a cover charge on weekend nights, especially during high season.

VILLAGE PUB
266 South Palm Canyon Dr.
(760) 323-3265
www.palmspringsvillagepub.com
The Village Pub, in downtown Palm Springs, features nightly entertainment, three full bars, a cigar bar upstairs, and a large tented patio. This is a rowdy, college-age crowd that often spills out onto the sidewalk and gets downright crazy on weekends. Open until 2 a.m.

SPAS

aken from the name of a celebrated watering hole in Belgium, "spa" technically refers to a mineral spring or any place with a mineral spring. The European spas that became enormously popular in the early 20th century were elaborate resorts where people came to "take the waters," sipping and bathing in natural hot mineral springs for a variety of health objectives. A hundred years later, the word has evolved dramatically—today it's not unusual to find hotels with no more than a hot tub and a sauna advertising their "spa."

To help you find exactly what you're looking for—from a simple soak in a natural hot mineral spring, to pampering massages and facials, to the most comprehensive health and fitness evaluations in an atmosphere of extreme pampering—we've compiled a representative listing of the desert's many excellent spas, along with some tips on getting value for your vacation dollar. To qualify as a spa for our listings, the establishment must either offer a variety of body and skin treatments that go well beyond what one would find in a typical beauty salon or day spa, or feature a genuine hot mineral springs pool for soaking. In the desert the most luxurious spas generally are located within large resort hotels, and they offer everything from medical screening to fitness classes and exotic body treatments.

To help you choose a favorite from the Coachella Valley's many options, we've grouped spas in two categories: Resort Spas and Hot Mineral Spring Spas.

Resort Spas are located within full-service hotels or resorts and offer a complete range of body and face treatments, as well as use of swimming pools, saunas and/or steam rooms, and fitness centers.

Hot Mineral Springs Spas, as the name states, have a natural mineral spring to supply water for the soaking/swimming pools. Hot mineral springs abound in the nearby city of Desert Hot Springs, and many small to midsize hotels are built around one or two pools that are filled with hot mineral water from the hotel's own underground wells. In this group there are midsize hotels with moderate prices and amenities, as well as those hotels whose only claim to spa fame is the water itself. These hotels can offer excellent value for long-stay visitors who enjoy simplicity and the reputed healing properties of the water.

Just like rates for hotel rooms, prices for spa services vary with the seasons, and visitors can get the best values in the hot summer months. Spa-accommodation packages are also a good way to save money in season. If you're staying at a resort with a spa, use of the spa, but not spa services, may be included in your room rate—always ask when you make reservations.

Prices for standard services such as a basic massage and facial do not vary much among the larger resorts, which are all in competition for the same customer—it's not unusual for a resort spa to have at least 30 percent of its clients come from the local population or from other hotels without spas. You can count on paying top dollar for the spas with the most elaborate facilities, such as large fitness centers, extensive "wet" facilities, on-site medical services, and top beauty salons. That said, these places may offer the best value if you are going to bundle up services during one visit, so always ask about package pricing. Prices for standard facials will run around $80 to $95, a half-hour massage will cost from $50 to $65, and a one-hour massage will cost from $95 to $150.

Spa 101

Reservations are de rigueur for all but some express services in some spas.

Most spas limit their services to guests who are 18 years or older.

Keep your appointment and be on time. Many spas will charge full price for skipped appointments. If you are 10 minutes late, expect your service to be 10 minutes shorter, in order to accommodate the guest following you.

You can request either a male or a female therapist; it's your treatment and you need to be comfortable. However, therapists are health care professionals so they give it no never mind and you should follow suit. We think the best strategy is to request whichever therapist excels at the chosen therapy, regardless of gender.

Leave your cell phone and pager behind—this is quiet time for everyone.

You'll be given a locker, robe, and shower shoes. Wear the robe in the relaxation room or lounge, to move about co-ed areas and to your treatment. Shower shoes should be worn everywhere, except in the pools and plunges.

If it's a sex-segregated facility it's up to you if you want to wear a bathing suit when using the steam, sauna, cold plunge, whirlpool, or whatever combo of goodies is offered. If you choose to skip the suit, always use a towel when seated in the sauna and steam room, in the locker area, etc.—just use your common sense.

Always tell your therapist if you have an injury, an area needing special attention or if anything is making you uncomfortable. A lot of therapies can be done with you wearing nothing but what you came into the world in, and that's for a reason. Therapists are skilled in draping. If you're still uncomfortable you can wear loose-fitting undergarments or something similar.

Allow extra time before and after your scheduled treatment to use the spa amenities, even the pool if there is one. This is YOUR time.

Ask, ask, ask, at any time before or during your experience. The spa wants you to be happy and comfortable.

Enjoy!

If you want just a basic massage, facial, or nail service, you will probably get the best deal by booking your appointment at a stand-alone day spa or beauty salon that doesn't offer the extra luxury of soaking tubs, saunas, pools, and a fitness center. A good source of recommendations is your hotel's concierge or front-desk staff. If the hotel has a spa, they'll certainly tell you about it and will also give you tips on where else to go.

Unless otherwise noted, the resort spas and mineral springs spas offer their services to non-hotel guests and include use of the adjacent fitness facilities, wet facilities, and other amenities when a service is purchased. Depending on whether the hotel has a "full house," some also offer day rates for use of the pool and fitness facilities without purchasing a service. Make sure to call ahead, because these policies are subject to change.

A note on "day spas": These facilities, often part of a beauty salon, do not offer lodging or such amenities as a fitness center, sauna/steam room, or swimming pool. They vary widely in scope and quality of service, and because most offer only basic massage and facial treatments, we have not included these in the listings below.

Readers should assume that all of the establishments listed accept major credit cards, unless otherwise noted.

RESORT SPAS

Resort spas offer all the amenities of a traditional vacation destination, including a complete selection of spa services, programs, and dining.

DESERT SPRINGS, A JW MARRIOTT RESORT & SPA
74-855 Country Club Dr., Palm Desert
(760) 341-2211, (800) 808-7727
www.desertspringsresort.com
One of the biggest convention and business hotels in the Southwest, Desert Springs has 450 acres, 884 rooms, two championship 18-hole golf courses, 18-hole putting course, 20 tennis courts, 10 restaurants and lounges, shopping arcade, and stunning, nearly brand new spa and fitness center.

Spa Desert Springs was wholly gutted and rebuilt in 2007, and what had been a venerable and at-one-time trend-setting facility jumped forward several evolutionary levels. The facility is massive, 38,000 square feet, yet totally embracing, with a guiding principle being the concept of "spa together," making the spa experience that much more inviting for couples and groups. Couples can book the Revive Suite, which has a hydrotherapy tub for two. The elite can snag the Spa Sanctuary, complete with private entry, butler, fireplace, and multiple tubs. There's even a spa within the spa for groups. There are same-sex and co-ed relaxation lounges—guys, yours has a 50" TV in it!—and the wet facilities include saunas with windows looking out over the golf course. The spa also has its own pool, and 4,000-square-foot fitness center.

Treatments remain familiar, which is good since Desert Springs has always been into Ayurveda in a big way. Ayurveda is an Indian healing system and under it spa treatments are personalized to match with each patron's dosha or energy pattern. Good stuff. If you just want to work things out with deep tissue, you can get that too. And there is a full-service salon.

DORAL DESERT PRINCESS RESORT
67-967 Vista Chino, Cathedral City
(760) 322-7000, (888) 386-4677
www.doralpalmsprings.com
A private condominium and hotel development, the Desert Princess has a 27-hole golf course and a beautiful location on the north side of Cathedral City near its border with Palm Springs. The Body Center'd Spa here is a small, well-kept facility with a limited array of massage and body treatments, plus basic salon services for hair and nails. Women's and men's saunas and a coed hot tub and lap pool are also available. The resort's small fitness center is located separately.

HYATT GRAND CHAMPIONS RESORT AGUA SERENA SPA
44-600 Indian Wells Lane, Indian Wells
(760) 341-1000, (800) 554-9288
www.aguaserenaspa.com

THE MEDICAL AND SKIN SPA
44-600 Indian Wells Lane, Indian Wells
(760) 674-4106
www.medicalandskinspa.com
When what today we call the BNP Paribas Open tennis tournament grew too large for the stadium at the Hyatt Grand Champions, Hyatt embarked on a major remodeling, updating rooms, enlarging their meeting space, and creating the remarkable Agua Serena Spa. This is one of the desert's top spas, in terms of both aesthetics and the variety of services they offer.

The 30,000-square-foot facility includes a spacious fitness center with modern equipment and free weights, personal training, and classes in yoga, aerobics, and Pilates. Every resort guest and spa patron gets to enjoy the center, as well as the steam room, sauna, and whirlpool adjoining the private locker rooms. The men's retreat area features a cold plunge pool, and the women's area has a private entrance to the realm of the Medical and Skin Spa. There is also an exceptional beauty salon.

The retreat, or relaxation, areas are much more than just a place to wait for a massage. Carrying out the decorating theme of rich wood, sleek tile and glass, and smooth stone, these lounges have indoor and outdoor areas with reclining teak chairs, reflecting pools, and aromatic herb gardens filled with the spa's signature scents of grapefruit and sage. Each of the spa's treatment rooms has a walled terrace and floor-to-ceiling windows overlooking beautiful garden areas and allowing each guest to have as much fresh air and natural light as desired. Eight of the treatment rooms also have private outdoor showers. There are also outdoor treatment rooms, a couples massage room, and a Vichy shower room.

The Desert Sage and Date Sugar Scrub is one of the spa's signature treatments, using organically grown Medjool dates from the date grove down the road, along with sage, juniper, grapefruit, and date sugar. These edible treats are whipped into shea, cocoa, mango, and kukui nut butters for a super-rich exfoliating and moisturizing treat.

Other original treatments include the Stone Facial, using smooth basalt stones, warm mud, and botanicals, and Fit2Golf, which combines a fitness consultation and training session, 18 holes of golf with swing analysis, and a one-hour sports massage.

The Medical and Skin Spa is a true medical office with all the luxurious trimmings and atmosphere of the spa next door. Specialties here are many of the most currently popular cosmetic procedures, such as Botox® and Restylane®, which are performed by the spa's founder and medical director, Dr. Richard M. Foxx. All clients have a personal consultation with the doctor, who also supervises the laser treatments for skin rejuvenation, hair removal, and spider veins. Microdermabrasion and all types of medical peels

are on the menu, as well as comprehensive health and lifestyle evaluations, hormone evaluations, and diet and vitamin analyses.

LA QUINTA RESORT & CLUB
49-499 Eisenhower Dr., La Quinta
(760) 777-4800, (800) 598-3828
www.laquintaresort.com

The doyen of the desert resorts, La Quinta Resort & Club opened in 1926 and has grown into a true destination, with sprawling, beautifully manicured grounds that contain both hotel rooms and plush casita-style lodging, five golf courses, 23 tennis courts, 41 swimming pools, and 53 hot tubs, plus three full-service restaurants, a fitness center, and the 23,000-square-foot Spa La Quinta, which was added in 2002. The Yamaguchi Salon (760–777–4800; www.yamaguchibeauty.com) and the WellMax Center for Preventive Medicine (800–621–5263; www.wellmax.com) are both part of the spa facility (see below).

One of the highlights of the spa is its outdoor Sanctuary Courtyard, a lushly landscaped extension of the spa itself. Here, guests can sign up for the Celestial Shower, a private open-air Swiss shower treatment with sprays of varying strength; soak in a private tub; or have a massage alfresco before or after a delicious health-conscious lunch. The soaking baths include the Seawater Soak, Citrus Soak, and Desert Rose Bath, all nice by themselves or as a prelude to a massage or one of the exotic body treatments, such as the cleansing/moisturizing Orange Blossom Special Body Facial. Men's facials and sports massages that target the specific muscles used in golf or tennis are also a specialty.

Adjacent to the spa is the Yamaguchi Salon, a top-notch hair and makeup spot, featuring hair and nail treatments based on each person's feng shui, as well as makeup applications and lessons.

The WellMax Center for Preventive Medicine, located off the resort plaza, is a one-stop medical testing and evaluation office that offers extensive physical examinations, including such components as CT scans of the lungs, conventional or virtual colonoscopy, hormone level testing, and on and on. Staff physicians are also available at Eisenhower Medical Center, the desert's largest and most respected hospital and research facility.

WellMax clients can spend as little as a half day and as much as four days getting all the tests and evaluations, and that's where the benefit of a spa next door is really seen. Somehow, having your blood drawn is a little more palatable when it's followed by a massage and facial.

ℹ **The rule of thumb on tipping is the same as it is for dining out: A 15 to 20 percent gratuity that reflects your satisfaction for the service is considered appropriate. Many resort spas automatically add a gratuity to the bill, so get a handle on that when you check in so you don't double up. If the locker room attendant is more involved with your experience than tossing you a towel while seated behind a desk, glued to the TV, tip accordingly.**

LE PARKER MERIDIEN PALM SPRINGS
4200 East Palm Canyon Dr.
(760) 770-5000, (800) 543-4300
www.parkermeridien.com

Ranked by *Condé Nast Traveler* as one of the top 10 spas in America for four years running, the Parker's Palm Springs Yacht Club spa began its life when the former Autry Hotel became the Givenchy Resort & Spa. Now under new ownership, the hotel has undergone a complete transformation. What was once a kitschy Versailles look-alike is now a popular and trendy retro hideout, complete with croquet and bocce ball courts, Joseph Adler-designed furniture and decor, and a tongue-in-cheek attitude. This, plus great service, is also the reigning atmosphere at the new spa, which has shed its French frosting look for a trim, nautical theme, and a lighter, breezier, more tongue-in-cheek attitude about itself. Thai-assisted stretching and massage is dubbed "Voodoo We Do." Get-down-into-those-muscles deep tissue is aptly "the Wringer." Stone massage is "Rock Star." Light. Breezy.

Student Aid

Savvy spa-istas know to do some homework before heading out on vacation. The subject matter? Massage school. Not in terms of enrollment, rather enjoyment. How do you think would-be therapists become therapists without a little hands-on training?

The Milan Institute's Student Spa in Indio offers the full range of "standard" massage therapies—Swedish, reflexology, shiatsu, sport, deep-tissue, pregnancy, therapeutic—performed by its student-practitioners. (Sounds a lot better than hitting the student practicum at the local dental school, eh?) And since it is part of the (supervised) curriculum the prices are nutty low, as in $35 for a 60-minute session and only $50 for 90 minutes. Sure you don't get the Watsu pool or the Perrier Inundation Shower or the free-range Dungeness and organic Tibetan whole-grain barley wrap option in the trendy spa cafe. But back-to-school never looked this good growing up.

Services are provided 1-6 p.m. Tues, 10 a.m. to 6 p.m. Wed through Fri, and 9 a.m. to 5 p.m. Sat, 45-691 Monroe St., Suite 5, Indio (760-347-9079; www.milaninstitute.edu).

Wraps, scrubs, facials, and waxing round out the spa offerings, and include "The Matriarch" and "Creature from the Beautiful Lagoon." Breezy. Light. An on-site beauty salon provides full hair and nail services.

Men's and women's areas are completely separate and clothing-optional. Each side has its own indoor swimming pools, Jacuzzi, and steam and sauna rooms. The 24-hour fitness center is also in the spa building and has a good selection of weights, machines, and classes—yoga, tai chi, chi gong, Pilates, and croquet classes are available throughout the day, both indoors and outdoors.

MIRAMONTE RESORT & SPA
45-000 Indian Wells Lane, Indian Wells
(760) 341-2200, (800) 237-2926
www.miramonteresort.com
A luxurious, midsize resort hotel with a Tuscan theme and 11 acres of winding gardens, Miramonte added The Well Spa in 2004. Right in step with the current trend of indoor/outdoor treatments, The Well Spa has a Watsu pool and a Vichy shower with tables made from 100-year-old acacia cedar. In the shallow spa pool, smooth stone benches make for "natural chaise lounges" and encourage lingering.

There are nine indoor and 10 outdoor treatment rooms; men's and women's steam, sauna, and locker facilities; a swimming pool and whirlpool; as well as a full-service beauty salon and 24-hour fitness center. The fitness center offers two outdoor pools with hot tubs, machines, free weights, and fitness classes. Personal trainers are available by appointment. Waxing is available in the spa, and nail services are also offered.

One of the spa's signature services is the Pittura Fiesta, or mud-painting party. Guests paint themselves or their partners with colored mud and clays, then let the sun bake the mud dry while aestheticians deliver a scalp massage and personalized pressure-point facial. A Swiss shower is the finale, rinsing off the detoxifying mud and leaving the skin soft and refreshed.

Italian-themed treatments are the signature here and include such services as the Wine Bath Cobblestone Massage, Mediterranean Veggie Organic Wrap, and Monticelli Mud Wrap.

RANCHO LAS PALMAS RESORT AND SPA
41-000 Bob Hope Dr., Rancho Mirage
(760) 836-3106, (877) 843-7720
www.rancholaspalmas.com

Spa Las Palmas, like the resort, is a bit of an overlooked gem tossed in with others that pack more carats. It's a great spa for newbies because it is very low on the intimidation scale. The facilities are complete yet manageable. There's the Spa Café so you lunch right there, in between, say, napping beside the spa-patrons-only pool and the restorative desert cactus wrap. Staff and therapists are low-key and attentive, and that's a winning combo. And that pool, well, there's music piped in underwater. For those who are really driven there's a fitness center and when it's all done the adjoining Yamaguchi Spa can get you ready for the night's activities (760-834-2170; www.yamaguchibeauty.com).

RENAISSANCE ESMERALDA RESORT AND SPA
44-400 Indian Wells Lane, Indian Wells
(760) 836-1265, (866) 236-2427
www.renaissanceesmeralda.com
Completed in 2002 and really not looking any older than a newborn, this comforting spa radiates ease the moment you enter across cool marble accompanied by the sound of trickling water. Spa Esmeralda checks in with a svelte assemblage of a dozen-plus treatment rooms and a while-away-the-day Spa Garden, where waterfall soaking pool and private treatment cabanas await. If traveling in tandem, several rituals will get vacation started just right, or send you off in bliss mode: Couples Retreat rounds up a rose elixir bath for two, mud masks, and twin-massage performed in your private spa suite. The spa of course offers the full roster of massage, body, and skin treatments, as well as a salon.

THE RITZ-CARLTON, RANCHO MIRAGE
68-900 Frank Sinatra Dr., Rancho Mirage
(760) 321-8282, (800) 542-8680
www.ritzcarlton.com
The Le Prairie Spa at the Ritz-Carlton opened recently when the property itself emerged from a lengthy, needed remodel and rebranding.

THE WESTIN MISSION HILLS RESORT AND SPA

71-333 Dinah Shore Dr., Rancho Mirage
(760) 328-5955, (800) 228-3000
www.starwoodspacollection.com

The new spa in this Spanish–Moorish theme resort is medium-size (13,000 square feet) with an intimate, cozy boutique atmosphere. All of the treatments are indoors, and guests have the use of steam rooms, hydrotherapy rooms, lockers, Jacuzzi, and a full fitness center. Classes include yoga, the WestinWORKOUT®, cardio fitness, weightlifting, and personal training.

The menu isn't exhaustive but it covers enough bases with clay and aloe wraps, several scrubs, facials, and a variety of massages. One thing the Westin does have is Lomi Lomi, a Hawaiian modality of long rhythmic strokes of forearms or hands, and not always working the same area at the same time. Another signature treatment is hot and cold stone reflexology. The salon offers makeup, waxing, and nail services.

i Aside from a killer massage or facial or wrap, another great benefit of a spa service is being allowed to use the spa, all day if you'd like. Soaking, steaming, swimming, working out, even having some healthful victuals, it's a package deal. And resort spas almost always allow daily access for a relative small fee—$20, $30, $40, lunch not included—and think about how much money you won't be spending not out ambling about El Paseo Drive. At times this privilege is extended to non-hotel guests.

HOT MINERAL SPRINGS SPAS

No single culture has a corner on the market of seeking out and using hot mineral water. In fact, long before the once-every-Saturday bath became such a smashing rage, it's not hard to imagine some enterprising Cro-Magnon opening Mastodon Cave & Spa, in between bouts of painting Spanish caves, that is. The "waters" have been thought to cure a whole lot of stuff, and even if most of it was bunk, a date with Mother Nature's Jacuzzi is not a bad thing.

Most of "Palm Springs'" hot mineral springs are in Desert Hot Springs, the sprawling but not densely populated city at the northwest end of the valley. Unlike some of what bubbles up in Yellowstone or Mt. Lassen, these waters are odorless, tasteless, and colorless, something like that little bottle of Pellegrino the ristorante charged you eight bucks for at dinner last night. Because of these qualities, you can soak in it for hours without turning into a prune and you don't run the risk of coming out smelling like egg salad.

If you're looking for a soak in natural hot mineral springs, Desert Hot Springs is the place to be. The mineral springs well up from a hot-water aquifer, often rising to the surface at temperatures as high as 180 degrees, then cooled for use in the hotel pools, which keeps Little Jimmy from going the way of Larry the Lobster.

Few of the hotels listed here have full-service spas; many are modest accommodations built around the hot mineral springs, and their rates often reflect that fact.

AGUA CALIENTE HOTEL & MINERAL SPA

14-500 Palm Dr., Desert Hot Springs
(760) 329-4481, (800) 423-8109
www.aguacalientehotel.com

One of the best features of this little spot is the in-room mineral water Jacuzzis, although the outdoor pool is large and attractive as well. Many of the rooms have kitchens, and the hotel also offers monthly rates for retired individuals. The spa includes a fitness center with personal trainers; provides services such as massages, facials, wraps, and polishes; and has a beauty salon.

A fairly recent addition is the Desert Cruise Detox and Weight Loss Package, which includes lodging, meals, vitamin and mineral supplements, therapeutic treatments, detox baths, personal training, and nutritional classes.

DESERT HOT SPRINGS SPA HOTEL
10805 Palm Dr., Desert Hot Springs
(760) 329-6000, (800) 808-7727
www.dhsspa.com
This medium-size hotel features eight natural hot mineral pools and is set up for family use, with a lot of locals coming for the day just to soak and take it easy. There are separate men's and women's saunas and lockers rooms. In the less busy low season, the hotel often offers a special day rate for rooms and spa admission. It's always a good idea to call for availability. There is no fitness center, steam room, or beauty salon.

HOPE SPRINGS
68-075 Club Circle Dr., Desert Hot Springs
(760) 329-4003
www.hopespringsresort.com
Ten rooms, three pools—90 to 105 degrees—and a determined-to-be-hip attitude that comes straight from the hot mid-century architecture have transformed this little old motel into a favored destination for Southern Californians looking for the next new thing. Clean, light, and oh-so-retro in style, it offers three varieties of salt rubs, three different wraps, and nine types of massage. Meals can be arranged in advance and served poolside or in the rooms.

LIDO PALMS SPA RESORT
12-801 Tamar Dr., Desert Hot Springs
(760) 329-6033
www.lidopalms.com
An immaculate little mineral springs motel, Lido Palms has 10 remodeled one-bedroom king or double-queen guest rooms with full kitchens, wireless, Tempur-Pedic beds, robes, TVs and foot-cooling slate tiles.

One large swimming pool, two jetted hot tubs, one indoors and a just minted facility with three treatment rooms are what put "spa" in the name. There's an exercise room and a sauna, as well. Children and pets should be left in the care of their loving grandparents or others.

LIVING WATERS SPA
13-340 Mountain View Rd.,
Desert Hot Springs
(760) 329-9988, (866) 329-9988
www.livingwatersspa.com
This was a custom-made "spa-tel" in the 1960s and has been completely renovated. The owners kept the original neon Kismet Lodge sign, and the nine guest rooms also show a retro flair, but with a modern twist and amenities such as free Wi-Fi. Most come with full kitchens. There are also six two-bedroom units.

Be warned—this is one of the desert's clothing-optional places, and most guests take the no-clothes option. The hotel is designed to cater to couples, and there are no facilities or provisions for children. A covered soaking pool and outdoor swimming pool are, of course, full of hot mineral water. Lockers are available for day-use guests, who must bring their own towels.

MIRACLE MANOR SPA RETREAT
12-589 Reposo Way, Desert Hot Springs
(760) 329-6641, (877) 329-6641
www.miraclemanor.com
A six-room jewel furnished in a "desert Zen from the '50s" style, Miracle Manor has been featured in just about every travel publication in the country. The privacy, ambience, and attention from the owners are unbeatable, the rooms are clean and stylish (many also have kitchens), and the water is hot. This little place books up very quickly, so it's wise to check on reservations early in your vacation planning.

A single hot mineral pool is the center of the inn, and there are two separate treatment rooms situated at the opposite end of the property, for maximum privacy and quiet. Several different types of massage and facials are on tap. A signature treatment, Water Miracle, combines Thai and acupressure techniques while you float in a warm mineral pool.

MIRACLE SPRINGS RESORT & SPA
10-625 Palm Dr., Desert Hot Springs
(760) 251-6000, (800) 856-3174
www.miraclesprings.com
Something rather unique for the Desert Hot Springs hot water scene, Miracle Springs is of very recent vintage. The resort features eight mineral pools and a full-service spa with a complete range of massages, facials, body scrubs, wraps, nail services, and waxing.

The specialty here is the great variety of packages. A favorite of locals and guests at other hotels is one that includes day use of a hotel room, brunch, a massage, facial, wrap, and manicure/pedicure. After all that, you may be so relaxed that you decide to spend the night in one of the quiet, simply furnished rooms.

NURTURING NEST
11-149 Sunset Ave., Desert Hot Springs
(760) 251-2583, (888) 557-0066
www.nurturingnest.com
A little seven-room retreat newly renovated in the increasingly popular minimalist Zen style, Nurturing Nest is operated by its owners, holistic health practitioners Dr. Sandra and Ramesh Guné. Their specialty is three- to seven-day retreats tailored to each individual's needs and wants. A wide range of physical and counseling-oriented therapies, including energy healing, Ayurvedic treatments, yoga classes, and basic spa services, are on the menu for anyone taking the retreats or just staying for a few days. Breakfast is complimentary, and five of the rooms in the inn have full kitchens for those who want to prepare their own meals, the remaining two have small fridges.

SAGEWATER SPA
12-689 Eliseo Rd., Desert Hot Springs
(760) 220-1554
www.sagewaterspa.com
Originally built in 1954, the seven-room Sagewater has been beautifully restored and now offers top-of-the-line amenities such as European zillion-thread count linens, DSL connections, flat-screen TVs, DVD players, and kitchens stocked with designer coffee and coffee cakes. Guests can choose from a wide selection of massage and body treatments performed in their rooms, as well as Watsu massage in the outdoor mineral pool, the chemical composition of which is broken down on the resort's home page.

SAM'S FAMILY SPA
70-875 Dillon Rd., Desert Hot Springs
(760) 329-6457
www.samsfamilyspa.com
Built as a family park in 1971, Sam's has 50 acres available for tents, campers, travel trailers, and motor homes and also offers a small selection of motel rooms and mobile homes for rent. It's meant for long stays, though they are happy to accommodate those travelers who are just passing through and want to soak in the springs for a few days. The pools are fed from three wells on the property. This is the epitome of simple, laid-back, anything-but-stylin', family-oriented vacationing.

SPA RESORT CASINO
100 North Indian Canyon Dr.
(760) 778-1772, (888) 999-1995
www.hotwatercasino.com
It's a resort, it's a casino, and it's a spa. And it's also the desert's original spa and first casino. Located in the heart of downtown Palm Springs, the spa is built on top of the city's namesake hot springs, a sacred site to the Agua Caliente (hot water) Band of Cahuilla Indians, who are owners and operators of the resort and casino. An integral part of any visit to the spa is Taking of the Water, an experience that includes stops in the steam room, sauna, eucalyptus inhalation room, and mineral soaking tubs. An all-day pass to the spa includes this, as well as access to the fitness center, outdoor whirlpool, and swimming pool. Men's and women's spa areas are separate, and each includes these amenities as well as a number of treatment rooms. The fitness center offers machines, free weights, personal training, and a range of activity classes.

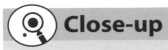 **Close-up**

The Spa Resort Casino

In Palm Springs there is no spot that has had a more pivotal role in the city's history and fame than the hot spring that now feeds the soaking tubs in the Spa Resort Casino. Considered a sacred place by the Agua Caliente Band of Cahuilla Indians, the spring was the heart of the tribe's winter social life for hundreds of years.

When Dr. Welwood Murray built the town's first hotel in 1887, he made sure to erect it as close as possible to the hot spring, which was reputed to have considerable curative powers. The water came out of the ground at around 104 degrees and had a distinctly sulfurous smell, unlike the odorless waters of the hot mineral springs in Desert Hot Springs.

Murray leased the site from the tribe for $100 a year and built a bathhouse and dressing rooms directly over the spring. It stood there until the tribe razed the shabby wooden building in 1916 and built their own bathhouse, which in 1939 charged just 25 cents per visitor. This bathhouse was an improvement over the older one, with the corners of four separate rooms intersecting over the spring, but it was still little more than a simple wooden building.

In 1957, as the tribe gained the authority to offer their property on long-term leases, developer Sam Banowit convinced the Tribal Council that he could build a hot springs bathhouse that would finally make a profit for them. As part of the agreement, he relocated the palm trees, sacred to the tribe, to another site on the property. Banowit later negotiated the first 99-year lease on Indian land and built the five-story Spa Hotel next to the bathhouse. With a slick modern hotel and tile-lined spa, the bathhouse once again became a center of social life for the entire town.

In the 1980s and 1990s, as the tribe worked for financial independence, they were eventually able to buy back their land lease and become full owners of the most prominent piece of land in Palm Springs. Sitting in the heart of the city, the new Spa Resort Casino has undergone near-constant renovation and enlargement and is the centerpiece in the tribe's impressive economic engine. As part of their long-range plan to create financial stability for all their members, the Agua Caliente Band of Cahuilla Indians currently owns and operates multiple business ventures in the Palm Springs area, including a bank, golf course, the Indian Canyons, the Agua Caliente Casino in Palm Desert, the Spa Resort Casino, and the Indian Canyons Tours.

Spa treatments run the gamut of different massage therapies, facials, scrubs, wraps, and waxing. Packages are generally a good value, particularly if you can persuade a group to join you for a day or half day of pampering. A full-service beauty salon offers hair, makeup, and nail services.

THE SPRING

12-699 Reposo Way, Desert Hot Springs

(760) 251-6700

www.the-spring.com

The Spring is one of the small treasures of Desert Hot Springs, with nine rooms and two suite accommodations and three mineral pools. Hammocks, sunbathing spots, and a massage cabana ring the main pool. Six of the rooms have kitchens, and all have courtyards with privacy panels. Service is exceptional, including meal delivery from the area's top restaurants.

A central lounge area serves continental breakfast and is a good spot to read or relax before spa treatments in the separate spa building, an elegantly simple facility decorated in cool neutral tones with lots of natural light. Services include a variety of massages, wraps, scrubs, and facials. Simple non-polish manicures and pedicures are offered poolside on weekends. Five- and seven-day fasting and cleansing retreats are offered at different times during the year.

TWO BUNCH PALMS RESORT & SPA
**67-425 Two Bunch Palms Trail,
Desert Hot Springs
(760) 329-8791, (800) 472-4334
www.twobunchpalms.com**

Two Bunch Palms has been a magnet for stressed-out celebrities and wealthy businesspeople almost since it first opened in the early 1920s. It's one of the few desert resorts that can truthfully say it's never advertised—word of mouth is just amazingly strong. And, despite its obsessive rules on guest privacy, the place has been featured in a number of movies. Readers of *Condé Nast Traveler* and *Travel & Leisure Magazine* have consistently rated it among the world's top 10 spas, the centerpiece of which is the Grotto, Two Bunch's natural lithium-rich mineral pool.

The facility is located behind private gates, and accommodations are a mixture of casitas, villas, spa suites, suites, and guest rooms spread out over 256 acres. Dedicated to de-stressing and pampering, this is an unusual place that emphasizes quiet and serenity. Guests are cautioned about using cell phones in public areas and asked to speak quietly to preserve the peace.

The dozens of spa treatments run the gamut: Watsu and other water therapies, Ayurveda, Thai (table or mat), a variety of offerings for expectant mothers, mud baths, breathwork (using breathing techniques to rid the head and body of "blocked energy"), reiki…the list goes on.

SHOPPING

Survey after survey of American travelers tells us that there are three activities that are always at the top of the "must-do" list: dining out, shopping, and sightseeing. Even people who do little shop-hopping at other times feel the need to buy something when they're in a new place—a memento of their visit, a gift for people back home, a hard-to-find item at a great price, even vacation necessities such as flip-flops or swimsuits. Though Palm Springs doesn't measure up to such Southern California shopping meccas as Los Angeles, Santa Monica, San Diego, or south Orange County, it has its share of national stores, specialty boutiques, and places that are unique to the desert.

Jewelry is a big deal here, as is the type of bright, glittery, casual women's clothing known as resort wear. It's telling that the Eddie Bauer store closed its doors and vacated its prime spot on El Paseo after only a few years. Its style of simple, rugged sportswear and plethora of sweaters and coats in the winter always seemed out of place in the perpetual sunshine and highly groomed surroundings, though under the guise of "value" as an outlet at Desert Hills in Cabazon, a northwoods/desert alliance ultimately was forged. On the other hand, St. John has a flagship store here, as does Tommy Bahama, and they sell lots and lots of clothing.

To help you in your hunting and gathering, we have included a brief rundown on the major shopping areas in the valley and the general type of merchandise you will find there. Otherwise, shopping options are presented by category of goods, making it easy for you to find antiques, toys, books, and more. Chain stores are not listed in the individual categories, but we do note where they can be found.

MAJOR SHOPPING AREAS

Palm Springs

In the past decade, the city has developed its own antiques and art gallery section known as the Uptown Heritage District. Covering several blocks beginning in the 300 block of North Palm Canyon Drive, the area is a charming collection of historic buildings housing consignment stores, gift shops, galleries, restaurants, and home-decorating boutiques. This area really got its start when the mid-century modern craze hit Southern California. Suddenly, movie types and hipsters from Los Angeles discovered a few furniture consignment stores offering amazing bargains on well-preserved furniture and bric-a-brac from the 1940s and '50s. The bargains are no longer amazing, but astonishing finds

still turn up, and spending the day wandering through the shops can be quite entertaining. This area also puts on First Friday Art Walk on the first Friday of each month. Stores stay open until 9 p.m. and offer music and entertainment. In the heart of downtown, a host of galleries, retailers, and restaurateurs have kept civic life moving in the city's urban heart, and First Friday takes the guise here of VillageFest, held Thursday evenings, a convivial gathering of shopping and dining late, street entertainers, and a pause now and again for an adult beverage.

Yet for all the retail and commercial vibrancy that has re-embraced downtown since at least the turn of the millennium, for all the busy storefronts and strip centers, what Palm Springs lacks and has for years is a major regional shopping complex. Downtown's Desert Fashion Plaza went adios in 2001, and except for a short-lived flirtation with a Cirque du Soleil-type production, it remains as moribund as an ethics conference in Washington, D.C. And the Palm Springs "Mall," while providing useful retail services, consists of office supply, pharmacy, grocer, hardware, and a discount clothier.

Cathedral City

This is car-shoppers' heaven, with a large auto mall along Highway 111 and an adjoining supporting service-commercial area. Other than that and scattered specialty retail, the city's merchant offerings consist of small neighborhood and larger community shopping centers comprised of the usual suspects—big-box retailers, office supply, discounters.

Rancho Mirage

Until The River opened a few years ago, Rancho Mirage was renowned for high-end furnishing, art and home boutiques and shops, and nothing in the way of "typical" retail. This new open-air lifestyle and dining complex—often referred to as "retailtainment"—is more geared to food and entertainment than "shopping," but specialty retail has been part of the formula since day one, and it is doing well. Rosters always change, but the list includes Cohiba Cigar Lounge and Tulip Hill Winery (both listed later in this section), Borders Book & Music, M.A.C. and Ulta cosmetics, Diane's Beachwear, and Bang & Olufsen.

Palm Desert

This city is the valley's undisputed retail king. Westfield Shoppingtown is a midlevel enclosed mall anchored by JCPenney, Sears, Macy's Robinsons-May, and a huge Barnes & Noble. Built in the early 1980s, it was the first enclosed mall in the desert and was the start of the retail boom for Palm Desert. There are around 150 of the usual small mall shops, kiosks, and food court stations, plus extras such as a shopping concierge, valet parking, parking services for pregnant women, package carry-out, and new covered parking areas to stash the car out of the heat.

> **i** Though the department stores, national retailers, and most of the merchants in Palm Springs stay open late at least one night a week—Friday—many of the independent shops on El Paseo Drive still stubbornly close their doors at 5:30 or 6 p.m.

El Paseo Drive is the "Rodeo Drive of the Desert," a land of facelifts trailing tiny dogs with diamond-studded collars and searching out every upscale service or trinket imaginable, from cashmere blankets to jeweled bracelets, cosmetic surgery to designer furniture, hand-engraved stationery, sequined baby booties, couture gowns, grand art and is-that-art? art, and because the guys deserve something, custom-tailored suits. National designers with signature shops include Escada, Oilily, Ralph Lauren, and St. John. (Please accept that the late-in-the-decade economic meltdown had a serious affect upon the complexion and makeup of the Cactus Rodeo.)

The street's contribution to "mall" shopping is The Gardens on El Paseo, a two-story open-air complex with covered parking and a desert landscape that's the envy of all homeowners trying to nuke the lawn and go water-friendly without ending up ugly and austere. During the winter season there are free concerts and frequent benefits for local charities. It's anchored by Saks Fifth Avenue and features such national stores as Ann Taylor Loft, Banana Republic, Brooks Brothers, Coach, Cole Haan, Harry & David, L'Occitane Tiffany & Co., and Williams-Sonoma. Other national stores, include Aveda, Johnston & Murphy, Pottery Barn, and Tommy Bahama's Emporium, a do-it-all-in-vivid-florals combo clothier, home decor store, and eating establishment. If the desert was a sit-com with edgy/cool yet angst-riddled characters, they'd shop here.

In the Desert Crossing shopping area at Highway 111 and Fred Waring Drive, big-box retailers abound. There are Target, TJ Maxx, Payless Shoes, and about a dozen more. Just across the street you'll find Pier I Imports, Best Buy, Cost Plus, and other recognizable chains.

Once you leave Palm Desert and head east, the shopping options decline dramatically through Indian Wells, though The Village certainly beats your typical strip mall; it is tres toney Indian Wells, after all. There's an upscale Ralph's Grocery, medical offices, a couple clothing boutiques, service commercial, florist, housewares, and a few eateries including one of the desert's toppest top-end restaurants, Le St. Germain.

i Palm Desert offers a free "Shopper Hopper" shuttle. It runs a continuous loop, with stops at most of the major hotels and shopping areas. For times call SunBus at (760) 343-3451.

La Quinta and Beyond

If there's a commercial up-and-comer in the desert, it's La Quinta. Long stretches along Highway 111 that were unused or under-used since the days when Ike would pop in for a round of golf and a cold one have been churned into a good-sized auto center, grocer- and big-box-anchored centers, galleries, notable restaurants and many more quite standard, medical and office space, and two spots sure to warm any heart, Costco and Bevmo.

A work-in-progress, deep down in the cove, in an area that time had left behind, Old Town La Quinta has been springing back to life. There have been fits and starts, and the renaissance is nearer its birth than full flower, yet life there is. Restaurants, new service-commercial, a new resort and spa, and a stucco-and-tile complex of buildings that screams old California and that's slowly filling in with resort wear, kitchen gadgetry, jewelry shops, and the like shows the city is on a good path.

Back out of the cove and heading east on Highway 111 … well, there's not a lot of reason for vacationing shoppers to head much past Roger Dunn Golf Shop. The Indio Fashion Mall is a dinosaur surviving on a diet of discounters, street wear, beauty supplies, and fast food. The parts of town recently developed as planned residential areas sport the usual array of national big-boxes, grocery, and suburban retail, but none of it functions as a destination.

Not so long ago most of the independent shops would close their doors for the summer, celebrating a "grand reopening" in Sept. Some still do take off for a few months, particularly high-end establishment whose lifeblood is the resort seasonal trade, but the majority are open year-round. By the same token, many shops that closed on Sundays a few years ago are now open every day in season. What we're saying is always call ahead to check on hours, and remember that the retail world in this resort is almost as fickle as the restaurant world, so some shops may have moved, closed, or changed the type of merchandise they offer.

ANTIQUES AND CONSIGNMENT STORES

ANTIQUE COLLECTIVE
798 North Palm Canyon Dr.
(760) 323-4443
Just as the name suggests, this is a collective endeavor of dozens of individual antiques dealers, offering everything from Bakelite bracelets to beautifully preserved furniture from a variety of eras. The building that houses the collection is exceptionally well kept, with the look and feel of glossy retail stores. The staff has all been in the business for years and is knowledgeable about all the goods. If you're looking for unusual, high-quality gifts or a piece to round out a collection, the collective might be a good place to start.

BRAM'S
461 North Palm Canyon Dr.
(760) 416-2667
This is a real specialty store, featuring antique furniture, art, and accessories from the Arts and Crafts period, roughly 1890 through 1930. There is also a good collection of handmade Mexican sterling silver jewelry of the hefty, rough-hewn variety found decades ago.

ESTATE SALE COMPANY
4185 East Palm Canyon Dr.
(760) 321-7628
www.theestatesalecompany.com
This is the store that brought high-end, professional consignment retail to the desert about 15 years ago. A family-owned business, it's expanded twice and is known as the best place for locals to sell furniture, quality accessories, furs, jewelry, and art quickly. The inventory changes rapidly, and the prices are reasonable for a wide selection that ranges from apartment-grade couches to unusual pieces that were custom-designed and have lost their appeal to the original owners. For some locals a stop at the Estate Sale Company to check out the new stuff is a regular Saturday stop.

HEATHER JAMES ART & ANTIQUITIES
73–080 El Paseo Dr., #5, Palm Desert
(760) 346-8926
www.heatherjamesartandantiquities.com

HEATHER JAMES FINE ART
45-188 Portola Ave., Palm Desert
(760) 346-8926
www.heatherjames.com
Twin galleries specializing in fine cultural and ethnographic art from all over the world, with emphasis on African, Asian, pre-Columbian, tribal, and classical pieces. At any time, you might find a fine 500 B.C. Attic ware vase, a pair of ancient pottery tomb figures from Jalisco, 19th-century Tantric Buddhist art, or a mask worn by Borneo shamans in healing ceremonies. Heather James also offers art buying and consultation and has access to sources for fine art from the masters—Van Gogh, Matisse, Monet, Renoir, Degas, Hassam, and many others. You can count on finding museum-quality pieces here, as well as top service.

PHYLLIS WASHINGTON ANTIQUES
73-960 El Paseo Dr., Palm Desert
(760) 862-0021
www.maisonfelice.com
From its opening in 1999 to the summer of 2007, this masterful gallery was known as Maison Felice. Following a major do-over, Phyllis Washington Antiques—recognize a name continuation in there?—emerged, specializing in 18th- to pre-war 20th-century European, antiques, art, and furnishings. The shop itself is worth a short visit, if only to admire the tasteful merchandising and elegant interior. In season a series of "Style of Life" lectures is presented.

ROBERT KAPLAN ANTIQUES
469 North Palm Canyon Dr.
(760) 323-7144, (888) 277-8960
www.desert-life.com/kaplan.htm
A Sotheby's associate, this shop specializes in small items such as clocks, watches, music boxes, fine jewelry, silver, china, and glassware, as well as Tiffany pieces, old paintings, and art objects. There is also a selection of extremely fine furniture and old Russian items. The layout and display are clean, attractive, and easy to navigate. Don't even go in the door unless you're prepared to fall in love with a lovely Art Nouveau brooch, a perfect Russian icon, or an exquisite little writing desk.

STEWART GALLERIES
191 South Indian Canyon Dr.
(760) 325-0878
www.stewartgalleries.com
Stewart's has a huge inventory of paintings by well-known artists in the California Impressionist and Plein Air schools, featuring original oil paintings by artists from the past as well as up-and-coming new talent. Their buyers are also well respected in the art world and often are first on the scene to acquire notable estate paintings from the Modern and Surrealist movements, theory schools, and much more. The antiques side of the business is one of the most popular in the desert, with a changing inventory that includes crystal chandeliers, oriental figures, classic marble statues, fine antique furniture, and decorative accessories. There is always a large selection of bronze sculptures as well.

MID-CENTURY FURNISHINGS AND ACCESSORIES

Although you will find an occasional piece of mid-century furniture or decor at another shop in the valley, this era is almost exclusively represented in Palm Springs. The following shops all feature collections of furniture, home accessories, and memorabilia from the 1940s through the 1970s. The quality and specific items vary greatly from time to time, but they are all quite competitively priced. Most of the goods are on consignment, so you may be able to pick up a piece that has some valley history. Also, the specific area of Palm Canyon Drive where these shops are located has gotten the reputation throughout Southern California as being the place to find interesting, unusual, and high-quality mid-century pieces, as well as those that are simply kitschy and fun. If this is the era that interests you, take a few hours browsing the shops before you make your selection—the comparison may help you find a better price on a particular piece or an example that's in better condition. To help in your walking expedition, we've arranged the stores by location, starting with the ones that are closest to downtown Palm Springs and moving north, and as all are in Palm Springs the city is not noted in the entries. Economic attrition, sadly, has significantly thinned the ranks.

ℹ️ Jonathan Adler is the 21st century's answer to an updated mid-century style. A noted ceramicist, he recently turned his considerable design talents to the decor of the Parker Palm Springs, creating a variety of vases, tabletop items, and furniture. Get a catalog from the hotel's concierge or order from www.jonathanadler.com.

VINTAGE OASIS
373 South Palm Canyon Dr. Studio A
(760) 778-6224

MODERN WAY
745 North Palm Canyon Dr.
(760) 320-5455
www.psmodernway.com

20 FIRST
1117 North Palm Canyon Dr., Suite A
(760) 327-5400

STUDIO ONE 11
2675 North Palm Canyon Dr.
(760) 323-5104
www.studio111palmsprings.com
High-end and rare mid-century furnishings and accessories from the 1930s through the 1970s.

BOUTIQUES/GIFT SHOPS/ SPECIALTY SHOPS

THE BOOK RACK
78-329 Hwy. 111, La Quinta
(760) 771-3449
The Internet and national retailers have killed the independent bookstore. While no one will mistake this place for a bookseller just off Harvard Square, if you happen to be in the neighborhood—say heading to the Beer Hunter for a game and a pint or teeing up it down at PGA West, and you like pulp fiction or you have a bunch of old paperbacks to trade, give it a look.

CLOCKWORKS, A CLOCK GALLERY
160 East Tahquitz Canyon Way
(760) 327-2475
New and streamlined, old and elegant—this shop has them all, along with some very nice watches and a reliable repair service for heirloom pieces.

COHIBA CIGAR LOUNGE
71-800 Hwy. 111, Rancho Mirage (The River)
(760) 346-4748
www.theriveratranchomirage.com
Not only can you buy a fistful of premium cigars, but you can settle down and smoke them here as well. Smoking accessories and handmade cigars from Nicaragua, Honduras, and the Dominican

Republic are the highlights. Cuba? Soon, one would think, soon.

COLD NOSE WARM HEART
189 South Palm Canyon Dr.
(760) 327-7747
www.coldnosewarmheart.com
It's like Home Depot for Bowser featuring everything imaginable for dogs and even the people they own. Handmade dog bowls, organic dog treats, fine leather collars, high-quality beds, goofy little sweaters, cards, and gift items are all doggone charming.

FAME TOBACCONIST
155 South Palm Canyon Dr., A-3
(760) 320-2752
This shop has what they bill as the largest cigar humidor in Southern California, stocked with all manner of exotic cigars from all over the world. Of course they have a wide selection of other smoking goods, including pipes, lighters, cigar and cigarette cases, and as is often the case with tobacconists, a fine grouping of murderous-looking knives from internationally known knife makers.

HOME 101
392 North Palm Canyon Dr.
(760) 318-9886
www.home101store.com
A fun little catchall gift shop with a huge array of high-end bath and body products, plus interesting but not expensive jewelry, cards, books, lighting, and some home furnishings. If you're looking for a tasteful but trendy gift for your host or a last-minute birthday party, this shop will offer a lot of excellent and interesting choices.

KITCHEN FANCY
73-930 El Paseo Dr., Palm Desert
(760) 346-4114
Located on El Paseo Drive since the late 1970s, Kitchen Fancy features a wide selection of unique home accessories, gifts, table linens, greeting cards, candles, barware, and paper goods. They will also gift wrap and ship. This is great place for hostess gifts and hard-to-find items for serious home chef-ers.

MUSICIANS' OUTLET
44-850 San Pablo Dr., Palm Desert
(760) 341-3171
www.musiciansbestfriend.com
For professional and serious amateur musicians, this store stocks a wide selection of different instruments—specializing in guitars, keyboards, and drums—as well as a good amount of amplifiers, PA systems, karaoke, tapes, and sheet music. There are a lot of musicians in the valley but, oddly enough, very few stores that cater to their needs. With the outlet local musicians need not beat feet for LA to stay in tune and in gear.

SPECTACULAR SHADES
73910 El Paseo Dr., Palm Desert
(760) 568-4500, (800) 800-9067
If there's one person in the desert who knows fabulous sunglasses, it's owner Sonia Campbell, who's been stocking the largest selection of upscale shades for many years. Brand names include Oliver People's, Carrera, Dior, Armani, Persol, Fendi, Diva, Kieselstein-Cord, Picasso, Nicole Miller, Calvin Klein, and a lot more. Gosh, whatever happened to good old Ray-Ban and Vuarnet?

TABLETOP ELEGANCE
73-470 El Paseo Dr., Palm Desert
(760) 674-9234
For the detail-oriented host and hostess, this shop features a large selection of china, glassware, flatware, and accessories for creating fashionable tabletop settings. The gamut runs from silly paper goods for eating by the pool to supremely elegant collections for those state dinners.

ULTA
71-800 Hwy. 111, Rancho Mirage (The River)
(760) 836-3381
www.theriveratranchomirage.com
This is a national store, but worth mentioning because of its huge inventory and single-minded

focus. As many a hairdresser will say, "It's all about the product." The product here includes every hair potion around, dozens of perfumes, bath and body products, nail polishes, and what seems like an acre of mascara, eyeliner, blush, foundation, lipstick, and gloss. They also have a walk-in beauty bar where you can get a manicure, quickie facial, or bang trim and be out the door for dinner in less than half an hour.

CHILDREN'S CLOTHING AND TOYS/HOBBIES (ALL AGES)

DOLLSVILLE DOLLS & BEARSVILLE BEARS
296 North Palm Canyon Dr.
(760) 325-2241
www.dollsville.com
From highly collectible and fragile dolls to those that are meant for a long, happy life of being dragged from playground to bed, this little shop has them all. There is also a wide selection of stuffed animals, including many collectible lines and future cuddly friends.

MR. G'S FOR KIDS
180 North Palm Canyon Dr.
(760) 320-9293
www.mrgstoys.com
This shop is crammed full of toys for all ages, model kits, books, unusual gifts, and even the classics like yo-yos and paddleballs. They have a small selection of collectibles, plus coloring books, games, and cards. The latest, hottest electronics and large toys aren't here, but it is a charming place with lots of little treasures.

OILILY
73-545 El Paseo Dr., Palm Desert
(The Gardens on El Paseo)
(760) 837-9356
www.oililyusastores.com
This shop is an explosion of color and features its own signature line of bright, graphic flower prints done up in girl's dresses, tops, shorts, pants, and hand-knit sweaters. There is even a small section

for women. The colors are gorgeous, and the workmanship is excellent. The styling is faintly Icelandic, but the vivid pinks, oranges, blues, and greens are anything but staid.

UNCLE DON'S HOBBIES & SUPPLIES
44-250 Town Center Way, C–8, Palm Desert
(Corner of Town Center Way and
Fred Waring Drive)
(760) 346-8856
www.uncledonshobbies.com
Uncle Don's was a fixture in downtown Palm Springs for years and after moving to Palm Desert found itself in larger, more updated quarters. Mainstays here are electric and gas RC planes, boats and vehicles, trains of all scales, plastic and wood models, kites, rockets, puzzles, you name it. There's just about everything to keep a young (or old) hobby enthusiast busy and happy. And Uncle Don consigns.

COLLECTIBLES

CRYSTAL FANTASY ENLIGHTENMENT CENTER
268 North Palm Canyon Dr.
(760) 322-7799
www.crystalfantasy.com
Owners Joy and Scott Meredith are known in town for both their community spirit and their unfailing eye for the best fantasy collectibles and art—representing Harmony Kingdom, faeries, mermaids, dragons, and other magical creatures. There is always a new treasure—incense, candles, gems, jewelry, herbs, oils, stained glass, books, and music— including a new, expanded home store.

i Historically, the best sales of the year are in late May and early June, when storeowners know the slow days of summer are just ahead. Few shops advertise, so call your favorite to find out when the big markdowns are scheduled.

UNIQUE COINS

655 North Palm Canyon Dr.
(760) 320-3140

This well-respected local shop sells rare coins and currency, as well as fine silver, china, and a small selection of estate jewelry and collectibles. The staff is quite knowledgeable and can find sources for specific coins and rare pieces of jewelry. Many visitors have come to rely on the shop to build their collections over the years.

GARDEN SHOPS

GUBLER ORCHIDS

2200 Belfield Blvd., Landers
(760) 364-2282
www.gublers.com

One of the country's largest orchid growers, Gubler's set up shop in the high desert in 1975. With temperatures that are 10 to 15 degrees cooler than in the Coachella Valley, year-round sunshine, and the controlled climate of green-houses—at 155,000 square feet this spot is ideal for these exotic beauties. Gubler's propagates their own orchids and gives tours of the grow-ing areas where they nurture an Eden of orchid hybrids and carnivorous plants; and you thought the kids would be bored. The selection is huge, and they will ship just about anywhere—even Alaska. Prices are excellent, and the plants are top quality. Gubler's also stocks special potting soil, fertilizer, pots, and baskets, as well as cards, T-shirts, and small gift items.

THE LIVING DESERT'S PALO VERDE GARDEN CENTER

47-900 Portola Ave., Palm Desert
(760) 346-5694
www.livingdesert.org

As befits a nursery inside one of the country's finest living museums of desert biotic communi-ties, this garden center features hundreds of rare and hard-to-find desert plants from all over the Southwest and Mexico. In addition, you'll find seeds, books on desert landscaping, and a good selection of attractive pottery.

MOORTEN BOTANICAL GARDEN

1701 South Palm Canyon Dr.
(760) 327-6555

A Palm Springs Historical Landmark, Moorten Botanical Garden has been in the same spot since 1938, cultivating an astounding variety of cacti, succulents, and other desert plants. There are more than 3,000 varieties here, and something is always in bloom. This is truly a taste of old Palm Springs. Clark Moorten—son of the garden's founders, "Cactus Slim" and Patricia Moorten—is there every day. Just like his parents, he has a true love for the desert and an encyclopedic knowledge of its plants. Take a stroll through the grounds, where specimen plants tower hundreds of feet high and the sounds of doves and other desert birds fill the air. Pick up an exotic plant as a gift for a local or have it shipped back home. Moorten has done the consulting for many of the desert's most stunning landscapes, and he'll give expert advice on what will work for you.

JEWELRY STORES

B. ALSOHN'S JEWELERS

73-585 El Paseo Dr., Palm Desert
(760) 340-4211

With a master jeweler and GIA-trained gemolo-gist on staff, this shop features designer jewelry in silver, gold, and platinum; individual gems ready for setting or collecting; and fine watches.

DELUCA JEWELERS

73-655 El Paseo Dr., Suite F, Palm Desert
(760) 773-1763
www.delucajewelers.com

Joe DeLuca has owned this business for decades and is one of the desert's most respected jewelry designers. Featured items include original gold pieces, fine diamonds, designer sterling silver, and estate pieces.

DENISE ROBERGE

73-995 El Paseo Dr., Palm Desert
(760) 340-5045

All designs are created and manufactured in

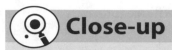 Close-up

Moorten Botanical Garden

As every desert old-timer knows, Palm Springs just wouldn't be Palm Springs without Moorten Botanical Garden, a labor of love created by Chester "Cactus Slim" Moorten and his wife, biologist Patricia Moorten.

Nicknamed "Slim" for his tall, lanky form and work as a contortionist, Chester was one of the original Keystone Cops, worked as the stand-in for Howard Hughes, and played parts in many other movies over the years. Poor health led him to the desert in the 1930s with his young wife Patricia, a biologist with a special interest in botany. Together they explored this desolate landscape and worked the Rainbow's End Gold Mine in the high desert. They began collecting desert plants, historic artifacts, and minerals early on and sold them at their shop, located near the site of today's Spa Resort Casino.

As the city attracted socialites, Hollywood royalty, and tycoons in the 1940s, Slim and Patricia created elegant desert gardens and became known for engineering naturalistic waterfalls and pools. They designed and installed landscapes for Frank Sinatra and set up the spare, meticulously "wild" desertscapes at Walt Disney's nearby Smoke Tree Ranch. Disney consulted them in the design of the western-themed Frontierland for the brand-new Disneyland.

The Moortens were also well traveled and packed up their only son Clark for trips down Baja California and into Mexico, collecting plants as far south as Guatemala. These adventures were extensive, and they became familiar not only with the plants but also with the indigenous people and local wildlife. Many rare plants in the Moorten Botanical Garden were collected on these trips.

The Moortens' Mediterranean-style home, "Cactus Castle," sits in the middle of the Botanical Garden, which the Moortens began building in 1938. The setting for many movie scenes and countless weddings and garden parties, the home is a sprawling affair built for the weather, with concrete walls 2 feet thick to keep out the desert heat. For years, the Palm Springs Chamber of Commerce has held its last mixer of the season here, a much-anticipated event that marks the unofficial end of "season" and beginning of summer.

Clark is now the curator of this botanical wonderland. He is an authority in his own right and among the most knowledgeable experts on succulent plants in America. He tends the garden and propagates many of its plants for sale and is there to greet visitors almost every day. Clark also consults on desert landscaping for clients all over the world.

this elegant space, which is an extension of the Roberge art gallery and Augusta restaurant. The distinctive designs recall classical pieces from Greece or Rome, using 22k gold and large cabochon, colored stones.

DIAMONDS OF SPLENDOR
73-400 El Paseo Dr., Palm Desert
(760) 568-6641
Two GIA graduate gemologists own this cozy little space and will create just about any design you have in mind. Originality and quality are

watchwords here. They specialize in unusual cuts and faceting, as well as designs that are more traditional and European in style.

EL PASEO JEWELRY
73-375 El Paseo Dr., Palm Desert
(760) 773-1040
This is a trendy jewelry boutique featuring diamond and gemstone pieces at bargain prices. Designer knockoffs and basics in the latest styles are the specialty.

EMRICK JEWELS
73-896 El Paseo Dr., Palm Desert
(760) 568-4522
Emrick offers a selection of antique and contemporary jewelry that includes Victorian, Art Deco, Art Nouveau, and retro '50s along with a finely edited group of sleek modern works. They also offer appraisals and repair.

ESTATE JEWELRY COLLECTION
73-470 El Paseo Dr., Suite 4, Palm Desert
(760) 779-1856
www.estatejewelrycollection.com
The prices are low enough to keep the pieces moving, and you're likely to find outstanding values from Cartier, Bulgari, David Webb, Tiffany, Van Cleef & Arpels, and other famous designers.

FRASCA JEWELERS
73-560 El Paseo Dr., Palm Desert
(760) 568-5848
One of the valley's oldest jewelry sellers, Frasca has been on El Paseo Drive for 20 years. A full-service store offering high-end gold pieces and platinum, they also offer watch and jewelry repair, pearl restringing, and engraving.

GAIL JEWELERS
73-525 El Paseo Dr., Palm Desert
(760) 776-7150
www.gailjewelers.com
Gail specializes in diamonds and platinum, with a sophisticated selection of designer goods, watches, and gifts. Repair, estate purchases, and appraisals are also available. One of the desert's most respected jewelers, Gail always stocks high-end platinum and high-carat gold in classic as well as contemporary styles.

HEPHAESTUS JEWELERS
132 La Plaza
(760) 325-5395
www.hephaestusps.com
Named for the Greek god of artisans, as well as other trades and things like fire and volcanoes, this shop focuses on designer jewelry and

also does custom orders and designs. It has a good reputation for quality work and imaginative design using the client's own gems or supplying them from reputable sources.

LEEDS & SON
73-670 El Paseo Dr., Palm Desert
(760) 568-5266
www.leedsandson.com
A family-owned business that's been adorning desert residents since 1947, Leeds spotlights classic designs from such masters as Harry Winston. Custom work features fine diamonds and colored gems, and the timepieces include beauties from Rolex, Damiani, Patek Philippe, Panerai, and more.

ROBANN'S JEWELERS
71-800 Hwy. 111, Rancho Mirage (The River)
(760) 341-8142
www.theriveratranchomirage.com
Robann's is another longtime desert jeweler, family owned and operated for more than 30 years. They specialize in custom pieces and one-of-a-kind original items. They pride themselves on doing all the work on the premises. A certified gemologist appraiser is also on staff.

MEN'S AND WOMEN'S CLOTHING/SHOES/ ACCESSORIES

4 SEASONS SWIMWEAR
73-400 El Paseo Dr., #4, Palm Desert
(760) 340-2490
Swimwear of most every type for every body shape, style and size, with all the requisite cover-ups, pool shoes, and accessories.

BLONDE
71-800 Hwy. 111, Rancho Mirage (The River)
(760) 836-3366
www.theriveratranchomirage.com
Blonde is the sister to Z Boutique in Palm Springs and offers a bit dressier selection of trendy, California-girl wear. Still, there are racks and racks

of great T-shirts and jeans. The presentation is a bit jumbled, but it's worth a little bit of extra time to hunt out that new outfit.

CACTUS FLOWER SHOES
73-640 El Paseo Dr., Palm Desert
(760) 346-6223

This shop has a good selection of dressy men's and women's shoes, with the emphasis on casual, resort styles. The women's side always has fun, embellished sandals, heels, and mules, as well as nifty belts, purses, and other accessories.

COMPLIMENTS
74-907 Hwy. 111, Indian Wells
(760) 836-1570

Stop in here for what may be the desert's best and most reasonably priced selection of "Palm Springs babe" jeweled and crystal-encrusted sandals, belts, T-shirts, handbags, jewelry, and resort clothes. You'll always find a good sales rack and a very pleasant staff.

DOT
73-575 El Paseo Dr., Palm Desert
(The Gardens on El Paseo)
(760) 346-5825
www.dotpalmdesert.com

Of all the clothing stores in the desert, DOT is the one most resembling a high-end, low-key shop in Los Angeles. It features a beautifully edited collection of men's and women's casual clothes in quality fabrics and subdued colors—rather unusual in Palm Springs. You'll find brands such as Isda, Puma, Three Dots, Big Star, Donald J. Pliner, Isabella Fiore, Magaschoni, and new stars in the design world. Very sophisticated.

DRAPER'S & DAMON'S
73-930 El Paseo Dr., Palm Desert
(760) 346-0559

42-396 Bob Hope Dr., Rancho Mirage
(760) 568-1165
www.drapers.com

When it opened in Palm Springs in 1927, this was the desert's first department store, carrying a dizzying amount of both men's and women's clothes, from tuxedos to walking shorts and everything in between. They're national now, but history allows us to keep it, and times really haven't changed much—it's still stuffed full of clothing that's a bit on the fuddy-duddy side, and the service is still excellent.

GREG NORMAN
48750 Seminole Dr., Cabazon
(Cabazon Outlets)
(951) 849-6884
www.cabazonoutlets.com

Indeed, it's an "outlet" store. Don't be deterred. The outlets of yore hawking never-would-sell disasters and "seconds" are a distant memory at this shop. Deeply-discounted closeouts indeed abound, and you'd have no problem wearing 'em at the member-guest. However, most of us wouldn't have a clue if the majority of in-stock shirts, slacks, belts, shorts, and those trademark Shark hats were all the rage at retail just last week or last season. There's a limited supply of women's wear, as well.

JOY! A MATERNITY BOUTIQUE
73-170 El Paseo Dr., Suite 1, Palm Desert
(760) 773-5450
www.joymaternity.net

What a joy it is to find well-made casual fashions, lingerie, and sleepwear, as well as good-looking diaper bags, gifts, and baby footwear.

i Didn't bring your swimsuit? Brought your old faded one because it's winter and the stores back home are only showing sweaters and coats? You can find a great selection of swimwear, shorts, and warm-weather clothes year-round in the major department stores, most of the trendy boutiques, the outlets in Cabazon, the sports-oriented retailers, and if you're not too worried about being voted off Too Chic Island, places like Costco, which are particularly good for togs for the little ones.

MACMILLAN'S RESORT WEAR
899 North Palm Canyon Dr.
(760) 323-2979

This shop specializes in colorful, cotton and rayon resort clothing for women—bright sundresses, skirts, tops, and shorts by Jams, Reyn Spooner, and Tommy Bahama. If you want the hot "island" style at good prices, this is the spot.

RANGONI OF FLORENCE SHOES
73-130 El Paseo Dr., Palm Desert
(760) 346-6646
www.rangoni.it

Women's high-end brands include Rangoni Firenze, Amalfi, Cole Haan, Donald J. Pliner, Anne Klein, and more, with a specialty in narrow sizes. Men' footwear includes Rangoni, Morescho, and Cole Haan.

ROBERT'S FINE SHOES
73-725 El Paseo Dr., Palm Desert
(760) 340-2929, (800) 833-5299
www.robertsfineshoes.com

Offerings here are at the upper end of quality and price. Men's shoes include styles by Bruno Magli, Lorenzo Banfi, and Cole Haan. For women, there's a wide array of shoes, handbags, and accessories from Salvatore Ferragamo, Bruno Magli, Stuart Weitzman, Cole Haan, Icon, and Judith Leiber.

ST. JOHN BOUTIQUE
73-061 El Paseo Dr., Palm Desert
(760) 568-5900
www.sjk.com

This is a St. John "flagship" store, meaning that the selection is more complete than just about anywhere else in the country. You will find some St. John items in Saks Fifth Avenue down the street, and a nice grouping of off-season pieces at the outlet store in the Desert Hills Premium Outlets, but this is the place for the real deal. Shoes, jewelry, sportswear, evening wear, suits, perfume—it's all here.

TRINA TURK BOUTIQUE
891 North Palm Canyon Dr.
(760) 416-2856
www.trinaturk.com

Trina Turk is a well-known sportswear designer whose retro-chic designs turn up in Saks Fifth Avenue and other high-end national stores. Trina's second home is in Palm Springs, and she's opened this cool little shop to keep herself entertained while she's in town. Pieces here represent the complete line and are strong on women's outfits that would be perfect by the pool or out for cocktails on a warm spring evening. A bonus—you'll find a few choice vintage pieces and a selection of menswear designed exclusively for the Palm Springs shop.

TROY
73-255 El Paseo Dr., Palm Desert
(760) 776-1101
www.troypalmdesert.com

Troy is one of the El Paseo Drive merchants that helped cement the street's reputation as a high-end fashion destination. This lovely shop highlights women's clothing by Oscar de la Renta, Bill Blass, Basier, David Josef, Bob Mackie, and other designers known to offer ornamentation and feminine fit. Troy also has its own private label.

THE WARDROBE OF PALM SPRINGS
108 South Indian Canyon Dr.
(760) 325-4330
www.psthewardrobe.com

A desert institution, this is a favorite stop for women who want a glamorous black tie look without the El Paseo prices. There's also a good selection of jewelry, lingerie and fun handbags, and excellent end-of-season sales.

GIFT SHOPS IN ATTRACTIONS

These all offer items specific to their nature—often things that can be found nowhere else in the desert. Be sure to check the shops out when you visit.

CHILDREN'S DISCOVERY MUSEUM

71-701 Gerald Ford Dr., Rancho Mirage
(760) 321-0602
www.cdmod.org

Educational toys and games, museum logo merchandise, and a lot of very fun, very unusual featured items—such as chicken socks, stunt magnets, goofy puzzles, and motorized bubble lights—are available here.

LIVING DESERT ZOO AND GARDENS

47-900 Portola Ave., Palm Desert
(760) 346-5694
www.livingdesert.org

The shops here offer goods from Africa, including pots, baskets, jewelry and gift items, and other warm-dry climes; books, cards, and trinkets with animal and plant themes; and native desert plants, as well as pots, bird feeders, and wind chimes.

PALM CANYON TRADING POST

The Indian Canyons
(No street address)
(760) 416-7044

This little shop specializes in Native American crafts and arts from tribes across the country. Merchandise includes paintings, pots, jewelry, leather, sculpture, a variety of crafts, and a good selection of books and cards. To get to this store, follow South Palm Canyon Drive in Palm Springs until it dead-ends, just a few minutes from downtown.

PALM DESERT VISITORS INFORMATION CENTER

72-567 Hwy. 111, Palm Desert
(760) 568-1441, (800) 873-2428
www.palm-desert.org

This city-run facility offers a good selection of Palm Desert "promo" gear—logo'd clothing and the like for adults and kids.

PALM SPRINGS AERIAL TRAMWAY

One Tramway Rd.
(760) 325-1391, (888) 515-8726
www.pstramway.com

This is the only place to find a replica of the tram and tram logo gifts, and maps, books, and posters pertaining to the of San Jacinto Mountains.

PALM SPRINGS AIR MUSEUM

745 North Gene Autry Trail
(760) 778-6262
www.palmspringsairmuseum.org

Everything to do with World War II airplanes and pilots is the specialty, with models, maps, books, stickers, posters, and more. There are also some pieces that relate to air warfare since World War II.

PALM SPRINGS ART MUSEUM

101 Museum Dr.
(760) 325-7186
www.psmuseum.org

The small gift shop here offers art jewelry as well as gifts, books, and posters that focus on the latest exhibits, a good children's section, stationery, and some very high-end original pieces such as Dale Chihuly glass.

PALM SPRINGS VISITORS CENTER

2901 North Palm Canyon Dr.
(760) 778-8418, (800) 347-7746
www.palm-springs.org

This center offers a wide selection of books on architecture and the city's history, plus good-quality logo merchandise and souvenir items. If you're trying to find an out-of-print or rare book on the city's past, this might be the place to shop.

SPECIALTY FOOD AND BEVERAGE STORES

BEVMO

79-715 Hwy. 111, La Quinta
(760) 342-3277
www.bevmo.com

"Specialty?" Indeed. This national chain is the Costco of hops, distilled grains, and fermented grape juice. By any store's standards, the diversity of beer, wine, and spirits is, for lack of a better word, diverse. If putting in for a long weekend or just getting in for the season, consider stocking up here. The arsenal includes mixers, nonalcoholic beverages, stemware, a diverse menu of cocktail-hour eats, and a good range of cigars. It should be noted Bevmo doesn't beat everyone on every price, but it excels for one-stop shopping.

JENSEN'S FOODS
78-525 Hwy. 111, La Quinta
(760) 777–8181

73-601 Hwy. 111, Palm Desert
(760) 346–9393

42-150 Cook St., Suite A, Palm Desert
(760) 837-1877

2465 East Palm Canyon Dr.
(760) 325-8282

69-900 Frank Sinatra Dr., Rancho Mirage
(760) 770-3355
www.jensensfoods.com
Like many other popular stores in the desert, Jensen's got its start in Palm Springs and expanded to the rest of the area, even adding four locations in the San Bernardino and San Gabriel Mountains, and the quick-stop "Minute Shoppe" on Cook Street in Palm Desert. This is a combination of grocer, butcher shop, bakery, wine store, and gourmet foods emporium. You probably want to buy your laundry soap and dog food elsewhere just to save some money, but the food here is absolutely the best, freshest, and tastiest.

PASTRY SWAN BAKERY
68-444 Perez Rd., Cathedral City
(760) 202-1213

73-560 El Paseo Dr., Palm Desert
(760) 340-3040
www.pastryswan.com
This bakery offers exquisite cakes and cookies, pies, and angelic-looking pastries, plus fresh breads, rolls, and all things yeasty and sugary—the desert's favorite for birthdays, brunches, and special treats. The specialty cakes are elegant and glamorous and can be made up with very little notice for special occasions. Stop by early in the morning for the hot, crusty French bread or a croissant and steaming coffee. The Cat City facility is both a retail outlet and the swan's baking facility.

TRADER JOE'S
67-720 East Palm Canyon Dr., Cathedral City
(760) 202-0090

46-400 Washington St., La Quinta
(760) 777-1553

44-250 Town Center Way, Palm Desert
(760) 340-2291
www.traderjoes.com
This quirky discount specialty grocer has a cult following, although cult might be too limiting given its mainstream standing in so many places. The trader sources an immense array of quality products that it then brands under its own labels—including some chucklers like Trader Giotto's for Italian goodies, Trader Jose's, Trader Jacque's, Trader Joe-San's—and of course the singular wine in America, Two Buck Chuck (Charles Shaw). Organics, earth-friendly products, a growing array of fresh meats, ready-to-eat and frozen staples and entrees, a UN of coffees, a forest of nuts, and a veritable dairy of cheeses and yogurts, it's a regular low-cost smorgasbord. TJ's cannot fill every corner of every cupboard or fridge, but it does a lot of things the national chains and some of the fusty gourmet shops cannot, and that's not just make you laugh and save you money.

TULIP HILL WINERY
71-800 Hwy. 111, Rancho Mirage (The River)
(760) 568-2322
www.tuliphillwinery.com
This lovely little shop features a tasting bar for Tulip Hill wines, a small winery in Northern California. The limited-release wines have won numerous awards and are highly regarded in culinary circles. There's also an olive oil-tasting bar, specialty gourmet foods, chocolates, gifts, wine glasses and accessories, and all kinds of gift items for entertaining.

VAN VALKENBURG HAUS OF CHOCOLATES
73-655 El Paseo Dr., Palm Desert
(760) 341-8558
The chocolates here are made in the best European tradition—using the finest chocolate, hand-dipped and finished with distinctive shapes and flavors. A gift box of these chocolates will surely earn you major points, no matter who receives it.

SPORTING GOODS

GOLF ALLEY
42-829 Cook St., Palm Desert
(760) 776-4646, (877) 781-4646
www.golfalleypreowned.com
This is heaven for gear-head golfers, a storefront jammed to the rafters with golf clubs of every name, every style and nearly every vintage. It's all used, some quite little given the peculiarities of some players, and on consignment. Pricing is very fair as while everyone turning something in thinks that that particular club is worth more than Tiger's haul on a typical Sunday in April, the guys who run the joint do a fine job talking 'em out of the trees. It's a mish-mash so if you need a particular needle you might have to dig through many haystacks, but clubs are generally sorted by type and manufacturer. And beware trying to buy something you've put on consignment as a certain writer from the area recently did. There's a full-service repair shop on site.

i If going to either of the outlet centers in Cabazon, stop by the mall offices and inquire about promos or coupons presently being offered, and if you have a few more laps around the sun than most, see if the higher mileage is good for any discounts or specials just for you and others with a similar odometer reading.

LADY GOLF SPORTSWEAR
42-412 Bob Hope Dr., Rancho Mirage
(760) 773-4949, (888) 215-5855
www.ladygolf.com

Lady Golf fills a much needed niche: a clothier for women who golf. So forget two rounders in the corner at the national (men's) retailer. The inventory is varied and stylish, with a good selection of shirts, shorts, hats, gloves, and shoes from well-known designers such as Escada, Lauren, Nike, and Tail. The prices are often discounted at the end of the season, which is the best time to shop for all types of golf wear and equipment. Golf shoes and colorful golf bags are big here as well. Another standout feature is the wide selection of sizes, from 2 all the way through 20.

LUMPY'S GOLF
67-625 East Palm Canyon Dr., Cathedral City
(760) 321-2437

46-630 Washington St., La Quinta
(760) 904-4911
www.lumpys.com
Lumpy's is one of the Big 3 of Coachella Valley golf retailers, and likely the most balanced over the years in inventory, expertise, and customer service; the shoe salespeople are of particularly high note. Like everyone else, Lumpy's will work with you on trade-ins and there's a repair facility. And just so to cover the other side of the continent, there's a Lumpy's in Ft. Myers, Florida.

PETE CARLSON'S GOLF & TENNIS
73-714 Hwy. 111, Palm Desert
(760) 568-3263
With nearly three decades in the desert, Pete Carlson's is the oldest of the large golf retailers, and tennis is about as important to the operation as the Scottish obsession. The shop itself, has grown like a parasite expanding, taking over other hunks of its host strip center a piece here and a piece there; at this rate Pete just might have an address in Rancho Mirage and an address in Indian Wells. From a merchandising standpoint the shop is packed like Golf Alley, although this stuff is shiny new. Service, unfortunately, runs the gamut, and whether it's the changing weather or just particular folks, one's sales associate can be a polished diamond and another a lump of coal.

ROGER DUNN GOLF SHOPS
69-048 Hwy. 111, Cathedral City
(760) 324-1160

80-555 Hwy. 111, Indio
(760) 775-1414
www.worldwidegolfshops.com
Dunn's always had more of the warehouse look to its shops than the competitors; put it this way, the newer Indo outlet is in a former Smart & Final. That's neither good nor bad, it just is. All the needed goodies and manufacturers are represented, and with more elbow room you can actually walk around without taking out a display, or another patron. This place always has seemed accepting of customers kicking the tires, and they have a great supply of previously loved gear. Dunn operates as part of a larger regional chain with other-named shops—Van's and the Golf Mart—under the corporate wing, which can't hurt if needing help back home with something purchased in the desert.

THRIFT SHOPS AND RESALE CLOTHING

AMERICAN CANCER SOCIETY DISCOVERY SHOP
42-446 Bob Hope Dr., Rancho Mirage
(760) 568-5967
Run by volunteers from the American Cancer Society, this is a pretty ordinary secondhand shop, though you might get lucky and find a nice piece of jewelry, designer clothing, or items from an estate. Then again, isn't it really about the charity?

ANGEL VIEW
454 North Indian Canyon Dr.
(760) 322-2440
www.angelview.org
This is the flagship shop of the Angel View Crippled Children's Foundation, one of the valley's leading organizations. This "boutique" features the better-quality donations of men's and women's clothing and accessories. There are an additional half-

dozen foundation-supporting thrift stores across the valley (and several outside the area).

CITY OF HOPE
35-688 Cathedral Canyon Dr., Cathedral City
(760) 321-2266
The City of Hope is a national cancer research insti-tute in Southern California, and this shop is one of many that sell items to benefit the organization. There's always something here—antiques, books, jewelry, household items, and clothing. The atmo-sphere says "thrift store," so you'll have to hunt a bit, and the selection varies from day to day.

EISENHOWER MEDICAL CENTER AUXILIARY COLLECTORS CORNER
71-280 Hwy. 111, Rancho Mirage
(760) 346-1012
This well-run shop often gets high-end items of furniture and accessories. They also have a small selection of men's and women's clothing, housewares, and odds and ends. Overall, the presentation and quality are good, though some might find the prices are a bit steep for used mer-chandise. Be sure to call ahead, as their hours are somewhat erratic and they do close for a period in the summer.

REVIVALS
68-100 Ramon Rd., Cathedral City
(760) 328-1330

68-401 Hwy. 111. Cathedral City
(760) 969-5747

73-608 Hwy. 111, Palm Desert
(760) 346-8690

611 South Palm Canyon Dr.
(760) 318-6491
www.desertaidsproject.org
All of the proceeds from the Revivals stores go to the Desert AIDS Project, one of Southern California's most progressive and active organi-zations helping individuals living with HIV/AIDS. Donations come from all over, and you can find just about anything here—cowboy boots, dinner

glasses, furniture, art, you name it. The prices are very good. The volunteers also accept and handle donations earmarked for the benefit of the local Shelter from the Storm, a shelter for abused women and their children.

OUTLET SHOPPING

The two desert outlet centers are in Cabazon, which is to the west of the Coachella Valley on I–10. Assuming you're not trying to get there on Sunday of Thanksgiving weekend, it's about a 10 minute drive from where Highway 111 intersects I–10 west of the windmill farms, so add another 15 or 30 minutes depending on where you are in the valley. You can exit at Apache Trail by Morongo Casino—not a great idea with traffic—or a mile or so farther west at Fields Road (which will still be a disaster on holidays).

i **Want the best deals at factory outlets? Shop late in the day before a major holiday such as Thanksgiving. Merchandise will already be marked down in anticipation of the sale after the holiday, and you'll be able to beat the hordes, or at least a throng or two.**

CABAZON OUTLETS
48-750 Seminole Dr., Cabazon
(951) 922-3000
www.cabazonoutlets.com
This is the smaller outlet, with 18 or so stores, Starbucks, and a snack shack. What it lacks in size to the bruiser next door it offsets with some great draws, including Greg Norman, Adidas, Columbia Sportswear, Brighton, Crate & Barrel, and Le Creuset, in case you want to get that 13-quart French roaster past TSA.

DESERT HILLS PREMIUM OUTLETS
48-400 Seminole Dr., Cabazon
(951) 849-6641
www.premiumoutlets.com
Desert Hills Premium Outlets is an attraction

unto itself, and the largest sales-tax generator in Riverside County. If you're planning a trip, better make it early on a weekday before the busloads of tourists and day-trippers show up like locusts to the Salt Lake Valley. Depending on the state of the economy and which designer's stuff is hot, or not hot, you can count on some 130 shops, covering most every type of consumer good that doesn't require special federal licensing. But seriously, the Fab 5 are clothing, shoes, home, jewelry, and "beauty" products. You also can eat here but nothing's of any particular note.

The quality of the stores is high, with international names such as Gucci, Ralph Lauren/Polo, Hugo Boss, St. John, Bose, Calvin Klein, Tag Heuer, Nautica, Nike, Lacoste, Saks Off 5th, Salvatore Ferragamo, Tourneau. In all such endeavors, it's your money, so pay attention to what you are buying.

There are two parts to the complex, east and west. The west end is much more user friendly, with parking behind, and the shops arrayed along either side of a pedestrian-only arcade; it's a mall with the top off. The east end is shaped a bit like Talladega Superspeedway—that would be an oval with one malformed side protruding. The center is all parking, and it's a mess.

OUTDOOR MARKETS

COLLEGE OF THE DESERT STREET FAIR
43500 Monterey Ave., Palm Desert
(College of the Desert Campus)
(760) 773-2567
www.codstreetfair.com
This event is run by the College of the Desert Alumni Association to benefit the community college, and it's been a profitable venture since its beginning, to say the least: Some $7 million raised to date. Hundreds of vendors set up for this weekly event on the COD campus just north of Highway 111 in central Palm Desert. The parking lots are clogged with shoppers by 8 a.m., so it's a good idea to get there early. The competition for vendor space is fierce, and the rules are strict. It's a very well-run event with free admission and free entertainment. Wear your walking shoes and

bring cash for small purchases such as produce and food. Most vendors accept credit cards, but do you really want to use your Visa for that tie-dye souvenir T-shirt? The street fair runs both Sat and Sun year-round, starting at 7 a.m. both days. It closes at noon from June through Sept and at 2 p.m. Oct through May.

PALM SPRINGS VILLAGEFEST
North Palm Canyon Drive between Amado and Baristo Roads
(760) 320-3781
www.villagefest.org
Up through the 1980s, Palm Springs was a place that rolled up the streets after 6 p.m. Stores closed, restaurants opened late only on the weekends, and there wasn't a darn thing to do at night. That left both visitors and locals feeling like farmers or kids with a curfew—early to bed and early to rise.

That changed when the city started Village-Fest in 1991 as an attempt to bring life to the streets and encourage weekenders to come on Thurs rather than Fri. Today this weekly street fair attracts thousands of people on the quietest, hottest summer night. During high season, attendance easily tops 10,000. It took several years for local merchants to get on board, but now virtually all the shops on the central part of Palm Canyon Drive stay open past 6 p.m., new restaurants have bloomed with outdoor seating,

and the event has become an integral part of the city's personality. In 2005 VillageFest received a series of upgrades, including a certified organic farmers' market, elimination of the kiddie rides, better live entertainment, and strategies to make it more accessible for wheelchairs. Organizers have also decided to strictly enforce rules that all crafts must be handmade and that the artists themselves must work the booths. This is one event that's a must, with music spilling from the nightclubs, shoppers walking their dogs—VillageFest is very dog friendly—and picking up art, street entertainers, an extensive farmers' market, and the added bonus of being able to wander in and out of all the shops on the street.

i The height of the date harvest is in February, and this is the optimum time to get fresh-from-the-palm dates. Check out vendors at the Thursday-night VillageFest in Palm Springs and the weekend-morning College of the Desert Street Fair in Palm Desert. Better yet, if you're in town during the Riverside County Fair & National Date Festival, go right to where the lovely date is the center attraction. The fair is held annually beginning the Friday of President's Weekend and runs for 10 days (www.datefest.org).

ATTRACTIONS

Like any other resort destination, the Coachella Valley has its fair share of attractions and diversions, campy or profound, for visitors looking for a change from the endless round of sun and play. But don't expect a string of amusement parks or cookie-cutter playgrounds. With a few exceptions, the attractions here are representative of the forces that have defined the desert and shaped its character: its Native American and western heritage, its natural resources, its weather, and its free-spirited pioneers.

If you're on a limited schedule or visiting for the first time, there are four "must-see" attractions that are suitable for all ages and will give you a deep appreciation of and respect for this area's personality.

If you've ever thought to yourself, "Oh, Palm Springs is just swimming pools and golf courses," you'll think very differently after a visit to the Indian Canyons, Joshua Tree National Park, the Palm Springs Aerial Tramway, and the Living Desert. Each of these spots offers a highly individual look at the interaction between man and nature here in this desert. Each place is nearly unique, and, above all, each one is great fun. You can use your visit as an opportunity for education and wonder or just have a good time petting Nubian goats, hiking to waterfalls, and enjoying a view that stretches from snow-tipped peaks to below-sea-level desert bottoms, and all the way to Mexico. Put these four on the top of your list and make room for a few more each time you visit.

Opening and closing hours can vary, so be sure to call ahead or check the Web sites for last-minute information.

Although most of these attractions can be seen and visited perfectly well on your own, several tour companies provide guides and programs that are outstanding. Depending on how you like to travel, taking at least one trip with one of these outfits could be more than worth the price many times over in the knowledge and appreciation of the desert that you'll gain. Because the prices and hours of the tours can change dramatically depending on the operator and time of year, we suggest you always call ahead to make sure you won't be disappointed.

Unless otherwise noted, all establishments accept major credit cards.

Price Code

Prices are given only as a range and are per person, using the following code.

$	Less than $15
$$	$15 to $30
$$$	$31 to $50
$$$$	More than $50

ATTRACTIONS

AGUA CALIENTE CULTURAL MUSEUM FREE
219 South Palm Canyon Dr.
(760) 323-0151
www.accmuseum.org

This small and beautifully arranged space is the center of the tribe's growing efforts to preserve the Cahuilla history and culture. Permanent and changing exhibits display just some of the museum's Southern California basketry collection, as well as contemporary arts and artifacts from the Tahquitz Canyon Archaeological Collection, one of the most extensive excavation projects in California.

With some of the world's best examples of the work of Cahuilla basket weavers and their neighboring tribes, the full collections are available to researchers and students on request. More baskets, artifacts, and archival photographs are displayed in the lobby of the tribe's Spa Resort Casino at 100 North Indian Canyon Dr. in Palm Springs. The museum is open Wed through Sat from 10 a.m. to 5 p.m. and Sun from noon to 5 p.m. in season, and the same hours and days in the summer, except Wed and Thurs.

i The Palm Springs Aerial Tramway offers a summer pass, good for unlimited rides May through August—$60 for adults and half that for kids. If you're planning to ride up at least three times over a summer stay, you're money ahead. Winter time passes are $150 and $90 for the respective age groups.

CABAZON CULTURAL MUSEUM   FREE
84-245 Indio Springs Parkway, Indio
(760) 238-5770
www.cabazonindians-nsn.gov
This small museum adjacent to Fantasy Springs Resort Casino on Cabazon land in Indio has been a work in progress for some time. It lacks the ethnographic and historiographic detail of Agua Caliente but is worth some of your time if out in the east valley. Hours are 1 p.m. to 5 p.m. Tues, Wed, Fri, and Sat.

CABOT'S PUEBLO MUSEUM   FREE
$ (GUIDED PUEBLO TOURS)
67-616 East Desert View Ave.,
Desert Hot Springs
(760) 329-7610
www.cabotsmuseum.org

A California state historic site, this is one of the oddest attractions in the area, verging on the creepy. Built in the style of a Hopi pueblo, the building is the work of Cabot Yerxa, the man who "discovered" hot mineral water in Desert Hot Springs.

A wanderer and explorer who grew up in a family of Indian traders, Yerxa headed for the Klondike in 1899 when he was just 16, following other prospectors searching for gold. He became fascinated with the Inuit culture, collecting curios and artifacts and learning the language. When his father bought land in Cuba, he joined him and later set up a cigar factory in Key West. The family moved on to Riverside and invested in orange groves, and Cabot established a homestead on 160 acres on the present site of Desert Hot Springs. His search for reliable water led to his discovery of the first hot mineral springs in the area.

He later enlisted in the army and finally returned to the desert in 1937. Two years later he started building his life's work, a reflection of his personal interpretation of Indian belief.

Cabot believed that symmetry retains evil spirits, so the doorways and floors slant, the walls are uneven, and the windows form puzzles of multishaped glass. He learned how to make adobe bricks and scavenged most of the building materials from abandoned homesteads. The result is a four-story, 35-room maze with 150 windows, 5,000 square feet, and innumerable narrow staircases and winding halls.

Touring Cabot's Old Indian Pueblo is not for those who are claustrophobic, but it's a fascinating look at one man's obsession. It's open Fri and Sat from 10 a.m. to 3 p.m. and is closed July through Sept.

CHILDREN'S DISCOVERY MUSEUM
OF THE DESERT $
71-701 Gerald Ford Dr., Rancho Mirage
(760) 321-0602
www.cdmod.org
Kids will be in their glory at this hands-on heaven. In "Today I Want To Be" kids can indulge the skills

ATTRACTIONS

they'll need down the line, whether that's shopping in the "Grocery Store" or experiencing life as a veterinarian in the SPCA-sponsored "Furs, Fins, Feathers & Fun" section. Physical activity is stressed in "Let's Get Physical," with a rope maze and rock-climbing challenge. There's also "Art Is Versatile," where smock-wearing tikes take paint and imagination and apply it to a real live VW Bug. Parents must stay with their children and are encouraged to join in the activities. Check the Web site for such events as free family fun nights, toddler parties, and holiday activities. Classes and special programs are planned throughout the week.

If you're looking for a safe, inexpensive place to spend quality time with the family, this is one of the desert's gems. The museum is open Mon through Sat from 10 a.m. to 5 p.m. and on Sun from noon to 5 p.m. It is closed on Mon from May through Dec, and some holidays. For more information, check the listing in the Kidstuff chapter.

COACHELLA VALLEY PRESERVE   FREE
Thousand Palms Canyon Road,
north of Palm Desert
(760) 343-2733
www.coachellavalleypreserve.org
Way back when in the mid-1980s, a plan was put in place to save about 20,000 acres of desert dune, hill and palm oasis because a little lizard was in danger of going away. Some scoffed at setting aside three disconnected hunks of desert for a reptile. Today, the habitat management plan remains an icon for other jurisdictions and communities seeking to resolve preservation/development conflicts.

Aside from happy critters and plants, we all gained something, and not just open space. The most easterly of the three blocks of turf, the Thousand Palms Preserve is one of those right-in-your-back-yard charmers that most locals don't even know about. The preserve's visitor center and a small museum are housed in a homesteader's cabin set within a magical natural garden of artesian springs and native palms. Three hiking trails fan out from there, taking in other oases here in

the San Andreas-created folds between I-10 and the mountains. Of the three we go for the Pushawalla Palms Trail, a six- to nine-miler depending on if walked as an out-and-back or a loop. There's a bit of climbing at various spots but the reward is a pristine oasis of nattering birds, towering palms, and surface-flowing water even in the depths of summer. Free admission, but please make liberal use of the provided donation box.

GENERAL GEORGE S. PATTON
MEMORIAL MUSEUM $
Chiriaco Summit (I-10 30 miles east of Indio)
(760) 227-3483
www.generalpattonmuseum.com
In early 1942 Major General George S. Patton Jr. was chosen to set up the Desert Training Center and start an emergency mission to train men and machines to stop Germany's advance into North Africa. He selected a site of almost 18,000 square miles, making it the largest military installation and maneuver area in the world. Joseph Chiriaco, one of the first area residents Patton met when he came to the desert, donated the site where the museum now stands.

The Desert Training Center became operational in early April 1942. Four days later, General Patton and the troops took their first desert march. Within 15 days, all units at the center had been on a desert march. Within 23 days, he had conducted 13 tactical exercises, including some with two nights in the desert. As Patton explained to his men, "If you can work successfully here, in this country, it will be no difficulty at all to kill the assorted sons of bitches you meet in any other country." The bravado with which Patton approached taking on the Germans on another continent an ocean away based on two nights of bivouac several hours east of Hollywood is a testament to his steely resolve and the spunk of his men.

Patton was at the Desert Training Center for less than four months before he was sent overseas to start planning the North African campaign. More than a million troops eventually trained for desert warfare here. The facility houses an eclectic assortment of memorabilia and armament, and someone on staff might be able to direct you to spots in the desert where Patton's tank tracks are still visible.

The museum is open daily from 9:30 a.m. to 4:30 p.m., except Thanksgiving and Christmas. It's located at Chiriaco Summit, 30 miles east of Indio on I–10.

i If you book a tour that involves much more than gawking at where Bob Hope once got his hair cut, leave the flip-flops at the pool and wear close-toed shoes. Even well-trod paths such as those at the Living Desert can smack a toe.

THE INDIAN CANYONS $
38-500 South Palm Canyon Dr.
(760) 323-6018
www.theindiancanyons.com

TAHQUITZ CANYON $$
500 West Mesquite Ave.
(760) 416-7044
www.tahquitzcanyon.com

Located on Agua Caliente tribal land, just a few minutes' drive from downtown, Andreas, Murray, and Palm Canyons are true, natural palm oases, with waterfalls, streams, and cool canopies of towering palm trees. To reach the canyons, follow South Palm Canyon Drive in Palm Springs until it dead-ends. Palm Canyon and Andreas Canyon also have the world's largest stands of naturally occurring palm trees. This is one of the desert's four "must-see" attractions, along with the Living Desert, Joshua Tree, and the aerial tramway.

Listed on the National Register of Historic Places, the canyons are the ancestral home of the Agua Caliente Band of Cahuilla Indians and are owned and operated by the tribe. Andreas Canyon was the largest gathering place, the center of social life during the hot summer months. Here you can spot faint petroglyphs and an impressive stone outcropping where the women of the tribe used to grind grain. Picnic tables and a parking lot

are as far as most visitors go, but make the effort and take a short hike to nearby Murray Canyon. This small palm oasis is the access point to the area's famous "Seven Sisters" hiking spot, where waterfalls tumble down from the mountains, going through seven immense natural stone bowls before settling into a peaceful stream.

Palm Canyon is the largest of the three canyon-oasis areas. It stretches through palm-lined canyons and streams for 15 miles, and at the top it intersects Highway 74 on its way to Idyllwild. You can drive right up to the trading post and take a stroll to a lovely waterfall, or you can put on your hiking boots and venture out for a full day of wandering and dreaming. This truly is one of the most beautiful spots in the entire desert and an absolute must for those who want to get close to the true heart of Palm Springs. Be warned, though: It's easy to lose your bearings, and the rocks can be slippery and treacherous. Always let people know where you're going, take a map and cell phone, and wear the right shoes and clothes.

If you're staying around the trading post, be sure to check out the maps, books, and fine-quality Native American arts and crafts from tribes around the country. Have a cold drink and strike up a conversation with the people behind the counter—they're a wonderful resource for tales and inside information about the canyons.

Tahquitz Canyon, just a few blocks from downtown Palm Springs, is also on the National Register of Historic Places. For years the area was scarred by graffiti and littered with trash. Then, with income provided from the Indian Canyons and the new Spa Resort Casino, the tribe fenced the canyon land, cleaned it up, and built the Tahquitz Interpretive Center, where visitors can learn about the area's history. This is the place to sign up for a guided hike that leads directly to Tahquitz Falls, a breathtaking spot with a huge waterfall that runs year-round and figured prominently in an ages-ago film classic, Frank Capra's Lost Horizon.

The Indian Canyons are open daily from 8 a.m. to 5 p.m. Oct through June and 8 a.m. to 5 p.m. Fri through Sun during the summer months. Tahquitz Canyon is accessible 7:30 a.m. to 5 p.m. daily Oct through June, and the same hours Fri, Sat, and Sun during the heat of summer. The Tahquitz hike is moderately difficult and takes approximately two hours. Reservations are required.

THE INTEGRATRON $
2477 Belfield Blvd., Landers
(760) 364-3126
www.integratron.com
A sun-bleached dome about 20 miles from Joshua Tree National Park, the Integratron is a legendary site in UFO circles. It's just down the road from Giant Rock, a freestanding boulder that's seven stories high, covers 5,800 square feet, and has a place in Native American lore as a site where elders received teachings from spirits.

The Integratron began to take shape in 1947 when George Van Tassel, a Lockheed engineer and former test pilot for Howard Hughes, left his job, leased four square miles around Giant Rock, and moved his family to a campsite by the boulder. He claimed that his weekly meditations led to an encounter with aliens from the planet Venus who invited him onto their ship and gave him tips on rejuvenating living cells with sound.

Combining these tips with theories involving the earth's magnetic field and the locations of both the Great Pyramid in Egypt and Giant Rock, Van Tassel started building his "rejuvenation chamber" in 1954.

For the next 18 years, UFO conventions and donations from thousands of believers kept the family afloat, but when Van Tassel died in 1978, the Integratron was not fully finished and the work was abandoned.

The Integratron still stands, a pristine white dome looking as if it was painted yesterday. The 38-foot-high, 50-foot-diameter structure was built without nails, screws, or any metal framing to enhance its magnetic properties. The upper level is engineered to amplify sounds, with a central spot on the wooden floor that creates an almost living vibration. Here, two sisters who bought the property a few years ago give sound baths using Tibetan crystal bowls and explain the workings of "the Dome."

Although the Integratron has been featured on many TV shows, including one on the Discovery Channel, very few locals even know of its existence. This is truly an "insider place" and for those of the right frame of mind and persuasion, well worth the visit. Be sure to call or visit the Web site for driving directions, as the street address will be of little help.

Self-guided tours, private group tours, sound baths, retreats, and workshops are held throughout the year. Because of ongoing restoration and times when the facility is rented to large groups, opening times vary. Check the Web site for updates.

JOSHUA TREE NATIONAL PARK $
Joshua Tree National Park Visitor Center
74485 National Park Dr., Twentynine Palms
(760) 367-5500
www.nps.gov/jotr/index.htm
Joshua Tree National Park is the jewel of the California desert, even if it lacks the fame and infamy of Death Valley or the shrouded intrigue of the Providence Mountains' Mitchell Caverns. Straddling two different deserts and both ringed and cleaved by mountains the park is larger than Rhode Island.

Joshua Tree can be done as a drive park, though to do that to the exclusion of getting dust on your boots would surely have the late Edward Abbey tuning in his grave. The park is accessible via car from two points on the higher-elevation north side and from the south off I–10 about a half hour east of Indio. It's a through-route slashing across from top-left to bottom-right, essentially. (Two other access points dead end in the park from the north: the Black Rock Visitor Center, camping, and picnic area at the northwestern corner, and Indian Cove, with individual and group camping, and a picnic area, in the center.) We think starting down south is the preferred angle of attack, for the very simple fact that the lower desert portions of the park aren't as gutturally drop-dead gorgeous, and concluding up top is exactly why dessert comes last. So if you do this, just drive through in Abbey's hated "industrial tourism" mode, please at least promise us you'll obey the posted limit and roll down the windows once in a while. Then either turn around and return the way you came or loop back to the valley through the high desert.

Rock-climbers—this is a world-class climbing destination—equestrians, dayhikers, stargazers, backpackers, campers, and even four-wheel drivers know the park is best experienced by being experienced. On foot, or above hoof, the desert screams life, from barrel cactus blossoming in a riot of purple in spring through the forests of Joshua trees that stand sentinel over time to the Flintstone heaps of granite that exceed anything a cartoon could ever hope to over-embellish. Of the host of "musts," several jump out, and these are all day-use options; if you backpack, you already know the whys and hows.

Lost Palms Oasis is a seven-plus mile out-and-back hike starting from the natural springs at the Cottonwood Visitor Center a few minutes inside the south entrance. A moderate hike traversing desert wash and ridge ends at about frond level above the lush oasis, a cleave in the rumble-tumble desert wilderness where plate tectonics conspires to bring water to the surface. Scramblers can scurry down into the oasis and access another canyon and oasis. Pack water and wear sturdy shoes or boots, and think about bringing the youngest dust-kickers back in a couple years.

For the car brigade, Keys View brings a stunning view back into the Coachella Valley, stretching from the Salton Sea on your left to the San Gorgonio Pass in the west. The overlook is accessible and a quick walk up a little ridge enhances the scene just a tick. For orientation purposes, if you're out about Indio look northward, up into that folded mass of terra firma called the Little San Bernardino Mountains, Keys View is in there somewhere.

At any number of spots around the park, nature trails lead to the monoliths that are such a draw for climbers. With names like Skull Rock,

Arch Rock, and the no-kidding Jumbo Rock, you know you're gonna wanna have a look.

Finally, the park service puts a lot of heart into its interpretive centers. Kids weaned on the Internet mind find it all so quaint—it is—so show them what vacation used to be all about, when seeing the relief map and the stuffed bobcat was almost as cool as the time you made dad waste six hours of pay taking you to Rattlesnake World Safari just off the Interstate. Each of the centers mentioned have displays and information, and the main Oasis Visitor Center in Twentynine Palms has a wealth of books, the works of local artisans and as elsewhere across the park, rangers who just want to share. Hours vary from center to center, but most open at 8 a.m. and close at 5 p.m.

Joshua Tree is open year-round, and know that it can snow from time to time at the park's higher elevations. However you "do" the park, please just do it. With several campgrounds, day-use picnic spots, easy nature trails and a bounty of hikes, even dedicated trails for equestrians and off-roaders, there is something in the park for everybody. And bring your camera, and tons of memory, and if you've never really seen the Milky Way, come out some night.

KNOTT'S SOAK PALM SPRINGS $$
1500 South Gene Autry Trail
(760) 327-0499
www.knotts.com

A full-fledged water park with nearly two dozen slides and rides, Knott's is an exceptionally clean, well-run facility that caters to all ages. The 800,000-gallon wave pool is as close to the beach as you can get in Palm Springs, and the waves are actually big enough to get in a little boogie board action.

Toddlers are well served here as well, with the gentle Gremmie Lagoon and Kahuna's Beach House, a family water playhouse. Tubes and life vests are provided at no charge. There are extra fees for locker rentals and parking. Leave your chairs, barbecues, food, and drink behind, because they aren't allowed inside; small hand-held coolers with water are acceptable. Likewise, come in appropriate swimwear—long pants and denim aren't allowed in the pool or activity areas.

This is a fine place to spend an afternoon, particularly if the kids are chafing under orders to keep the noise down at the hotel pool. Knott's is open Mar through Sept. For more information, check the listing in the Kidstuff chapter.

i Despite its harsh appearance, the desert is an extremely fragile environment, so if out hiking or four-wheeling, stay on the path given. Straying across the desert can leave marks that last decades, even centuries And don't pluck any flora and leave the rocks for others to see just as you did. Take only pictures, leave only memories.

THE LIVING DESERT $
47-900 Portola Ave., Palm Desert
(760) 346-5694
www.livingdesert.org
Another of the must-sees, the Living Desert is a unique combination of zoo, botanical garden, and wildlife education/breeding/recovery center. There are so many different activities and events going on that it's a good idea to call before you visit or check the daily schedule on the well-conceived Web site for updated events, programs, special tours, demonstrations, or lectures.

The Living Desert is dedicated to showcasing the animals and plants of the world's different arid regions. Many of the animals here are threatened or endangered species. The Living Desert has been successful in increasing the world's population of slender-horned gazelles, sand cats, addax, and Arabian oryx, and this is one of the few places in the world where these beautiful creatures can be seen up close. The medical facility is state-of-the-art and docent-led tours are offered and animal lovers of all ages can watch critters needing extra care in one of five special care units.

The animals live in exacting re-creations of their natural habitat, with room to roam. Along with the African wildlife—including cheetahs—the park showcases North American animals and birds of prey in Eagle Canyon and the peninsular desert bighorn sheep habitat is singular. The After Sundown exhibit features locals such as bats, scorpions, owls, mice, and snakes that are active only after dark. Coyotes, wolves, mountain lions, badgers, and bobcats are all part of the crowd, as they live wild in the mountains surrounding Palm Springs.

Village WaTuTu is an authentic replica of a North African village, with grass-thatched huts around the Elder's Grove, where storytellers weave tales from African and Native American folklore. There are a Petting Kraal, African domestic livestock, and leopards, hyenas, camels, birds, and plants from the region.

The Wortz Demonstration Garden gives homeowners and landscape architects ideas for using drought-resistant plants in their own homes or projects. The Palo Verde Garden Center offers a variety of cacti, succulents, flowering ornamentals, wildlife food, desert plants, and arrangements, as well as landscaping and horticultural books, videos, and garden ornaments.

You should plan on at least three to four hours to see everything. This place has thought of everything to make a visit pleasant, including lots of shade trees and misted rest spots, two excellent gift shops, restaurants, first aid stations, baby-changing stations, and ATMs.

One of the "star" attractions at the Living Desert is the periodic Starry Safari Overnight Adventure. This features a wildlife presentation, nighttime walk around the park, dinner, and tales around the campfire. Participants bring their own sleeping bags and tuck into the park's four-person tents for the night. The program is tailored to adults and children older than eight. Singles and couples without children are welcome. Reservations are required.

The Living Desert is open daily from 9 a.m. to 5 p.m. Sept 1 through June 15, with the last admission at 4 p.m.; it is closed on Christmas. It's open daily from 8 a.m. to 1:30 p.m. June 16 through Aug 31, with the last admission at 1 p.m.

Regular, non-narrated shuttle service is available throughout the park for an extra charge. Parking is free.

MOORTEN BOTANICAL GARDEN $
1701 South Palm Canyon Dr.
(760) 327-6555

A living museum with nature trails that weave around 3,000 varieties of giant cacti, trees, succulents, flowers, birds, and turtles, Moorten Botanical Garden has been a Palm Springs landmark since 1938. The one-acre site is packed with rare and exotic plants, grouped according to the desert region where they naturally grow, including Arizona, California, Texas, Colorado, Mexico, South America, and Africa.

Perhaps the most striking feature of this quirky, slightly Wild West site is the age of its plants and their density on this small site. Specimens here reach monumental proportions and bloom in abundance just as they do in the wild. Monstrous agaves, crested Cereus, towering cardon and exotic boojum trees, a two-story Pachypodium, and more than a dozen different aloes from southern Africa and Madagascar are a few of the standouts. Turtledoves, hummingbirds, lizards, and other small wild creatures are at home in the gardens and add to the feeling of being enclosed in a magical dreamscape.

The Cactarium, a greenhouse that protects some of the most rare and unusual species from the brutal summer sun and cold nights, is a treasure house of world-class specimens found virtually nowhere else outside of private collections or their native habitat.

Many unusual botanical specimens are for sale, along with other souvenirs. No matter the day, one member of the Moorten family is always on hand to talk about the plants, the garden, and old Palm Springs. This is the most authentic, down-to-earth of all the man-made attractions in the desert. In fact, as Clark Moorten will tell you, it's not really man-made, just "man-maintained."

The botanical garden is open from 9 a.m. to 4:30 p.m. Mon through Sat and from 10 a.m. to 4 p.m. on Sun; it is closed on Wed.

OASIS DATE GARDENS   FREE
59-111 Hwy. 111, Thermal
(760) 399-5665, (800) 827-8017
www.oasisdategardens.com

A working date garden since 1912, Oasis is the oldest date grower in the valley. And it boasts the oldest date palm in the valley—planted in 1919, this giant towers 80 feet above the Oasis Ranch Store. In addition to hundreds of date palms in various stages of maturity, the 175-acre garden has a palm arboretum for propagation, a packing house, the ranch store, and a garden cafe. If you're taking one of the tours that goes to the eastern end of the valley, chances are good that it includes a stop at Oasis for free date samples, a rest break, and an opportunity for shopping.

Oasis ships its many varieties of fresh dates all over the world. Pick up a couple of packages for yourself and send some home to your friends. There's no souvenir that says "Palm Springs" more than a box of sweet golden-brown dates. The facility also gives daily tours at no charge. In season, Oasis is the home base for Camel Safari rides, so if you've harbored a desire to go a few blocks on top of the "ship of the desert," this is the place. Call for dates and prices. Oasis is open from 8 a.m. to 5 p.m. Mon through Sat.

> **i** Bring a sweater or light jacket if riding the tram. It's always 30 to 40 degrees cooler at the top than it is on the desert floor.

PALM SPRINGS AERIAL TRAMWAY $$
One Tramway Rd.
(760) 325-1391, (888) 515-8726
www.pstramway.com

This could be the must-see desert attraction—it's an "attraction," as some camp is allowed. The Palm Springs Aerial Tramway soars from above the desert floor in rugged Chino Canyon on the north edge of Palm Springs to the 8,516-foot Mountain Station. Temperatures at the top of the tram are generally about 30 to 40 degrees cooler than they are in the desert, and the pine-scented mountain wilderness is a bracing contrast to the flash down below.

The trip up takes about 15 minutes and offers a spectacular view from the world's largest rotating tramcars. The cars hold around 80 people and are very stable, though you'll get a little "lift" when they pass under the cable towers. At the top you can have a cafeteria-style meal inside or outside on balconies that give a view of the entire valley floor, or step up to finer dining in Peaks Restaurant. A short film about the tram's making is good for history buffs and helps to explain why tram promoters call its building "the eighth wonder of the world."

Twenty years after the tram opened for its first ride in 1963, it was designated a historical civil engineering landmark. Of five supporting towers, the first is the only one that can be reached by road. The other four and the 35,000-square-foot Mountain Station were all built with men and materials flown in place by helicopters—more than 23,000 flights in all.

In 2000 the original tram cars were replaced, and the entire facility—designed by famed mid-century architect and Palm Springs resident Albert Frey—was given a much-needed interior updating.

The top of the Tram is right in the middle of the Mount San Jacinto State Park and Wilderness and is the hub for 54 miles of hiking trails. The trails are clearly marked, so you can strike off on your own and pick a pretty spot to have a picnic lunch. Remember, you are more than a mile-and-a-half in the air, so the oxygen level won't be what it was down in the flats. Taking the tram is also a "cheater" way to summit Mt. San Jacinto, rather than the longer haul up from the Idyllwild side of the mountain. The free, guided nature walks are also a wonderful way to learn about the natural environment at the top of the tram.

One of the joys of spending a winter vacation in the valley is the choice of sunbathing by the pool or playing in the snow—or even doing both in the same day. Snow at the top of the tram is virtually guaranteed by Christmas. During the winter months the Winter Adventure Center offers cross-country ski and snowshoeing equipment rental; or you can bring your own. Sleds and cold-weather clothes are also for sale in the Mountain Station gift shop. Really hardy types even camp out in the snow.

Day permits are available at the Ranger Station in Long Valley, a short walk from the Mountain Station, and are required for any hiking or backpacking beyond Long Valley. Permits are also required for overnight camping at the primitive campsites in four designated campgrounds. Requests for advance permits can be made in person or in writing—no phone or fax requests are accepted. Check the Web site for details.

Tram cars depart at least every half hour, starting at 10 a.m., Mon through Fri, and starting at 8 a.m. on weekends and during holiday periods. The last car up is at 8 p.m., with the last car down being at 9:45 p.m. Ride 'n' Dine specials that give a discount for a ride and a meal are available after 3 p.m.

i Want the ultimate summer romantic date? Pick a full-moon night and get the tram's Ride 'n' Dine special. Have a leisurely dinner while the sun sets, then head for Lookout Point, about a half mile from the Mountain Station. With clear weather you can see the moonlight shining on the Salton Sea.

PALM SPRINGS AIR MUSEUM $
745 North Gene Autry Trail
(760) 778-6262
www.air-museum.org
The Palm Springs Air Museum is dedicated to World War II aircraft and has one of the world's largest collections of operable craft of that era. These planes are in perfect working condition and are pressed into service for flight demonstrations and hands-on exhibitions throughout the year, particularly on significant military anniversary dates.

The planes, along with rare combat photography, enormous murals, artifacts, and memorabilia, are grouped by theater of conflict, Europe or the Pacific. Ongoing history and education programs are part of the lure here, along with a remarkable group of docent volunteers, all of whom served in World War II themselves and make up the irreplaceable living history component of the air museum.

Large-scale model ships and gorgeous vintage automobiles are also displayed in the museum's air-conditioned hangars. There is a fine library, computers with flight simulators, and a gift shop stocked with models and flight-related souvenirs. The institution is on a 10-acre site that includes visitor parking, ramp access to the Palm Springs International Airport for visiting display aircraft, exterior displays, and an aircraft ramp for special shows and flight demonstration viewing.

The museum is open daily from 10 a.m. to 5 p.m., closed Thanksgiving and Christmas.

i **The Palm Springs Art Museum offers free admission from 4 to 8 p.m. each Thursday, during the weekly Village-Fest. Make an evening of it by touring the museum, having an early dinner, and shopping for fresh produce and crafts, all within a 4- to 5-block radius.**

PALM SPRINGS ART MUSEUM $
101 Museum Dr.
(760) 322-4800
www.psmuseum.org
Founded in 1938, the Palm Springs Art Museum is one of the country's best small fine arts/natural history institutions. Its patrons over the years have been the most affluent and famous of the desert's visitors and residents, from Walter Annenberg to Kirk and Anne Douglas, Steven Chase, and William Holden. All contributed large amounts of money, art, and love to building a world-class facility.

Named the Palm Springs Desert Museum for more than 50 years, the institution changed its name in 2005 to the Palm Springs Art Museum, more accurately reflecting its focus on the fine

and performing arts. The museum's permanent art collection features 19th-, 20th-, and 21st-century works focusing on contemporary California art, classic western American art, Native American art, pre-Columbian art, Mexican art, European modern art, glass studio art, American mid-20th-century architecture, and American photography.

In addition, the Annenberg Theater keeps an eclectic calendar from ballet to modern dance, opera to jazz, and comedy to drama. The museum offers art classes, special events, lectures, films, two sculpture gardens, a cafe, and a new online museum store filled with unique items you won't find anywhere else.

In the newly re-installed Denney Western American Art Wing, fans of classic western art such as paintings and sculptures by Charles Russell and Frederic Remington can view their works alongside contemporary works such as Alexis Smith's image of a modern-day desperado or Arlo Namingha's sculpture inspired by traditional Hopi kachinas.

In the spacious upstairs galleries, added with the museum's major expansion a few years ago, visitors can view a major survey of 20th-century art, with approximately 100 paintings, works on paper, and sculpture by well-known artists. From early modernists to the contemporary, some of the artists are Alexander Archipenko, Marc Chagall, Amedeo Modigliani, Alberto Giacometti, Henry Moore, Barbara Hepworth, Franz Kline, Sam Francis, Helen Frankenthaler, Frank Stella, Robert Motherwell, Robert Arneson, William Wiley, Dale Chihuly, DeWain Valentine, Peter Voulkos, and Edward Ruscha.

Along with outstanding traveling exhibitions of major artists, the museum is known for its natural history and science wing. Here the changing exhibits appeal to all ages and are always focused on learning through fun. Past exhibits have included the world of dinosaurs, nocturnal desert wildlife, earthquakes, and more.

Special children's and family programs are a recent addition to the museum during the summer months. Check the Web site for current events and activities. For more information on the Annenberg Theater, see the listing in the Arts and Entertainment chapter.

The museum is open from 10 a.m. to 5 p.m. Tues, Wed, Fri, Sat, and Sun; from noon to 8 p.m. on Thurs, with free admission after 4 p.m. Sponsored by the city to coincide with VillageFest. It is closed on Mon and major holidays. Docent-guided tours are available.

i During the winter season, Sunday Afternoon Concerts at the Annenberg Theater in the Palm Springs Art Museum are a bargain, showcasing top classical and jazz musicians and groups on their way to higher-priced dates in Los Angeles and San Diego.

SALTON SEA STATE   **$ (PER VEHICLE)**
RECREATION AREA   **$$ (CAMPING)**

SALTON SEA NATIONAL
WILDLIFE REFUGE
Riverside and Imperial Counties
(760) 564-4888
www.saltonsea.ca.gov
The Salton Sea is a massive inland sea created when irrigation canals bringing Colorado River water to the desert failed, flooding the low-lying Salton Trough over a several year period during the first part of the last century. For the past 80 years the sea has been primarily sustained by "rivers" carrying a toxic mix of agricultural residue, and with no natural outflow it has been increasing in salinity and nutrient levels, leading to a double-edged sword of becoming less hospitable to aquatic life acclimated to a briny-but-not-this-briny environment and being subjected to ever-increasing oxygen-stealing algae blooms

The Salton Sea is most famous for its role as a winter stopover for migratory birds. More than 400 species have been documented here, including 100 breeding species, giving this salty sump the second-highest concentration of avian life anywhere in the nation. Because of wildlife and general ecological concerns, lost recreational opportunities, and the economic primacy of agriculture in the two desert valleys that "feed" the

sea, the multi-interest Salton Sea Authority has been laboring since the mid-1990s to come up with a comprehensive restoration and management plan for the gravely endangered sea.

The area has a fascinating history and an uncertain future. One of the best ways to learn about both is to take a nature tour with one of the desert companies that specialize in this area. It will be an unforgettable experience and a rich opportunity for photos of bubbling mud pots, an inland sea, and the remains of Salton City, once touted as the desert's most exciting new recreation area. The 35-mile-long Salton Sea lies south of Indio and is accessible from Highway 86 or Highway 111.

THE VILLAGE GREEN HERITAGE CENTER   **$**
221 South Palm Canyon Dr.
(760) 323-8297
The Village Green Heritage Center sits in a well-groomed little park right in the middle of Palm Canyon Drive and features two 19th-century pioneer homes. The McCallum Adobe, the oldest remaining building in Palm Springs, was built in 1884 for John McCallum, the first permanent white settler. Although adobe was eminently suited for the desert climate, few people in the area knew how to make the bricks, and this was an oddity at the time.

Palm Springs' first hotel operator, Dr. Welwood Murray, built the second structure, Miss Cornelia's "Little House," in 1893. The house was constructed of railroad ties from the defunct Palmdale Railway and purchased by the sisters Miss Cornelia White and Dr. Florilla White in 1913. In 1961 the Palm Springs Historical Society acquired the home and furnished it with antiques donated by local residents.

Between the two old homes, there's a vast collection of photographs, paintings, clothing, tools, books, Indian artifacts, and furniture from the earliest pioneer days of the city. Also in the Village Green complex are the Agua Caliente Cultural Museum and Ruddy's 1930s General Store Museum, a re-creation of a turn-of-the-20th-century general store, complete with authentic

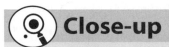 Close-up

Bruce Poynter, Desert Guide Extraordinaire

Every tour operator and hotel concierge knows Bruce for his endless store of knowledge and unfailing enthusiasm. Even though he's been taking visitors out on desert tours for more than two decades, he still gets genuinely excited about spotting a red-tailed hawk, reciting a mind-boggling assembly of geologic facts, or capturing a gentle rosy boa so the children and adults in his tour group can see one of the desert's most delicate and harmless snakes up close.

Right out of high school Bruce joined the Air Force and spent most of his enlistment working with the fire rescue crews in Vietnam at the height of the conflict, earning a Commendation Medal as sergeant. The experience sharpened his appetite for firefighting, and he joined the Indio Fire Department as soon as his military service ended.

The next 20 years were spent in emergency medical services as a fire department captain, emergency medical transport specialist, and instructor in first aid, CPR, and desert survival. Named Firefighter of the Year and Emergency Medical Technician of the Year, Captain Poynter was known all over the valley for his humor, daring, and professionalism. He'd probably still be there today if not for an injury he sustained while trying to move an accident victim out of oncoming traffic on a rainy night.

The injury ended his fire department career and opened the door for a new one. As Bruce was recovering, the first tours were beginning in the desert, and the organizers called on his expertise to help design scripts and find trails through the hills. A match made in heaven. Over his more than 30 years in the valley, Bruce has hiked or four-wheeled on every possible path from Joshua Tree to Mexico, exploring on his own, traveling with herpetologists from the University of California to round up rattlesnakes for their venom, and unraveling the history and barren beauty of the desert for his friends.

In his career as tour guide extraordinaire, Bruce has starred in travel programs for the Travel Channel, BBC1, BBC2, and Travel Tokyo. He's been quoted in *Sunset* magazine, *Men's Journal, Palm Springs Life,* the *New York Times, Los Angeles Times, Chicago Tribune,* and dozens of other publications.

Today he splits his time between training other guides and leading tours for families and Fortune 500 companies. Although he's often on call for VIP groups, he also consults with Big Wheel Tours and is their lead guide and trainer. It's practically impossible to name a natural desert attraction or sight that Bruce hasn't studied and burned into his brain—the Palm Springs Aerial Tramway, Indian Canyons, Joshua Tree National Park, Salton Sea, Mecca Hills Wilderness, Santa Rosa National Monument, the Living Desert, Idyllwild—and all come alive with insider tips and knowledge that he has amassed over a lifetime of living here.

You may be fortunate to take a tour with one of the guides who trained under Captain Poynter. If you're really lucky, you'll get the man himself.

fixtures and dry goods. The Village Green might be of greatest interest for its location, showing an immediate contrast between the city's modern air-conditioned shops and restaurants and the humble dwellings of the past.

From mid-Oct through May, the Village Green complex is open from noon to 3 p.m. on Wed and Sun and from 10 a.m. to 4 p.m. Thurs through Sat.

TOURS

Aerial Rides/Tours

**NOSTALGIC WARBIRD &
BIPLANE RIDES** $$$$
Palm Springs International Airport
(760) 641-7335, (800) 991-2473
www.nostalgicwarbirdrides.com

An FAA-rated pilot with more than 20 years behind the controls of every type of aircraft from gliders to fighters and Boeing 737s, Mike Carpentiero has been flying gliders since 1984 and operating this company since 2003.

The thrilling flights allow passengers to take the controls of a 1941 open cockpit World War II Stearman trainer or sit side by side in a 1928 TravelAir biplane. Rides are tailored to the individual—daredevil or serene—and can include acrobatics. A video of the adventure is optional. Considering that a one-hour flight can cost as much as $500, that's a souvenir worth having.

Rides are offered Oct through May, and reservations are required.

i Many tour companies either cut their programs drastically in the summer or just close down from June through early September. Always check the Web site or phone ahead to get the latest prices, tour details, and available times.

Balloon Tours

Floating above the desert isn't cheap. Neither was that $50 a la carte steak at dinner the other night or that foursome for golf. It's vacation, quit sniveling (save that for when you're in a tiny little basket dangling below a flamethrower while hundreds of feet off the ground). And there's something magical in floating largely silently over the sand and golf courses, and from up in the air you'll get a real appreciation for the extent of agriculture in this valley, and perhaps a little side show at someone's pool.

All of the balloon companies offer virtually the same experience, which includes optional transportation to and from the launch site, a chase vehicle to make sure your craft has help if you land away from the predetermined site, a pilot to guide the craft in the air, crew to assist the launch and landing, perhaps some bubbly at the end, and a lovely certificate as a memento of the trip. Be aware that high winds can cause pilots

to cancel flights at the last minute, which might very well be at oh-dark-30 since flights are done seasonally near dawn and dusk.

BALLOON ABOVE THE DESERT $$$$
(760) 347-0410
www.balloonabovethedesert.com

DREAM FLIGHTS $$$$
(760) 321-5154, (800) 933-5628
www.dreamflights.com

FANTASY BALLOON FLIGHTS $$$$
(760) 568-0997, (800) 462-2683
www.fantasyballoonflights.com

Bike Tours

ADVENTURE BIKE TOURS $$$$
(760) 328-0282
This outfit provides a mix of custom bike tours, and can supply all needed equipment. Please call to inquire about tour options and requirements.

BIG WHEEL TOURS $$$$
(760) 779-1837
www.bwbtours.com
Kinda makes you think of Creedence, no? Then what Big Wheel should conjure up is the sense of wind in your face as you descend from the high to low desert on a guided 20-mile trip on the paved and largely deserted backroads of the far eastern valley. The company also offers mountain biking and custom tours, and of course, provides all the equipment you'll need. (They also do jeep, hiking, and other tours.)

Nature and Sightseeing Tours

BIG WHEEL TOURS $$$–$$$$
(760) 779-1837
www.bwbtours.com
Each of Big Wheel's tours is meticulously researched, informative, and entertaining; the guides are first-rate, and the destinations show imagination and creativity. Hiking tours include at least a dozen of the best spots in the valley

or surrounding mountains. Off-road tours head into Joshua Tree National Park, through the San Andreas fault zone and other secluded areas, using SUVs or open-air Jeeps depending on location and customer preference. And of course tailor-made tours can be suited to your particular need for adventure and interests, be that the San Jacinto Mountains or a day spotting birds at the Salton Sea.

i Legitimate tour companies are licensed by the Public Utilities Commission, carry extensive insurance, and have guides who are CPR-certified. If you have any doubts, ask for these credentials up front.

CELEBRITY TOURS OF PALM SPRINGS $$$
(760) 770-2700, (888) 805-2700
This is the original tour company in the desert, taking visitors around in air-conditioned buses to gape at places where celebrities used to live. Call it the "Dead Star Tour" if you want, but some folks are really into this kind of stuff, even if the kids don't have a clue who the stars were. There's a geographically concentrated tour of Palm Springs and the so-called "Grand Tour" that heads farther afield in the valley so as not to miss the front-gate that guarded the home of the guy who dated the sister of the starlet who vehemently asserted she really should've made it past the first cut for the role ultimately given to the actress who won the best-supporting Oscar in '57. At minimum, it's a good way to get your orientation and see the neighborhoods that made Palm Springs famous way back when.

COVERED WAGON TOURS $$$$
(760) 347-2161, (800) 367-2161
www.coveredwagontours.com
Authentically built covered wagons pulled by draft mules and driven by guides who play to the "Wild West" history of the desert can be a delightful way to learn a little bit about the desert—a smidgen of history wrapped in a lot

of entertainment. High camp? You bet. And the kids'll love it. Barbecue cookouts over a campfire and country-western serenades as the sun goes down are part of the fun, and the wagons are equipped with padded seats and rubber wheels for a relatively smooth ride. The tours take place in the Coachella Valley Preserve, a lovely desert spot dotted with natural palm oases. Departure times and offerings vary, so be sure to call for information and directions.

ELITE LAND TOURS $$$$
(760) 318-1200, (800) 514-4866
www.elitelandtours.com
Elite Land Tours specializes in backcountry exploration from the air-conditioned comfort of Hummer's all-terrain H2. This is the tour that would be featured on *Lifestyles of the Rich and Famous*—it includes gourmet lunches and personalized DVDs for bragging opportunities back home. There's only one drawback: Although the Hummer is equipped to handle the gnarliest tracks, some patrons think the operators are a little hesitant to take their shiny toys into areas where the terrain might rough up the beautiful paint. Oh well. The tour guides are conversant in the area's history and up-to-date on current environmental issues, even if a K-rat or two becomes part of a Hummer's tread pattern. The tour menu offers good variety, including a "Nocturnal Treasures" adventure in Joshua Tree with special night vision equipment to spot the desert's elusive wildlife.

i Some tour companies include hotel pickup and drop-off in their prices; others do not. Some also provide water and snacks along the way. Find out before you book, as the cost of water, snacks, and hitching a ride across the valley can add up quickly.

JOSHUA TREE HIKING ADVENTURES $$$$
(760) 821-3227
www.joshuatreehike.com
If you have a hankering to see the park from foot

but don't relish the idea of trying to figure which hike to take or peak to bag, leave the guiding to someone else. Proprietor Mike Santine leads half- and full-day custom hikes for groups sized one to whatever. Since the leader's time costs are fixed, the more friends you take along the less each of you will pay, moving you well back down that price category above. The Web site lists hikes by category of difficulty, with all the boilerplate on length and elevation change, and a little narrative. Santine will also take you up your choice of several peaks in the park.

TRAIL DISCOVERY/DESERT SAFARI $$$$
(760) 325-4453
www.palmspringshiking.com
Company president and lead guide Scott Scott (nope, not a typo) has been hiking in the desert for years and is considered quite the expert. He's a delightful companion as well, adapting each tour to the participants' interests and ability levels.

Scott offers three main tours—Indian Canyons, Joshua Tree, and the forests above the tramway—and auxiliary excursions to the Coachella Valley Preserve and some outlying canyons. In winter he leads snowshoe trips. If you're in town when Luna is large, the full-moon hike is a must. All tours include transportation, loaner hiking packs, water, snacks, and admissions when needed.

i If the winter rains have been kind, the desert will be a carpet of wildflowers as early as February, lasting as late as May in the high desert. The Palm Springs Art Museum staffs a wildflower hotline and also does wildflower tours if the season warrants it. Call the museum at (760) 325-7186 in mid-February.

PARKS, RECREATION, AND SPORTS

With its near-constant sunny days and exceptionally low humidity, the Coachella Valley delivers the three things outdoor sports enthusiasts want: weather, weather, and weather. Even snow lovers can scratch at least a bit of the winter itch by taking a trip up the Palm Springs Aerial Tramway for snowshoeing and cross-country skiing, or by driving for a ways for downhill skiing in the San Bernardino Mountains.

There's so much for the golfer here that the sport gets its own chapter—with more than 100 courses throughout the valley, including some of the nation's most notable tracks, and perhaps its most infamous. Golf is the number one outdoor activity and the one that gets the most attention from the press.

Back in the early days of the desert, when movie stars and the wealthy "discovered" Palm Springs, golf was nonexistent. In those days tennis was the sport of choice, followed by horseback riding in the hills surrounding the town. Tennis continues to be popular, with the Indian Wells Tennis Garden hosting the fifth most important tennis tournament in the world, and most every hotel and scores of public parks have a couple and usually far more courts. Horseback riders, sadly from their position, have lost a lot of the open desert that used to be their roaming grounds, though the Desert Riders group is quite active in maintaining and building new trails in the foothills.

Polo is a major sport in the eastern end of the valley, and even if you've never picked up a mallet, it's a great spectator activity. You may even be tempted to sign up for a lesson or two so you can experience this "sport of kings" firsthand.

It almost goes without saying that if you're a swimmer, you've found your spot. Every hotel in the valley has a pool. For lap swimming and lessons, several of the cities offer Olympic-size pools and expert instruction. If you're a toe-dipper or a floater who thinks water is best used to make beer, you're in even better stead because the lazin' pools outnumber the workout ones about a gazillion-to-one.

Public parks for picnics, soccer, skateboarding, and just plain romping around are dotted throughout the desert. And for the furry travelers, off-leash dog parks are waiting for Spike and Fluffy.

To help you find your way around the sports side of the desert, we've grouped our listings by sport, with subcategories for geographic locations where appropriate. Sports activities with no address listed are companies that primarily provide tours and offer pickup and drop-off.

Keep in mind that many of the public parks and public pools have hours that vary by season. Public parks are free. Public facilities for such sports as tennis, fishing, and swimming usually charge a nominal fee. Always call the public spots to make sure you know their hours, available activities, and information about fees.

Well-marked bike trails in Palm Springs include the Heritage Trail and various loops around town and through the country club areas. Bike paths that connect among the other cities are works in progress but most major roadways are striped; Class II bikeways are far more prevalent here than Class I. Palm Desert, Rancho Mirage, and La Quinta are on board, as well. Is the desert two-wheeled nirvana? Weather-wise, yes.

From a systemic view, it's kinda in the middle. It's a helluva lot better, easier and safer—and more enjoyable—to bike the valley than Los Angeles or urban Orange County. Yet it's nowhere near a Boulder, Colorado, or Eugene, Oregon.

Price Code

Unless otherwise indicated, all credit cards are accepted. Price ranges apply to charges for one person in high season. No price ranges are indicated for public facilities, as many are free, and fees for others change with the season. Always call ahead to make sure the public facilities are open. Many close or curtail hours during the summer months.

$................. **Less than $15**
$$ .... **$15 to $30**
$$$ .... **$31 to $50**
$$$$ .... **More than $50**

BOWLING

FANTASY LANES FAMILY
BOWLING CENTER $
84-245 Indio Springs Parkway, Indio
(Fantasy Springs Resort)
(760) 342-5000
Located in Fantasy Springs Casino, this is a glossy alley with 24 lanes, neon pins, glowing lanes and gutters, laser lights, and fog machines. A snack bar, arcade, pool table, lounge, and proximity to more flashing lights in the casino make this a far cry from the dingy bowling alleys of days gone by.

FISHING

LAKE CAHUILLA RECREATION AREA $
58-075 Jefferson St., La Quinta
(760) 564-4712
www.riversidecountyparks.org
This 135-acre lake is an offering of the Riverside County Regional Park and Open-Space District. Fishing is allowed from the shore only, and the lake is regularly stocked. There is (mostly) full-service camping and a primitive camping area,

a seasonal swimming pool—the lake is no-body contact—and equestrian trails. Fishing licenses are required.

i Check the local newspaper, *The Desert Sun,* for organized bike rides and hikes throughout the week. Most are just a few dollars, and many are free. If your hotel has bikes to rent or loan—and many do—ask the concierge for a bike trail map and do some family exploring for a few hours.

HIKING

There are hundreds and hundreds of miles of hiking trails etched across the foothills and mountains around and above the desert cities. Most were originally created by the Cahuilla Indians for travel among bands, for hunting, and as trade routes, and modern-day explorers have added more than their share. Trail maps of varying quality are available online, from various tour vendors, the governmental agencies with jurisdiction over the area's parks and preserves, and the go-to USGS maps are of course always a good option. There are a number of very good hiking books on the market, perhaps the best of which is *140 Great Hikes In and Near Palm Springs* by Philip Ferranti.

Many of the attractions and notable sights we've highlighted to this point are fantastic places to hike, and not just the obvious ones like Joshua Tree and the San Jacinto park and wilderness; a very good trail leads out the back of the Living Desert, for instance. If you'd prefer not to head out on your own, contact any of the tour providers above.

As in all matters, it is advisable to check locally for trail conditions and closures.

i With so many trails right on the edge of the cities, you can spend a morning hiking and be down in plenty of time for lunch, a quick shower, shopping, and pool time.

HORSEBACK RIDING/POLO

COYOTE RIDGE STABLE $$$$
Morongo Valley
(760) 363-3380
www.coyoteridgestable.com
In a surprisingly verdant high desert valley north of Palm Springs, this stable offers a range of wrangler-guided rides for all skill levels.

ELDORADO POLO CLUB $–$$$$
50-950 Madison St., Indio
(760) 342-2223
www.eldoradopolo.com
The desert's original polo club, this sprawling facility offers lessons as well as regular international competitions and celebrity tournaments. Bring a picnic and enjoy the match up close from the grassy lawn next to the field. Admission to tournaments is usually just a few dollars. Polo lessons can cost as much as a good dinner, a very very good dinner.

THE EMPIRE POLO CLUB $–$$$$
81-800 Avenue 51, Indio
(760) 342-2762
www.empirepoloevents.com
Empire began life as the little kid on the polo block in Indio and is now best known for its special events, as well as many important international tournaments. The grounds are huge— even more extensive than Eldorado—and often host balloon festivals, concerts, rodeos, art shows, and other open-air activities in the winter. The restaurant is excellent. Lessons are also available for all skill levels. As is the case with Eldorado Polo Club, tournament admission is just a few dollars and polo lessons are more.

LOS COMPADRES STABLE $$$$
1849 South El Cielo Rd.
(760) 864-9626
This is one of the valley's oldest sports facilities of any kind. It's also home to the once-popular "Mink and Manure Club" where stars and the wealthy would saddle up for social trail rides and cocktails. Yes, we know, it's Palm Springs, another tale of old. Private and semiprivate lessons and boarding are available.

SMOKE TREE STABLES $$$$
2500 Toledo Ave.
(760) 327-1372
www.smoketreestables.com
This was once "out in the country." It's all citified now, out here on the range, or at least it's now part of the city. Smoke Tree is adjacent to Smoke Tree Ranch and has always been at the core of ranch life, stabling horses for the homeowners there and offering rides and lessons to the public. The crusty wranglers know their business, and it's not chatting up visitors, so just relax in the saddle and enjoy the ride through the wash and up into the Indian Canyons.

WILLOWBROOK RIDING CLUB $$$$
20-555 Mountain View Dr.,
Desert Hot Springs
(760) 329-7676
www.willowbrookridingclub.com
This 40-acre facility in Desert Hot Springs is tailored to arena/show riders but there's room to roam for trail riders.

ROCK CLIMBING

JOSHUA TREE ROCK CLIMBING SCHOOL $$$$
Joshua Tree
(760) 366-4745
For all the allure of Joshua Tree, one of the world's leading climbing spots, climbing's not a sport to be approached with the cavalier spirit with which you can take a stab at, say, golf, armed with no skill. Whether you are a rank neophyte or someone with loads of hang time, make the call, avoid the fall.

UPRISING ADVENTURE GUIDES $$$$
Joshua Tree
(888) 254-6266
Be it unique guided tours, group climbs, or good-

old-fashioned lessons, Uprising covers the desert and mountains from Joshua Tree to Tahquitz Rock.

i If you make your home in the desert for more than half the year and have the utility bills and other ID to prove it, you can get a resident card, which entitles you to amazing discounts on golf and other recreational activities owned/provided by the city in which you reside.

ROLLER HOCKEY/SKATING

BIG LEAGUE DREAMS SPORTS PARK $$
33-700 Date Palm Dr., Cathedral City
(760) 324-5600
www.bigleaguedreams.com
A handful of facilities across the country combine softball-/Little League-sized "replicas" of the Polo Grounds, Fenway Park, Wrigley Field, and some minor league joint called Yankee Stadium, with roller hockey and other sports venues in family friendly confines.

PALM DESERT SKATE PARK
73-500 Fred Waring Dr., Palm Desert
(760) 568-9697

PALM SPRINGS SKATE PARK
401 South Pavilion Way
(760) 323-8272

SOCCER

PALM DESERT SOCCER PARK
74-735 Hovley Lane, Palm Desert
(760) 568-9697
This offers five full-sized, lighted fields with picnic pavilions, tot and toddler lots with perimeter seating, horseshoe, basketball and shuffleboard courts, disc golf course, and paths for walking, jogging, biking, or in-line skating. Call the city to inquire about seasonal park maintenance.

SWIMMING

Indio/Coachella/Mecca

BAGDOUMA COMMUNITY POOL
84-626 Bagdad Ave., Coachella
(760) 391-9448

MECCA COMMUNITY POOL
65-250 Coahuilla St., Mecca
(760) 396-0257

PAWLEY POOL FAMILY AQUATIC COMPLEX
46-350 South Jackson, Indio
(760) 342-5665

i The desert wilderness is fragile and carefully protected. If you long to go off-roading within the valley, you'll have to do it as a paying guest with one of the local tour companies or at one or two approved vendor-run facilities.

La Quinta

FRITZ BURNS PARK
78-060 Frances Hack Lane, La Quinta
(760) 341-9622

Palm Springs

PALM SPRINGS SWIM CENTER
Sunrise Park, corner of Sunrise Way and Ramon Roads
(760) 323–8272

i Many of the desert's public parks make ideal places for reunion picnics, barbecues, and large get-togethers. Just make sure to check with the city's recreation department to get up to speed on rules and regulations, and to see about reserving a space.

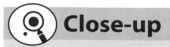

Close-up

Palm Desert's Family Parks ... and a Golfer's Paradise

Without a doubt, Palm Desert has the valley's best-planned and most extensive public parks and recreation programs. The city began with a plan and has adhered to a long-range vision as a balanced community that provides lots of amenities for its residents as well as super-high-end shopping and dining for visitors. Its serendipitous location right in the middle of the valley cities has made it a magnet for retail, which in turn has churned out sales tax revenue to help fund the parks and keep them in top shape.

The showplace of the city's parks is the Civic Center Park. With an extensive rose garden and sculpture walk, it is also a sprawling, green landscape with a meandering stream, picnic spots, lots of room to run and throw Frisbees, and walking paths that are lighted and well patrolled for a safe, fun outing. The park's huge amphitheater is filled with hundreds of families on hot summer nights, here to enjoy a picnic supper and watch the free movies and concerts. Lighted tennis courts, sand volleyball courts, two skate parks, baseball fields, and two dog parks are part of the complex, which always seems to be expanding and improving.

Licensed after-school programs, toddler classes to help kids make the transition from home to kindergarten, and camps for times when school is out of session are all available through the community center at Civic Center Park. (Brief jurisdictional sidebar: These services actually are provided by the Desert Recreation District, an overarching public entity that provides parks and/or recreational services, in varying degrees, to all valley cities except Palm Springs and Cat City.) Throughout the year, there are youth and adult basketball leagues, adult coed softball games, cross-country track meets, and girls' volleyball. The list goes on. And anyone can enjoy the parks and recreation programs, resident or not. Of course, fees are a bit higher for nonresidents, but they're still a bargain.

The city didn't stop with hoops, day-care, and free-form doggy recreation. It is almost a mandate from above that desert cities have their own golf courses, and more than half do. For all the mythology that Palm Springs equals golf in the desert and despite the Big Boys of Pro Golf teeing it up in Indian Wells and La Quinta, the alpha dog of true public golf (a course or courses owned by the public and open to the public) in the desert is Desert Willow Golf Resort, the city of Palm Desert's 36-hole magical kingdom.

TENNIS

Tennis has always been a big sport in the desert, owing somewhat to its consistently sunny and dry weather even in the dead of winter. The story has it that Charley Farrell and Ralph Bellamy founded the Palm Springs Racquet Club after they were kicked off the courts at El Mirador Hotel. The Racquet Club's main attraction, besides the cocktails and pretty girls around the pool, was its top-notch courts. Of course, that was a long time ago.

Today the Indian Wells Tennis Garden is the site of a major tennis tournament and has hosted every major tennis star in the world ever to play, or at least all players who know Borg-McEnroe as a quaint parental memory (their loss). Tournaments for seniors, juniors, and all skill levels abound during the season, and most large hotels offer courts for their guests. Public courts are plentiful in the desert, and though they may not be as luxurious as the ones at La Quinta Resort, they are well maintained and very popular. Court time is first-come, first-served, and players are asked to limit their court time to a few games when there are other players in line.

PUBLIC PARKS AND PLAYGROUNDS

CITY OF CATHEDRAL CITY

(760) 770-0340

www.cathedralcity.gov

Cathedral City has seven parks, ranging from passive memorials to full-on sports parks, three of which have tennis courts. The best of these is Panorama Park, the city's largest park and one of its oldest, located at the intersection of Tachevah Way and Avenida Maravilla. Panorama Park has a ball field, volleyball and basketball courts, walking track, play area, barbecues and shade structures, spray pool, and of course tennis courts.

CITY OF INDIO

(760) 391-4000

www.indio.org

Indio has eight public parks with a variety of amenities, including softball fields, basketball courts, barbecue areas, tennis, and playground equipment. As one of the most family-oriented cities in the desert, Indio has always put parks and public recreation near the top of its quality-of-life priority lists. The parks are well maintained and offer good equipment, spacious grounds, and a friendly environment for picnics, children's play, and basketball or tennis games. Two of the best are North Jackson Park just south of I–10 on Jackson Street, and South Jackson Park at the intersection of Jackson and Date Streets. Both parks have softball fields, barbecue areas, and playground equipment. North Jackson Park also has tennis courts.

CITY OF LA QUINTA

(760) 777-7000

www.la-quinta.org

www.playinlaquinta.com

La Quinta has grown in great bursts over the past 15 years, filling in open desert with residential tracts, country clubs, and huge retail and commercial complexes, and reclaiming some of the old. From a relative dearth of park space the city is now deep in grass. The 12-acre Fritz Burns Park at 78-107 Avenue 52 has a pool, tennis courts, skate and dog parks, and much more. La Quinta Sports Park (78-900 Avenue 50) has multiple soccer and baseball fields Added up, the city has some 11 active parks, extensive walking/hiking and biking trail system, a 100-plus-acre desert open space set back against the mountains, and its own golf complex—SilverRock—that hosts a PGA Tour event. And the county's Lake Cahuilla Recreation Area is at the south end of town. The city's informative and user-friendly Web site is about the best of any of the cities' Web sites and the affiliated www.playinlaquinta.com links you right through, just click on the "Play" tab.

CITY OF PALM DESERT

(760) 346-0611

www.cityofpalmdesert.org

Palm Desert has a dozen parks for humans and two off-leash parks; dogs are allowed on-leash at several other parks. Combined, the various non-canine parks offer facilities for just about every activity a family could wish for: baseball, softball, and soccer fields; basketball, tennis, shuffleboard, and horseshoe courts; two skate parks; picnic areas; tot and toddler lots; playground equipment; and a huge amphitheater for public concerts and movies. One of the most-used parks is Palm Desert Civic Center Park (Fred Waring Drive and San Pablo Avenue). Facilities here include softball fields, basketball courts, soccer fields, barbecue areas, playground equipment, tennis and racquetball courts, and walking paths. Hovley Soccer Park (74-735 Hovley Lane) has five lighted soccer fields; basketball, horseshoe, and shuffle-

i Although the weather truly is suitable for year-round sports, plan your activity for early in the day if you're here in the summer months. By 10 a.m. the temperature likely will be in triple-digits. And contrary to lore, only mad dogs and Englishmen will go out under the late-afternoon sun, as that is when temperatures are at their peak.

board courts; playgrounds for little children, and a concession stand. Dogs can roam at the mostly undeveloped/open-space Cahuilla Hills (45-825 Edgehill Dr.) and Cap Homme/Ralph Adams (72-500 Thrush Rd.) parks.

CITY OF PALM SPRINGS
(760) 323-8272
www.ci.palm-springs.ca.us
Palm Springs operates eight parks with a wide variety of amenities, including softball fields, batting cages, picnic shelters and barbecue areas, playground equipment, a skate park, a swimming pool, and tennis courts. The best of these are Sunrise Park (adjacent to the Parks and Recreation Department at 401 South Pavilion Way) and DeMuth Park (4365 Mesquite Ave.). Sunrise Park features the Palm Springs Swim Center and expansive park grounds with playground equipment and picnic areas. This park is also adjacent to the city's library and baseball stadium. DeMuth Park is in constant use, with several softball fields, tennis courts, picnic and barbecue areas, and playground equipment. The aptly named Dog Park is at 3200 East Tahquitz Canyon Way, right

behind city hall—now someone has a good sense of humor. The city's Web site ain't all that, but you can download a good schedule of recreational activities and events.

CITY OF RANCHO MIRAGE
(760) 324-4511
www.ci.rancho-mirage.ca.us
Rancho Mirage's park system is a true baby compared to those of any of the other valley cities, with minimal acreage and equipment. (The city's other, smaller parks have little to no recreational amenities and one is a desert open-space park.) On the other hand, Rancho Mirage probably has a smaller percentage of families than the other cities. Whitewater Park (71-560 San Jacinto Dr.) is the best of the lot, featuring four lighted tennis courts, two basketball courts, two racquetball/handball courts, an informal play area, picnic facilities, a children's playground, a life-size fire engine, a water feature, and walking paths. The city has a few short dedicated- and multi-use trails, and the city's Web site is quite informative as to the nature of each trail and its location.

GOLF

The Coachella Valley wasn't always a golf destination, let alone golf vacationland. In fact, when the movie stars first made this their preferred playground and hideaway spot, the only "sports" that mattered were tennis, pool-time, lighting the drinking lamp well before 5 p.m., and what can best be termed as a game that called for secrecy and discretion, neither of which seem to have been liberally applied. The first course popped up early enough, in the mid-1920s—the still-standing nine-hole O'Donnell Golf Club in Palm Springs. It was a step, the first step, but years would roll by before there was another, and then finally another, and there wasn't much in the way of a sprint until about the time some guy named Ike handed the office keys to some guy named Jack.

From the first post-war years into the 1970s, "Palm Springs" golf was private golf. This is the time that gave us the country clubs known as Thunderbird and Tamarisk and Bermuda Dunes and El Dorado. (You know, they held Ryder Cups at two of these, if you can believe it.) And the first clubs in turn provided a strong foundation for the Reserves and Vintages and Bighorns and Stone Eagles that came later.

Golf took the valley, in a very private way.

Then something happened. A man of the public who just happened to look Hollywood, play all-star, and knock elbows and likely a few tumblers with presidents and Rat Packers came to town. The hard-working down-to-earth son of down-to-earth hard-working Pennsylvanians took on the game of elites, gave his pants a hitch, and kicked ass, becoming arguably the greatest sport-transcending sports hero of all time. Arnold Palmer owned what we now call the Bob Hope Classic, winning five of them (in 14 years), and adding another desert victory in the tournament that evolved into the Bob Hope, the old Thunderbird Invitational. Fittingly, his last regular tour win was the '73 Bob Hope.

Arnie marched through the desert, bringing the public with him.

By the '70s, and mostly decidedly by the mid-'80s, Palm Springs and Co. could present a solid portfolio of public courses, and in time the valley was ready to check into a top-floor suite in the Pantheon of American Golf, and it's still doing a pretty good job of hanging around with the Scottsdales and Carolinas of the world. Some locales have more courses. Some have more expensive courses, if you can believe that. Some even have more "better" courses.

We have weather. We have Arnie.

Depending on the state of the economy and what's considered a golf course, there are 120 or so courses in the desert, from ramshackle nine-holers to the kind of places where the member-member looks like the Fortune 500. Most everybody who is anybody in course design has a project on the ground—Dye, Nicklaus, Arnie, Player, Hurdzan, Schmidt, and Curley (Faldo). Better yet, since most of us are regular old John and Joan Qs, the roster of notables extends to courses we can play. (Unfortunately we haven't seen Tom Doak on the public side yet, there's no sign of Jim Engh, and somebody please get on the horn to Ben Crenshaw and Bill Coore.)

And it's not just about playing the game. Golf fans have been treated to seeing the best of the best going back to when Thunderbird and El Dorado hosted Ryder Cups in the 1950s. Likely the second most important golf tournament in women's golf is a desert mainstay—the Kraft Nabisco Championship held every spring on Mission Hills' classic Desmond Muirhead track. Through various name changes and a throwback formula, the Bob Hope celebrated its 50th birthday in 2009. Silly and perhaps no more for the world, all but three of the on-hold-for-'09-and-maybe-forever Skins Games have been contested in the desert. At least one of the two major professional tours visits annually with some level of its qualifying tournament. Better yet, a number of courses used in these events are open to the public.

What follows is a listing of courses we think are notable, meaning worth your vacation time and your vacation dollar. It doesn't come close to covering every publicly-accessible course in the desert because some just aren't worth your time/dollars and, frankly, that's what phone books are for. We like to think of it as complete, not exhaustive, and highly representative. We've tried to hit all levels of the price scale. We didn't include courses that require membership or a secret handshake to get in. We've played all these courses, likely multiple times. Some are spectacular, coffee-table-book-cover-grade plays, some do exactly what they are supposed to do: deliver an enjoyable golf experience given how much someone wants you to pay for the privilege. All these courses are "comfortable" in their clothes, so to say. As for yardages, these guys mostly stretch to 7,000+ yards from the tees very few of us should play, and moving forward from there the stops typically come at some combination of two, three, or four of the following: 6700, 6,300, 6,000, 5,600, plus the really smartly designed courses have 5,200 or 4,900. And if it's a short or executive course, we tell you; Full-length courses generally par out on either side of 72. But since we play against par does it really matter if the number is 71 or 73?

Price is elusive. Most courses have multiple rates—weekday, holiday, low-shoulder, hotel guest, whatever. There are huge, massive spreads between winter and summer pricing. Third-party services negotiate varying discounts even with

the same property. It's like trying to decipher the Pentagon's budget. So for comparative purposes we list high season rack rate, the typical top-end weekend wintertime price you'll be quoted by the course/see on the course's Web site. This is typical high-season rack, so if the course in question offers a super special even-higher-on-this-holiday rate, it's not reflected.

You've probably already surmised that there will be times and ways to beat those prices, even at the source, and you are correct. The listed rates are for comparative purposes and since golf is a game of Scottish origin most of us who play are pretty good at finding thrifty alternatives where they exist. Prices crater during summer, most to the point that the cost will be within the range of the lowest price category below at even the swankiest swank palaces.

Price Code

Unless otherwise indicated, all credit cards are accepted. Price ranges apply to one round of golf for one person in high season. If you have the option of not taking a cart, and there's an upcharge to do so, that cost is not reflected. All the high-end properties include range balls with green fee. If those of you who've been hanging out in the desert for a while think that top ends starts a bit farther down the scale than in days past, you are correct. Whether because of competition, saturation, or the general economic malaise, "$199" looks to be the new glass ceiling, which is a distinct change from when it took nearly three Bens to play several of the big guns around here.

$.................. **Less than $75**
$$ .... **$75 to $125**
$$$ .... **$126 to $175**
$$$$ .... **More than $175**

CIMARRÓN GOLF RESORT— BOULDER AND PEBBLE $–$$
67-603 30th Ave., Cathedral City
(760) 770-6060
www.cimarrongolf.com

These sound like funny names for golf courses

but when you see the waste areas that are such an integral part of the play, you'll understand. Full-size Boulder is a play of angles, be that challenging doglegs or right-siding nearer trouble to improve or shorten an approach. It's a wide open, nearly austere scene, accented with outstanding vistas and really cool stack-faced bunkers. Pebble, as the play on words suggests, is a 3,200-yard, par-56 executive, and likely the best short course in the desert, demanding real-live thought and strategy in tee shot and making you pull every iron in the bag. Regardless which of the two John Fought designs you play, do it on foot as Cimarrón is one of the enlightened establishments that doesn't force you into a buggy.

THE CLASSIC CLUB $$$$
75-200 Classic Club Blvd., Palm Desert
(760) 601-3601
www.classicclubgolf.com

It was a perfect storm: the King, himself, working with the PGA Tour's in-house design team to craft a course that would host one of the game's longest-running professional events and the folks who owned the whole thing were willing to turn it over lock, stock, and barrel so that the charities benefiting from said tourney could benefit even more. Then the pros said no.

It's not a soap opera. It's the saga of the Classic Club, one of the most thoughtful designs anywhere to have Arnold Palmer's name on it. The course is a winner, built on a massive scale and shunning any and all sense of claustrophobia. It's a place where tournament-viewing crowds could pass with ease and players—pros for a week a year, the rest of us the rest of the time—would have great sightlines. They moved so much sand out here that every hole is a discrete little golf drama all unto itself, a mix of amphitheater greens and peninsular fairways and playing options galore, and you never have to worry about flinging a snappy-the-clown into the next fairway and beaning some poor lout.

The problem, however, was that all that sand that could be so wonderfully pushed around to make a magical golf course existed on the site in

You Can Play It

Public, daily-fee, resort, access privileges, semi private, what does it all mean? When you get down to the heart of the matter, not as much as you think. There's a ton of nonsensical crap tossed into golf-travel literature and particularly golf-marketing literature. A course may never have sniffed a tournament beyond the every-Tuesday four-ball with nothing more than an over-boiled hot dog in a crusty bun on the line, yet it's a "championship track." Bunk. And all this "who can play where stuff" is as bad. If a golf course has a listing in this part of the book, you can play it. We don't care if it's owned by a city or a private developer or a major corporation or as is often the case in recent financial times, a bank. If you can walk in, put down cash, and head to the first tee, it's public. It might be a "resort course," it very well could be "semi private," it might be owned by a municipality which truly makes it public, and some overzealous reservation clerk very well might tell you how lucky you are to be staying at Resort Splendifico because otherwise you would not be allowed to play their "championship track." If it's in this book, you can play it.

the first place because it's a hunk of land sitting smack-dab in the middle of a wind tunnel. Classic's not far from the windmills and how that escaped detection in the tournament's planning phase is mind-boggling. Wind's not a problem, per se, for the world's best players. The beef comes when the wind shows on some days and not others. The other courses used in the Bob Hope rotation are down in the coves, and largely immune to wind. So if you were part of the draw that was out by I–10 the day a ripper came through, you were behind the proverbial 8-ball. Hey, it's tough being a pro. Don't be sad that Classic was disenfranchised. Now the rest of us don't lose one of the valley's best courses for weeks every year.

"Hello!! We're back here!!!" Golf is not cricket. It's not played to the pace of a calendar. And you're not the only person on this course. Aside from cost, how long it takes to play a round is what's keeping the game's growth in the deep freeze. A Scotswoman with a bad knee and six clubs, walking, could get in 27 holes and a stop for haggis and a single-malt in the amount of time the typical American gets around the course while driving a car-ette. Being slow on the course is not a Great Society entitlement. Please keep it moving.

DESERT DUNES GOLF CLUB
19-300 Palm Dr., Desert Hot Springs
(760) 251-5370
www.desertdunesgolf.com

This is the first and so far only Robert Trent Jones II—when did he quit being Jr.?—public course in the desert. Desert Dunes closed in the spring of 2009 for a much needed greens reconstruction project, and was slated to reopen in Oct or Nov 2009. Conditioning and care long have been bugaboos at this most intriguing of layouts not far from the windmill farms. For all the "links this" and "links that" hyperbole so wrongly tossed about in conjunction with courses nowhere near linksland, like those great coastal locales, wind is a big part of the play here. The course runs through dunes, mesquite thickets, and stands of tamarisk, giving definition lacking in so many desert layouts. It's a joyful ball-strikers paradise as rich in wildlife as it is sparse in birdies, and if it is now getting the attention it has so long deserved. It is a Coachella Valley must-play.

DESERT FALLS COUNTRY CLUB $$$
1111 Desert Falls Parkway, Palm Desert
(760) 340-4653
www.desert-falls.com

Desert Falls is a private club that for seemingly eons has freely accepted outside play. It's a very friendly and collegial club, with members not worried they'll be sullied by such close association with the hoi polloi. It's also part of the ClubCorp network so if you are a ClubCorper elsewhere with Signature Gold, cash in on your two freebie rounds. The course sits right about where the south side of the valley tumbles away to the low-lying center, and as such there's a load of elevation change on both nines. It's a strategic design more so than brawny and heroic, with doglegging that puts a premium on where to hit driver (or often, something smaller), an easily reachable par 5 with a no man's land of chaotic bunkering usually determining if you are a stud or a goat, water everywhere, and two of the best returning holes—9 and 18—anywhere to be found and they're a bit of eye candy to boot.

DESERT SPRINGS (JW MARRIOTT)—
PALM AND VALLEY $$$
74-855 Country Club Dr., Palm Desert
(760) 341-2211
www.desertspringsresort.com

If you want to see desert "resort" golf at its pinnacle, head to Desert Springs. As we suggested above in the accommodations section, if there is a property here that could be plopped on the Las Vegas Strip and it would fit in without a single tweak—save adding the mandatory casino—this is it, from the eight-story atrium to the boat-filled waterways, and aesthetically the courses are exactly the same way. Rippling streams and island greens, blooms in every color of the spectrum in numbers that might exceed New England-in-fall maple leaves in number and radiance, soaring palms and pines, and deciduous evergreens that must tally in four figures; there's just a ton of show in these grounds and it seems no one wants you to have any clue you are in the desert. The Palm Course gets the attention because of a series of waterlogged and heavily adorned holes played along the resort's enticing entryway and then back to the house—in view of spa patrons lounging poolside, by the way. The rolling Valley Course may be the stronger test.

DESERT WILLOW GOLF RESORT—
FIRECLIFF AND MOUNTAIN VIEW $$$
38-995 Desert Willow Dr., Palm Desert
(760) 346-7060
www.desertwillow.com

Forget the Gardens on El Paseo. The most exquisite garden in Palm Desert if not the entire valley is right here at this city-owned two-course facility of immeasurable charm. Firecliff is ready, right out the chute, for any and all comers. The par 3s demand precision, whether going at them with a scoring club or a 3-iron. The par 4s exist in every increment of length to be found in the catalog of design, and some of the short ones are as much about controlling your emotions as those reaching to Trail of Tears duration. Some of the big holes might be better played with something other than driver off the tee, and how refreshing is it to find three-shot 5s where none of the three shots are kickaways? Yet for all the design supremacy displayed by Michael Hurdzan, Dana Fry, and John Cook, for every bit of three-dimensional play demanded, Firecliff catches the eye as much for the riotous bounty of what's growing as what was shaped. If you need a picture postcard to show the folks back home how verdant and how colorful the desert can be, forget the Living Desert and come out here. They've even re-created desert palm oases.

Mountain View is the baby brother, a genetic relation in look and feel, yet one who is more about play time than all-out athletic endeavor. The margins are wider, less desert and fewer things that sting you are in play, heck you can stumble and not hurt yourself nearly as badly. This is not an indictment; Mountain View is certainly much more in the wheelhouse of most visiting players. There's none of the same-old wall-to-wall carpets of green set between towering gum trees which in turn are set within rows of condos that is

the alternative at "classic old desert courses," and yet you need not buy every Bridgestone in the clubhouse to have enough ammunition to make it through the round. A course that is compelling and workable for the masses is about as much of a design victory as building the "perfect" course. Mountain View recently reconstructed the greens and bunkers and renovated the lakes.

In the land where most of the cities have built true public golf courses and some in the most grand fashion, Desert Willow takes the Mayor's Cup.

THE GOLF CLUB AT TERRA LAGO—
NORTH AND SOUTH $$$
84-000 Terra Lago Parkway, Indio
(760) 775-2000
www.golfclub-terralago.com

The valley's golf market excels for several reasons, one of which is the larger number of facilities that offer more than 18 holes. While that might be a head-scratcher to some, if you are reading this section you already know why that's a good thing. Formerly known as Landmark, this place hosted several Skins Game, including one with a certain incident involving a caddie and a camera. The Skins was played over a composite routing, which means to see the best of the best, you must play 36. Oh, darn. A ton of neat things went into this club, including risk-reward opportunities aplenty and funky railroad boxcar bridges. Nature played a hand, as well, offering up some eagle aerie tee boxes and vegetation-shrouded dunes at the foot of the Little San Berdoos.

HERITAGE PALMS GOLF CLUB $$
44-291 Heritage Palms Dr. South, Indio
(760) 772-7334

Heritage Palms is an extremely popular play with such a huge membership that while the joint isn't exclusionary, its popularity can make it hard for non-members to get in during the season. But do try. The asking price for this 6,700-yard, par-72 beauty is about as low as it gets in the desert for a course that's paid its water bills, understands golf is played on actual grass, and whose hazards don't qualify as Superfund sites. Part of an age-restricted community, Heritage Palms does not play like it's for the out-to-pasture crowd. Designer Arthur Hills is justly famous for purposeful-not-photo-op bunkering and some for the par 4s are flat-out bruisers.

INDIAN CANYONS GOLF RESORT—
NORTH AND SOUTH $$
1097 East Murray Canyon Dr.
(760) 327-6550
www.indiancanyonsgolf.com
Tucked into the south end of Palm Springs where the mountains peel back just enough to provide elbow room along with views, Indian Canyons' South Course provides an old-school hip scene with a Casey O'Callaghan/Amy Alcott dose of modernity that would do J. B. Holmes proud with its bomber's dream of five par 5s. North, a long-time mainstay of back-in-the-day golf is now open to outside play, as well.

INDIAN PALMS COUNTRY CLUB $$
48-630 Monroe St., Indio
(760) 347-2326
There is a wonderful convergence at play at Indian Palms. The course has roots in the valley that go so far back the Smithsonian might take note. It's founder is a true pioneer, not in the moldy-oldie sense rather the trend-setting-aviator/friend-of-Amelia Earhart sense. The club's first nine holes were put down two years after Hitler and Tojo gave up the ghost. It was a personal playground for Jacqueline Cochran, her Hollywood-studio-owing-hubby Floyd Odlum, and a big, warm circle of friends. In time the property passed through other owners, 18 more holes were added, and the private playpen became a country club of middling standing. Indian Palms isn't necessarily a must-play spot; it's actually somewhat forgettable in a golf capacity if looked at in terms of who might be a few streets over. But the price is right and history has immense value in and of itself; that's why grandparents are special.

INDIAN SPRINGS COUNTRY CLUB $$
79-940 Westward Ho, La Quinta
(760) 200-8988
www.indianspringsgc.com
Rejuvenation long has been one of the reasons why people have come to the valley. While the older, simpler way of taking the waters is quaint, romantic, nostalgic, sometimes a wee bit of surgery is demanded. For all the facelifts done around here, few patients have gained as much renewed youthfulness and vitality as Indian Springs. Before reconstruction at the beginning of the decade, this 1960s vintage track had become a third- or fourth-tier play, a last-second hey-let's-go-tee-it-up-because-it-beats-muckin'-out-the-stall option that wasn't too hard on the wallet, even as it beat on the irons. The new clubhouse is rocking, the grass never has been greener, and they lopped off entire body parts and attached new ones in other places. And look at that price, it's a buck under 100 at weekend high season peak.

INDIAN WELLS GOLF RESORT—
CELEBRITY AND PLAYERS $$$
44-500 Indian Wells Lane, Indian Wells
(760) 346-4653
www.indianwellsgolfresort.com
Since the big boom in resort and good public golf in the '80s, the city of Indian Wells-owned courses and private-sector allied resort hotels have presented a tough-to-beat package of fun golf and great stay. As the hoteliers stepped up their product in waves of reconstruction and improvement over the years, the course remained well maintained, horticulturally gorgeous, tee sheets humming, yet unchanging. Hello, change. The city has blown up the dreary, way-undersized clubhouse, tossed out the so-so dining, and bid adieu to the former West and East course.

The new clubhouse would be an absolute embarrassment of excess if not for the fact this is the desert and this is Indian Wells, and no one at City Hall has ever been pinched for so much as a jaywalking violation so that they spent 789 gazillion of their well-heeled citizens' dollars on perhaps the best clubhouse in the desert means nada—it's a brilliant edifice. (And the food rocks, too.)

Out back, right-proper Englishman and one-time Ryder Cupper Clive Clark took the old West Course, inverted a fair bit of its routing, kept its amazing trees, put a load of sensuous curves into the new and delivered to locals and visitors the Celebrity Course, aptly named because it might be the last place to ever host the Thanksgiving-staple Skins Game; don't hold a network's obsession with a long-tired, nobody-cares tournament against this place.

More profound is what John Fought did with the former East Course, always the mercy date play in these parts. With a piece of land that always had less to offer and, perhaps thankfully, not much of a road map to follow, Fought went yard with the Players Course, a some-time dance, some-time slugfest of here-it-is, have-a-go, straight-ahead smash-ball golf that wants to be twirled and floated like Ginger Rogers. That's a heady combo.

The range is still sub-standard for a resort of this caliber, but that's offset with a great nine-hole putting course and a Callaway Golf Performance Center.

The clubhouse doesn't bite, either.

LA QUINTA RESORT & CLUB— A DUNES AND MOUNTAIN $$$–$$$$
50-200 Avenida Vista Bonita, La Quinta
(800) 742-9378
www.laquintaresort.com

Years and years after opening, Pete Dye's Mountain Course still books annual passage on that train that is America's best golf courses. That's no small feat when you look at the roster of what's opened over the past 20-plus years, with an entire new cadre of young and truly inspired designers out doing their thing and most of the old dogs learning new tricks. Mountain breathes and achieves through its love affair with the Santa Rosa Mountains, where on both front and particularly back it heads into Rocky Land. If you've seen 15 through 17 when the Bob Hope

is played at PGA West's Arnold Palmer Private Course you have an idea of what's in store, except there's no irrigation canal at La Quinta and the holes are even more spectacular as they sweep in, cross and then dive out of terrain better suited for bighorn sheep than FootJoy-clad feet. The land is king here and Dye let it be, with no embellishments, though the holes that play at the foot of the mountains are sassed up with Dye railroad ties and his siggy-look par 3s. Dunes (Dye) is the weak chick in the La Quinta/PGA West brood, a resort-y routing played a good way around through floodways and forever constrained by look-alike housing.

MARRIOTT'S SHADOW RIDGE $$$
9002 Shadow Ridge Rd., Palm Desert
(760) 674-2700
www.golfshadowridge.com

Shadow Ridge is the handiwork of one Sir Nick Faldo—yes, he was knighted—and two guys who between them have worked for many of the best in the design game and who have for the past 10 or so years quietly placed themselves near the top of the golf architect pile, Lee Schmidt and Brian Curley. This course of one of the Forgotten Triad, three of the valley's best courses that no one really talks about that much, along with the Westin's Gary Player course and Desert Dunes, a trickster tucked away at the west end of the valley that has long needed the love it's now getting. Schmidt and Curley like to free-wheel as much as possible, and they've pulled off some remarkable tracks where residential and resort demands might've failed others. They're old school in the sense of not being tied to one way of doing things and they aren't put off by a blind tee shot, an obscured green, or collection areas. Their bunkering is wild, with ragged lines and footprints that would seem to have been originally traced by three Labs chasing two Frisbees, and there's a sense of the vertical at play which makes you realize that golf is not simply a down range endeavor. Faldo's worked with them on other signature courses, and the three have a good thing going.

THE OASIS COUNTRY CLUB $
42-300 Casbah Way, Palm Desert
(760) 345-5661
www.theoasiscountryclub.com

If you took one of the '70s or '80s era residential golf developments like a Sunrise or a Monterey, gave the golf course the Shrinky Dinks treatment and then hauled it over toward the east side of Palm Desert and plopped it down, you'd have Oasis. A par 60, 3,500-yarder executive routed through a nice mid-market housing project, Oasis is a legitimate play, with a bounty of lakes and smooth greens. Putting the package together—playing interest, conditioning, cost, and time necessary to get around—there is some high bang-for-the-buck going on here, and particularly if you don't need the full ensemble of 7,000 yards, 240-yard forced carries, par 5s, valley-wide vistas, and a major championship winner where the scorecard says "designed by."

ℹ️ The valley-wide convention and visitors authority—the cities have tourism departments and programs of varying degrees of effectiveness, as well—puts out a golf guide with course reviews, and the usual advertorial, and it's a handy resource. The 2009 edition includes a piece about Arnold Palmer and his ties to and affinity for the desert and desert golf. For more information go to www.giveintothedesert.com or call (800) 417-3529. The convention bureau puts out a whole host of other guides, as well.

PALM ROYALE COUNTRY CLUB $
78-259 Indigo Dr., La Quinta
(760) 345-9701
www.palmroyalecc.com

While Big Long Courses rule the desert, there are several shorter options available for those who want to play a little golf but not invest half a day of time and the equivalent of a car payment to do so. And then there are those of us who really need to work on our short games, and also those who are just cutting their teeth. Palm Royale spreads just under 2,000 yards across its 18 holes, and if you do the math that's an average of about a gap wedge for each, though there is variation. Because Ted Robinson laid it out there will of course be water. We don't want to oversell the place: it's a fun, friendly pitch-and-putt that management takes care of.

PGA WEST—GREG NORMAN COURSE $$$$
81-405 Kingston Heath, La Quinta
(800) 742-9378
www.pgawest.com

The Shark's first and still only desert course met with mixed reviews when it opened in 1999. The idea was to try to replicate the famous sandbelt course of his native Australia, and while few of us have played Royal Melbourne so as to have a point of reference to compare, many thought it just a bit chopped up. Since re-worked, the course flows much more evenly, while still retaining its shock of free-form bunkering and limited turf, and there's a hug-the-land simplicity to the course that's always been lacking at its heavily fabricated sister courses at PGA West. Norman's an interesting designer whose works seems to swing through the same wild arcs that defined his all-world playing career.

ℹ️ A good walk spoiled? Hardly. Except for a few of the most enlightened establishments, don't even think they'll let you actually step on the course. This is Cart Country. Because desert golf courses often are built as adjuncts to housing developments, a free-form and organic routing often takes a back seat to where best to put the residential "amenities," communal dumpsters, and access roads. This can lead to some green-to-tee-stretches that Lewis & Clark would be hard pressed to navigate. Add in the twin pillars of evil—the cart-as-revenue-stream fallacy and the driving-is-more-expeditious delusion—and, well, Samuel Langhorne Clemens would never recognize the game he so despised.

PGA WEST—JACK NICKLAUS
TOURNAMENT AND STADIUM $$$$
56-150 PGA Blvd., La Quinta
(800) 742-9378
www.pgawest.com

Stadium is perhaps Pete Dye's most infamous course, if not his most recognized. It's a torture chamber of 20-foot-deep bunkers, grass pits that could swallow a circus of elephants, a craters-of-the-moon complexion, pushed up greens that fall away to oblivion, and enough water to float the Pacific Fleet. And we've not specifically talked about the island green or the other insidious par 3s, yet. This is a tough course specifically designed to punish, and the hedonists show up in droves, AMEX at the ready. All of Dye's signature treatments are here, from railroad tie bulkheads and funky protrusions obscuring lines of play to really long par 3s that look just like cape holes, though they're par 3s. For all the crankiness, it turns out that this is a thinker's course, with strategy and right-siding as important as getting in no more than modest trouble when out of play. We learned one of our greatest Pete Dye tricks out here, after hacking it around for a couple years: play it backwards. Not literally, but look at every hole from green to tee and the angles show themselves beautifully and you figure out that there's a lot more visual than actual terror. It works here, it works at TPC Sawgrass. Now if only we had game to go with our brainy skills. The course has hosted several silly season events, appeared in one Bob Hope and ruined the lives of many a Q School attendee. Thankfully there is talk that it might make its way back into the tour's rotation

Jack Nicklaus's companion course, opened a year after Stadium, shows many of the attributes of the Golden Bear as an '80s and '90s designer. There's tons of room to bash it around, with sideboards a good way around, the greens are Jones-esque in size, and the long iron—at least as wielded more than 20 years ago—is an essential part of the game plan. Nicklaus is more imaginative, less cookie-cutter, and dare we say whimsical now, as he has truly honed his craft, yet Tournament retains enough challenge and interest to set it apart in a valley beset with lots of hit-and-giggle golf. The par 4s are killer.

i Great trumpet flourishes were heard over Palm Springs in 2006 when the first new course to open in the city since seemingly prohibition threw open its gates. Escena Golf Club was the centerpiece of a brand spanking new hip-retro-mod housing project, and that too was cause for a riff or three. The Nicklaus Design course didn't see a lot of play, closing down while still in its infancy owing to a dicey housing market. As more golf is always better than less golf, it's a pleasure to announce that the course was scheduled to reopen in fall 2009. Fingers crossed.

SILVERROCK RESORT $$$
79-179 Ahmanson Lane, La Quinta
(760) 777-8884
www.silverrock.org

The city of La Quinta went all-in when it set about to build a world-class golf-and-getaway facility in a town populated by the likes of PGA West, La Quinta Resort, and a smooth mix of residential-golf developments that read like so many wish-list entries for most. The getaway component is still a work in progress for the city, but the golf bona fides have been established.

SilverRock entered life bold and brash, with a date for a spot on the PGA Tour's calendar not long after it popped out. Youthful precociousness and some bad weather delayed the ascension for a few years, but in 2008 the course took its place as one of the four courses used in the Bob Hope. A true beast at nearly 7,600 yards when stretched to the max, what makes SilverRock unique is not sheer length, though that is in adequate supply, rather the way the design mixes length, angle, approachability, and guile. The paradox is best represented by the I-know-I-can-reach-it-just-go-over-the-trees/no-I-shouldn't-try-it, sub-300-yard, par-4 5th and the oh-man-I-gotta-hammer-it, 453-yard, par-4 15th (blue-tee yardages). It's fitting that Arnie gets the design credit on this one.

TAHQUITZ CREEK GOLF RESORT $–$$
1885 Golf Club Dr.
(760) 328-1005
www.tahquitzgolfresort.com

Yes, folks, there is golf in Palm Springs. The supply isn't deep, but as with Indian Canyons, it can be quite good, and if looking for the city champ, it's Ted Robinson's Resort Course at Tahquitz Creek. Opened in 1995, Resort is touted as a "desert links-style" course, which of course is one of the many meaningless phrases that pepper and pollute the golf lexicon. Rolling out in a mantle of green beside one of the major floodways in the desert, dressed up in an explosion of seasonal flowers and hazards of blue, the course is most nearly a somewhat standard Ted Robinson resort routing, but there are some teeth here not usually bared at a lot of the late sly fox's designs. Success in this game always seems to come back to the driver, but as much effort here needs to be directed toward iron play as you come into a variety of green configurations, some pushed up, some ringed by a necklace of sand, that are large and need to be hit in the correct quadrant for any hope. And recession-responding pricing makes it a killer deal. Legend is the facility's senior member, the product of Billy Bell back when we really did fear the Russians. Despite work to give the elderly guy a few more teeth, and 40 more bunkers, Legend remains true to its roots in the era of grass and trees, thinking over crushing.

WESTIN MISSION HILLS—
PETE DYE RESORT AND
GARY PLAYER SIGNATURE $$$–$$$$
71-333 Dinah Shore Dr., Rancho Mirage

70-705 Ramon Rd., Rancho Mirage
(760) 328-3198 (Dye), (760) 770-2908 (Player)
www.troongolf.com

"Resort" in the name should be somewhat of an indicator that this is not your peeved pro golfer's Pete Dye course. Sure many of Nightmare Pete's

---

Lions or Lambs?

They once played a PGA Tour event at PGA West's Stadium Course. The millionaires (OK, that was '87 so hundred-thousandaires) lasted one tourney, and they never went back. Refused to go back, actually. Accustomed to short, sporty members' courses where a round of two-under will lose a player 53 spots on the Bob Hope's leaderboard, Pete Dye's playpen elicited a collective "no mas" from the jet-set. During high season players with Furyk-meets-Freddy Kruger swings have stood 12 deep on the first tee, having willingly forked over nearly $300 for the honor. They lost sleeve after sleeve of four-dollar-each Titleists, put so many Xs on scorecards that it looked like a fund-raising tourney for former porn stars, and needed an assist from two CPAs and an MIT grad in the locker room just to add it all up. And they loved it. Wait, it gets better. The PGA Tour has deemed that Tiger and Co. don't have to play Stadium—OK, Tiger never plays the Bob Hope—but you get the point. However, the aspiring PGA Tour-ists seeking admission to the Promised Land of BMW courtesy cars and five-figure last-place checks have to face Stadium every couple years during the tour's qualifying tournament. As the tour says, the players are really good. They just don't look so tough.

---

trademark elements are in play, be they waste areas, double-jeopardy lakes, or railroad-tie bulkheads. But this one was specifically designed for play by the good guests of the adjoining Westin

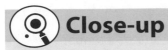

Close-up

Bob Hope Chrysler Classic

The Palm Springs Golf Classic—now the Bob Hope—was played for the first time in 1960, and its first winner was golf legend Arnold Palmer, who set a tournament record of 22 under par that remained unbroken for almost 20 years. That year, Arnie went on to chalk up eight more victories, dominating the field in his best year as a pro. Five months after winning the Classic, he shot a final round 65 to make one of the most dramatic comebacks in the history of the U.S. Open. That game made him a legend and elevated golf into the national consciousness as a top sport. Palmer won the Classic again in 1962, 1968, 1971, and 1973, and chalked up several runner-ups. The 1973 Classic was the King's last regular tour victory.

The Classic's early years determined the format and traditions, which remain to this day. Bob Rosburg is credited with creating the tournament's unique five-day format played over four different courses. The founding courses played were Thunderbird, Tamarisk, Bermuda Dunes, and Indian Wells Country Clubs. The tradition of the Classic Girls began in the event's early years, with the earliest tournaments having a Classic Queen. Debbie Reynolds, Jane Powell, and Jill St. John were early titleholders.

From the very first year, the Classic attracted Hollywood's hottest stars to compete in the tournament's pro-am competition: Bing Crosby, Burt Lancaster, Kirk Douglas, Phil Harris, Desi Arnaz, Ray Bolger, and Hoagy Carmichael. Dwight Eisenhower was the first former president to play in the tournament. Bob Hope, the biggest star of all, played in the early years, added his name to the tournament (the Bob Hope Desert Classic) in 1965, and later became the Classic's chairman of the board. The Classic had another huge draw—a $50,000 prize offered for a hole in one. For the first three years of the tournament, the Classic purchased an insurance policy from Lloyd's of London for a hole-in-one payoff—and the $50,000 was won in each of these years.

The combination of Arnie's victories and the hole-in-one bonanza were strokes of marketing genius and luck, and the Classic, which was televised for the first time in 1961, was a prime factor in launching golf into the sports mainstream. The annual tournament also brought images of the desert into homes all across the country, promoting the desert's sun and lifestyle in the winter when the rest of the nation was locked deep in ice and snow.

Frank Sinatra made his Classic debut in 1972. Other stars of the era who played often were Jack Benny, Andy Williams, Lawrence Welk, Sammy Davis Jr., Jackie Gleason, and Dean

resort, so it's Dye with a hug and a smile. Of course, there is a smirk in every smile and some hugs can get a wee bit too tight.

Now Gary Player's course, about a mile off site, long has toiled in the shadow of more famous desert tracks. And for valley insiders, that's both a blessing and an unfathomable concept. The course is a sleeper, an overlooked knockout where gnarled black mesquite build canopies of lacey green and rock-hemmed streams deliver the needed pucker, and for all the houses that trace the way, the architect's pen followed a surprisingly organic line.

CLINICS AND SCHOOLS

Is there another group that loves something as much as golfers love golf, yet does less in the way of actually trying to get better at it? And if we do practice, is it on the important stuff? Heck no. Beating driver is fun, putting bites. If you've reached the breaking point or you are reading this on January 2, here are some options for getting some help with your game, and in one case, your brain. Most are golf "schools," one is a venerable range where the type of curriculum is likely best suited to locals, and the last, at Des-

Martin. Gerald Ford joined the field in 1977, making him the second former president to play in the tournament. Willie Mays, Joe Louis, Johnny Bench, Merlin Olsen, John McKay, Maury Wills, and Bear Bryant were among the sports-world stars who teed it up in the Classic during the 1970s. Barbara Eden was the first Classic Queen of the '70s, reigning over a court that wore outfits with "Bob," "Hope," and "Classic" emblazoned across the front. Other queens during the decade were Gloria Loring, Brucence Smith, Linda Carter, Lexie Brockway, and Terry Ann Browning. The last four also held the title of Miss World USA. Beginning in 1975 the Bob Hope Classic Girls became the ambassadors of the Classic, as there was no longer a queen. By this time, Bermuda Dunes, Indian Wells, and La Quinta served as the host courses on a rotating basis. Eldorado and Tamarisk rotated as the fourth course in the lineup each year.

In the 1980s Chrysler, which had been a major sponsor for several years, added its name as title sponsor, increasing the total purse by 228 percent. A new course, PGA West, joined the rotation in 1987, then quickly departed when the pros complained about its difficulty, and the tourney became even more competitive, with 10 different winners in 10 years.

The biggest single news event at the Classic during the 1990s didn't even involve the world's top professionals. In 1995, the team of President Bill Clinton, President George H. W. Bush, President Gerald R. Ford, tournament host Bob Hope, and defending champion Scott Hoch teed it up for the tournament's opening round. This was the first time a sitting president had played during a PGA Tour event and perhaps the first time three presidents had played together—ever. As the first decade of the new millennium was starting to wind down, a short-lived and apparently very popular-with-the-public experiment to have comedian George Lopez host the tourney after Hope's death breathed some much needed life into an event on decline, but his style did not sit well with the Classic's powers-that-be, and he was sacked before the 2009 iteration. Another cloud passed overhead when Chrysler removed itself as title sponsor during 2009's financial meltdown.

Yet highs or lows, the Classic churns on, and has donated some $50 million to desert charities over its long life, helping support and sustain every good cause, from Guide Dogs of the Desert to Eisenhower Medical Center. Since its very first year, this star-filled sports event has been a vital player in the valley's life, bringing in tens of thousands of visitors, millions of dollars, and priceless publicity from all over the world. And helping one heck of a lot of folks who just needed a little help.

ert Willow, does it all, and then some. This is a volatile market niche, and while there are other quality programs in the desert, these schools have proven to have some staying power, and national/international chops. And never forget, at home or on the road, your friendly neighborhood PGA professional.

COLLEGE OF THE DESERT GOLF CENTER
73-450 Fred Waring Dr., Palm Desert
(760) 776-7486
www.collegegolfcenter.net
A large, lighted driving range offering individual and group instructions, and clinics; uses 3-D "motion capture" filming technology.

DAVE PELZ SCORING GAME SCHOOL
Cimarrón Golf Resort
67-603 30th Ave., Cathedral City
(760) 770-6060, (800) 833-7370
www.pelzgolf.com
Generally considered the foremost short-game instructor, this former rocket scientist offers one-day clinics and two- and three-day schools. Please check the Web site or call for sessions and dates.

EXTRAORDINARY GOLF

The Golf Club of Terra Lago
84-000 Terra Lago Parkway, Indio
(800) 541-2444
www.extraordinarygolf.com
If you think "Golf in the Kingdom" is the finest piece of golf literature, then the awareness programs of Fred Shoemaker's Extraordinary Golf are right up your alley. The core offering is a three-day program, and a variety of options are available, including ones for couples, women, and previous "graduates" of Extraordinary Golf. Call for specific offerings at this facility.

THE FALDO GOLF INSTITUTE

Marriott's Shadow Ridge
9002 Shadow Ridge Rd., Palm Desert
(888) 463-2536
www.golf-instruction.marriott-vacations.com
Multi-facet, multi-day schools for players of all ability levels. Can be done a la carte or in conjunction with a stay-and-play package through Marriott's Shadow Ridge time-share resort. Individual lessons are offered, as are programs for corporate or incentive groups.

JIM MCLEAN GOLF SCHOOL

La Quinta Resort & Club
50-200 Avenida Vista Bonita, La Quinta
(760) 777-4838

PGA West
56-150 PGA Blvd., La Quinta
(760) 564-7144
www.jimmclean.com
This is one of the top-rated programs, and include residency and commuter sessions, typically lasting two- or three-days, though one-, four-, and even intensive six-day programs are offered at times. Special programs include a "power school," group sessions and junior academies.

JOHN JACOBS GOLF SCHOOLS

Indian Palms Country Club
48-630 Monroe St., Indio
(800) 472-5007
www.jacobsgolf.com

John Jacobs is perhaps the largest provider of vacation golf school programs in the country. Two-, three-, and five-day sessions are offered for either commuters (instruction and materials only) or with a room-and-board package. Various Jacobs sites also offer specialty schools, junior programs, and individual or group lessons. School packages always include course time.

PALM DESERT GOLF ACADEMY AT DESERT WILLOW

38-995 Desert Willow Dr.
(760) 340-4057
www.desertwillow.com
An all-in-one shop offering clinics, private instruction, golf schools, video analysis, fitness and flexibility training, club-fitting, and an on-site Titleist Performance Institute. The practice facilities are superb.

TROON GOLF ACADEMY

Westin Mission Hills Resort
71-333 Dinah Shore Dr., Rancho Mirage
(866) 905-3300
www.troongolfschools.com
Two- and three-day schools with accommodations. Includes seven hours of instruction daily and on-course supervised play.

BOOKING SERVICES

Excluding those with more prurient interests, the Internet sure seems to have done more to revolutionize how we travel, learn about travel, and book travel than it has scrambled most any other endeavor. Yet a funny thing happened on the way to the Ethernet: Have we been parking our brains? While there are some very good, very legitimate information portals and more importantly third-party booking entities ("discounters") out there, just because it's on the Internet doesn't mean you're getting a great price. All this increased competition in many ways has lessened service/goods providers' need or desire to negotiate deals with arms-length vendors. Following are a number of operations that offer discounts, book your tee time(s), coordinate your

Desert Golf Rules

The days of galactic space-size voids separating playing conditions region-to-region are gone. Obviously cool-clime dwellers acclimated to bent grass need to adjust to bermuda. But let's not over-think all of this. We'd guess most avid recreational golfers—and we are avid recreational golfers ourselves—are more inclined to leave putts nowhere near the magic circle known as tap-in range than they are to lip-out low because the grass had 1.73583" inches more break than back home. Here are some thoughts about handling the desert's peculiarities:

It's hot here. And if it's not hot, it's dry. The wind blows, too. Drink plenty of fluids; nonalcoholic. Try to hydrate before you play, particularly during the summer, and drink every couple of holes. If you wait until you realize you are thirsty, you're done. Hopefully using sunscreen and wearing a hat goes without saying.

See all those mountains? Water runs away from them. Putts, all else equal, follow water. That's why the standard quip around here is: "It breaks toward Indio." That's because the watershed flows that direction, to the southeast. Of course what do you do if playing a course that's below Indio?

Grass: Bermuda grass has a good amount of "grain," owing to the way it grows. Advances in turfgrass have taken some of the coil out of the snake, so don't get all bound up looking at the first six-footer. Just know it might bend a little more than on your bent grasses back home. Where we think grain matters is in speed as down-grain putts will roll out much more than those into the grain. It's easy. Look at the green. Now do a 180 and look at the green. If it's shiny it's downgrain. Go get 'em, Crenshaw.

Mo' grass: Courses overseed in the desert. That won't affect most vacationers as the bulk of the process occurs when you least want to be here, late summer/early fall. In a nutshell, the water is turned off, the fairway grass croaks, it's shaven within an inch of its now-gone life, and winter-loving rye is sown. Turn the water back on and, voila, you have a golf course in about a month. It's actually kind of fun to play when the grass is going because the ball runs like Usain Bolt on 17 Red Bulls. But it's rough on the allergies. And don't get us started on paths-only during the grow-in.

group travel needs, serve as information portals/clearinghouses, or some combination thereof. Give 'em a look. And don't forget to sign the online guest books of courses that interest you and you might get discount offers.

GOLF À LA CARTE
(760) 772-7663
www.palmspringsgolf.com
The selling point here is 20-plus years of experience working with desert courses, so these guys can hook you up with a group tee time far in advance of what you'd be able to do through the usual channels. Of particular importance, smaller groups can cancel up to 72 hours before their scheduled tee times, groups with more than 12 players will have cancellation provisions negotiated into their contracts, and that usually means at best a 30-day window. With any type of third-party transaction, be it rooms or rounds,

clear, no-penalty cancellation allowances are worth their weight in gold. The Web site includes a rather complete matrix of course rates and overseeding schedules.

GOLF NOW
(800) 980-1226
www.golfnow.com

Golf Now is a nearly nationwide online booking engine covering 1,800 courses, and about 30 in the desert. The process is very similar to Stand-By Golf (below). Just for grins we put in some arbitrary dates and found PGA West's Greg Norman Course for about 20 percent less than the course was quoting. That's worth a couple sixers of Stone India Pale Ale. The discount percentage will change seasonally, and from course to course, and with any third-party discounter you often are drawing from a pool of limited tee time slots.

PAR-TEE GOLF
(760) 324-2222, (800) 727-8331

STAND-BY GOLF
(760) 321–2665, (866) 224-2665
www.standbygolf.com

These are affiliated enterprises, with Par-Tee coordinating advance tee-time reservations and golf packages. Stand-By will be of value to more players since it is the discounter. The roster changes over time, but Stand-By typically has a relationship with 40 or so courses, and not just the soiled doves. In-season discounts range from 10% to 50%. Historically players called the day of or the night before play to see what courses had what tee times available. A few courses allow advance discount booking up to 30 days out, and you also can now reserve online. Another great service is Callaway rentals for 30 bucks a bag. They're not the latest models but likely better than what a lot of us swing, and did we say they're 30 bucks a bag per day? The Web site has a very well maintained, easy-to-read overseeding schedule, and finally, the operation is located here in the desert, with affiliates in other markets. By the way, Stand-By would've saved us an additional two bucks at the Norman Course.

ANNUAL FESTIVALS AND EVENTS

Special events in the Coachella Valley follow the weather patterns—when it's hot, the pace slows to a crawl, but when the temperatures cool off, it's impossible to fit everything in. Dozens of fund-raising galas, golf tournaments, film festivals, art shows, and sporting events fill the calendar from late September all the way through April, tapering off dramatically in May.

There are lots of high-priced dinners and dances, to be sure, but most of the events in this section are geared to be affordable to the typical vacationing family. There are also ample opportunities for free entertainment, from concerts in the park to street fairs and art festivals to car shows and bike rides.

Despite its close historical ties to Hollywood stars, the Palm Springs area was never associated with "the industry" until Sonny Bono started the Palm Springs International Film Festival in 1990. Since then the slate of film festivals has grown enormously, and there seems to be a new specialty festival appearing every season. Many of these little festivals screen films that are virtually impossible to find outside of big-city art houses. And most of the festivals are held at the refurbished Camelot Theatre, close to downtown Palm Springs. A fixture in Palm Springs since its star-studded opening in 1967, the Camelot eventually closed and remained vacant for seven years until it was bought in 1999. Ric and Rozene Supple made upgrades and launched the Camelot as the desert's home for foreign and art films.

Golf tournaments are also popular in Palm Springs. The desert has more than 100 golf courses, and save an economic blip every now and again, there seems no end to the hunger for more, bigger, and fancier. Some of the biggest names in the sport, and the biggest himself (sorry Tiger, Arnie's still the man), maintain at least part-time residency here, and they've put there names on courses and even a restaurant. Combine the abundance of golf with the desert's many charities, and you have a lot of opportunities to raise funds, and the desert's residents do that in spades.

Each year there are tournaments that aren't successful enough to be repeated, and others that change names or lose sponsors. Because of this, our listings cover only those tournaments that have a proven track record. In this chapter we've also highlighted the most prominent and long-lived annual events, and some of the strong-running upstarts, knowing that more will pop up by the time this book is in your hands. The events are organized by month, with ongoing fairs and events grouped together at the beginning of the chapter. Some of the events may change months, duration, and location, and prices are sure to change. The prices given were current at the time of publication and are printed here for reference only. Use this chapter to help you plan your visit, but be sure to confirm the details with the listed phone numbers and Web sites.

ONGOING FAIRS AND EVENTS

Throughout the Year

COLLEGE OF THE DESERT STREET FAIR
43-500 Monterey Ave., Palm Desert
(760) 773-2567
www.codstreetfair.com
Every Sat and Sun from 7 a.m. to 2 p.m. (7 a.m. to noon June through Sept), locals and visitors crowd into this sprawling fair, which features more than 300 vendors selling everything from tacos to fine art and cheap sunglasses. The College of the Desert Alumni Association, an organization that carefully vets the vendors for quality and honesty, runs the fair. The farmers' market is a highlight—come early to get the freshest produce. The fair takes place in a large open area in the middle of the campus of College of the Desert. Enter the parking lot from Monterey Avenue, just south of Fred Waring Drive. Wear comfortable shoes and bring cash for food and small items. Free admission and street parking. For more details, see the listing in the Shopping chapter.

FIRST FRIDAY
North Palm Canyon Drive between Amado Road and Tachevah Drive
(760) 778-8415
On the first Friday of every month, the shops, restaurants, and galleries on North Palm Canyon's Heritage District stay open until 9 p.m., offering music, refreshments, and a festive atmosphere conducive to wandering and shopping. This area is full of consignment and antiques shops, boutiques specializing in real and faux retro items, and art galleries. Free admission and street parking.

INDIO OPEN-AIR MARKET
Riverside County Fairgrounds
46-350 Arabia St., Indio
(800) 222-7467
Every Wed and Sat night from 4 to 10 p.m., this flea market/street fair caters mostly to the Mexican-American population, with authentic food, Spanish-language music and videos, and new and used brand-name merchandise. The market takes place on the grounds of the Riverside County Fair and National Date Festival. Free admission and street parking.

PALM SPRINGS VILLAGEFEST
North Palm Canyon Drive between Amado and Baristo Roads
(760) 320-3781
www.palm-springs.org
Held from 6 to 10 p.m. each Thurs, VillageFest is the granddaddy of all the other street fairs and regular art strolls. The brainchild of City Councilman Tuck Broich back in 1991, it's been growing and attracting more shoppers every year. A good portion of downtown Palm Canyon Drive closes to street traffic on this night. Shops and restaurants all along the 4-block VillageFest strip stay open late, and the area becomes an absolute magnet for locals and visitors. Children and dogs are welcome, and there's lots of live music, interesting food, and good-quality arts and crafts, as well as a farmers' market. Free admission and street parking. For more details, see the listing in the Shopping chapter.

May through September

PALM SPRINGS INTERNATIONAL SHORT FILM FESTIVAL
2300 East Baristo Rd.
(760) 322-2930
www.psfilmfest.org
The largest competitive short-film festival in North America, this weeklong event showcases film, video, and animation shorts by cutting-edge filmmakers from all over the world. The event is also a marketplace for short films looking for distribution, and more than 45 films in the lineup have gone on to win Oscar nominations. The works are arranged into programs by subject matter and scheduled so that it's actually possible to see them all. You won't even have to skip a few meals to do so, because the Camelot has an excellent snack bar with fresh sandwiches, salads, and hot coffee.

Please consult the Web site for individual screening, block and all-access ticket pricing. The festival historically ran in late summer but has recently been held in June.

SUMMER OF FUN CONCERTS & MOVIES IN THE PARK
Palm Desert Civic Center Amphitheater
73-510 Fred Waring Dr., Palm Desert
(760) 346-0611
www.palm-desert.org
From the last Thurs in May through the first Thurs in Sept, the City of Palm Desert hosts free movies and concerts in the park. Concerts begin at 7:30 p.m. Movie preshow festivities with cartoons and prize giveaways start at 7 p.m. The movie starts at sunset.

This has become a huge community gathering, so get there well before the start times to get a good spot. You're welcome to bring all types of picnicking gear, such as food, soft drinks, low lawn chairs, and blankets, but alcohol is not allowed.

October through May
EL PASEO ART WALK
El Paseo Drive, Palm Desert
(877) 735-7273
www.elpaseo.com
From 5 to 9 p.m. on the first Thurs of each month from Oct through May, the dozens of art galleries and boutiques along El Paseo Drive stay open late for artist exhibitions, receptions, entertainment, and refreshments. This event offers even the most inexperienced art lover a good chance to view world-class art in a casual, friendly, no-pressure atmosphere. It's also a good opportunity to check out the menus and make a decision on where to eat later, as El Paseo is home to a great many restaurants, from white-tablecloth fancy to good family pizza places. Free admission and street parking.

WORLD AFFAIRS COUNCIL OF THE DESERT SPEAKER PROGRAM
Renaissance Esmeralda Resort
44-400 Indian Wells Lane, Indian Wells
(760) 322-7711
www.worldaffairsdesert.org
A nonpartisan and nonprofit group, the World Affairs Council focuses on noted international professors, political figures, and reporters discussing issues that have significance to U.S. foreign policy. Tickets for the evening are $45 for members, $55 for nonmembers. Held monthly on Sun evenings from Oct through May, the programs begin with a reception at 5 p.m., dinner at 6 p.m., and a speaker's presentation.

November through April
ART WALK AT THE ART PLACE
41-801 Corporate Way, Palm Desert
(760) 776-2268
www.theartplacepd.com
From 6 to 9 p.m. on the first Fri of the month, Nov through Apr, the many art galleries and design-supported businesses in the business park area of Palm Desert open their doors to welcome the public. It's similar in concept to the El Paseo Art Walk, but the atmosphere is less high-toned, and the art—much of it from artists who are showing in their own studios—can be a very good value. Free admission and street parking.

November through May
DESERT ARTS FESTIVAL
400 North Palm Canyon Dr.
(760) 778-8418
www.westcoastartists.com
Held on the last weekend of the month during daylight hours, this regular art event features fine art in all media, plus jewelry and other crafts by artists from throughout Southern California. The fair is on the grounds of the city's first park—Frances Stevens Park—and right in the middle of the action on Palm Canyon Drive. Park, explore the art, and have lunch or dinner downtown for an enjoyable, inexpensive day that's entertaining for most ages. Free admission and street parking.

JANUARY

PALM SPRINGS INTERNATIONAL FILM FESTIVAL

1700 East Tahquitz Canyon Way, Suite #3
(760) 322-2930, (800) 898-7256
www.psfilmfest.org

World and U.S. premieres, parties, lectures, and presentations and more than 100 new films are on the program, which often isn't finalized until very close to opening night. The black-tie gala awards program and dinner is one of the hottest events in an event-filled season in the desert, with everyone vying for tables close to the stars.

Screenings and other events take place at various movie theaters and hotels in Palm Springs in early Jan. Individual tickets are $9 for films before 5 p.m. and $10 after 5 p.m. Platinum Passes allowing the holder to view every movie are $350. Opening- and closing-night tickets are $50. Tickets to the awards gala are $350. There are also coupon books that offer package discounts.

KENNEL CLUB OF PALM SPRINGS DOG SHOW

Empire Polo Club
81-800 Avenue 51, Indio
(323) 727-0136
www.jbradshaw.com

The largest conformation show in the area is held annually in early Jan.

BOB HOPE CHRYSLER CLASSIC

PGA West Nicklaus Private and Palmer Private, La Quinta Country Club and SilverRock Resort courses, La Quinta
(760) 346-8184
www.bhcc.com

The Bob Hope has been the desert's biggest draw and sporting event since it began back in 1960. The value of the tourism promotion generated by the event is inestimable. The image, in mid-Jan, as seen by the snow-bound portions of the country, of perfect swings against a gorgeous backdrop of blue sky and immaculate emerald course is a hell of an enticement.

Traditionally, the tournament has been played on four courses, which varied at times as drawn from a short list of participating clubs. The courses remain 75 percent private, but city of La Quinta-owned SilverRock Resort now fills out the foursome after an experiment with another public track, the Classic Club in Palm Desert, went awry, owing to that course's location out in the wind tunnel that is the center of the valley. Classic Club's demise is a loss on two fronts, because it's a stellar course that all of us can play and it's always fun to see the pros on a course we might know, and it had been donated to the tournament outright, enabling even more money to go to desert charities. Oh well, the show goes on. And a good one it is, even if no one tosses up a 59 like Duval did in '99.

Clubhouse badges are $125. Grounds-only badges for the duration are $75 and daily tickets $25, with an additional $15 charge for clubhouse access. Parking is limited, so come early. Children under 12 are admitted free when a paying adult accompanies them. Discounts are available online if ordered before the end of the year.

SOUTHWEST ARTS FESTIVAL

Empire Polo Club
81-800 Avenue 51, Indio
(760) 347-0676
www.southwestartsfest.com

Typically held over three days late Jan, this judged and juried outdoor art fair features west-

---

i If you volunteer at one of the film festivals, you'll get free passes for some great movies. Lots of golf tournaments also have good deals for their volunteers, though most ask that you purchase your official tourney helper gear so as not to dip into the coin that goes to all the charities.

ern and southwestern-themed art and crafts in all media. The several hundred attending artists and craftspeople are primarily from the western United States, showing and selling works that range from the traditional to the contemporary. There is always lots of live entertainment, food, wine, and beer. Daily admission is $10 for adults, $8 for seniors, and children under 12 are free. Three-day passes are $18. Valet and self-park are available for $8 and $5, respectively.

FEBRUARY

STEVE CHASE HUMANITARIAN AWARDS
Palm Springs Convention Center
277 North Avenida Caballeros
(760) 323-2118
www.desertaidsproject.org
When renowned interior designer Steve Chase left his extensive art collection to the Palm Springs Art Museum, he also created a tradition of continuing support for his chosen charity, the Desert AIDS Project. This social event in early Feb began as a VIP cocktail party at the museum and has evolved into a glamorous all-out gala, attracting a guest list of the most affluent and influential names in the desert, as well as a lot of heavy hitters from Hollywood. Tickets are $425 per person for the cocktail reception, dinner, silent auction, entertainment, and awards show. Parking is free on-site or nearby on the street.

TOUR DE PALM SPRINGS
Downtown Palm Springs
(760) 770-4626
www.tourdepalmsprings.com
One of the largest charity bike rides in the country, the Tour attracts as many as 10,000 riders, so it's smart to get there early for sign-ups. Route maps for the different rides are given out on the morning of the event, so everyone starts out with the same level of knowledge. A spaghetti dinner the night before is great for carb-loading for the 5-, 10-, 25-, 50-, and 100-mile rides. Registration fees are $10 to $60, depending on length and age.

PALM SPRINGS MODERNISM WEEK
Various locations in Palm Springs
(760) 788-8418
www.dolphinfairs.com/palmsprings
This annual show and sale in mid-Feb features noted national and international dealers exhibiting vintage furniture and decorative arts and crafts from all design movements of the 20th century. The Friday-evening preview party gives collectors first dibs on their favorite items and benefits the Palm Springs Preservation Foundation, the organization that was instrumental in preserving and publicizing many of the city's most important mid-century buildings. Book signings and lectures are also scheduled for the weekend.

RIVERSIDE COUNTY FAIR & NATIONAL DATE FESTIVAL
Riverside County Fairgrounds
82-503 Hwy. 111, Indio
(800) 811-3247
www.datefest.org
This old-time combination of county fair, carnival, and Arabian Nights dress-up celebration opens the Friday of President's Weekend and runs for 10 days. Bring your camera and wear good walking shoes, because there's a lot to see. No outside food or drink is allowed, so make sure to bring extra cash for snacks, trinkets, and rides.

Some of the highlights are the Arabian Nights Pageant—a nightly re-telling of one of the *1001 Nights* tales—camel and ostrich races, nightly live concerts featuring popular, rock, country-western, and on the last weekend an entire slate of Mexican groups, and, of course, all the fried fair food and barbecued turkey legs you can eat. There are also cooking and art demonstrations, a livestock "nursery," a petting zoo for the little ones, and the mandatory date tastings. (Pssst, have a date milk shake.)

A large part of the event is typical county fair stuff, with thousands of exhibits: livestock, agriculture, horticulture, photography, fine arts, wood carving, crafts, and junior achievement dis

 **Close-up**

The Palm Springs International Film Festival and Sonny Bono

The late Sonny Bono created this 10-day event in 1990, midway through his term as mayor of Palm Springs. It began as an upstart festival focusing on emerging filmmakers and top international films not yet in general release. And it began on a shoestring, with seed money from the City of Palm Springs. Bono's name and film industry connections were the key to its initial success, though a lot of the city's longtime residents took a dim view of spending city money to support an unproven event.

At the time, the city had seen several years of retail and visitor exodus to newer shops and hotels in the other end of the valley, and its balance sheets were looking fairly anemic. But Sonny promoted the festival as a way of attracting the Hollywood heavy hitters and young stars who could make the city "hip" again and help reverse its slide into obscurity.

When Sonny went on to become a congressman, he continued his efforts with the festival, often putting his own money and staff to work when times were shaky. When he died in a skiing accident in 1998, his widow, now remarried, won a special election held to fill his vacated congressional seat. Mary Bono Mack was re-elected to that seat in 2008. Her support of the festival has never wavered, and she has been a key player in keeping sponsorship money flowing.

Seeing hotel rooms and restaurants full of visitors during the festival's run has validated the event as a real economic boon to the city, and Palm Springs has remained its primary sponsor, recently committing funds through 2010. As Mayor Ron Oden said in 2005, "This is our signature event. It gets our name out there to the international community."

As the festival has grown in prestige and name recognition, other sponsors have stepped up, including Tiffany & Co. (which presents the annual awards gala), the Cities of Indian Wells and Palm Desert, *The Desert Sun* newspaper, Mercedes-Benz, the Agua Caliente Band of Cahuilla Indians, and the National Endowment for the Arts.

Savvy programming and support from Hollywood insiders have helped the festival grow into one of the most prestigious and cutting-edge film events in the country, screening more than 200 films from 60 or more countries. Past honorees have included Kirk Douglas, Susan Sarandon, Sophia Loren, Nicole Kidman, Kevin Spacey, Samuel Jackson, and many others. Films premiered here have gone on to win dozens of Oscars and Oscar nominations. The festival has an attractive film sales and distribution record and is seen by American distributors as one of the best Academy Award campaign marketing tools.

Today Sonny Bono's little film festival has become the largest revenue-generating film festival in the country, with a box office of more than $750,000. In 2005 it scored 105,000 admissions, second only to the Seattle Film Festival with 157,000. In contrast, the venerable San Francisco Film Festival had 95,000 admissions, and Robert Redford's Sundance Film Festival racked up just 45,000.

In short, the Palm Springs International Film Festival has brought Hollywood back to Palm Springs, just as Sonny Bono envisioned it would.

plays. Adding to the often-frenzied atmosphere are lots of carnival rides and booths, multiple entertainment stages, off-track betting on horse races, and the nightly musical pageants featuring the fair's official Queen Scheherazade and her court. Past fairs have also included Mexican rodeos, monster truck demonstrations, and freestyle motorcycle contests.

Parking is plentiful and inexpensive around the fairgrounds. Admission is $8 for adults, $7 for seniors, $6 for children 5–12, and free for children under 5. A daily unlimited-ride pass is $25, and a season pass good for admission every day is $30. Fair-run parking is $7 per vehicle. Advance-sale tickets bring a $1 discount across the board.

FRANK SINATRA CELEBRITY INVITATIONAL
Fantasy Springs Resort Casino
84-245 Indio Springs Parkway, Indio
(760) 674-8447, (800) 377-8277
www.sinatragolf.com
This late-Feb event is two days of golf and three nights of entertainment, including a black-tie gala, plus a popular luncheon and fashion show. Held to benefit the Barbara Sinatra Children's Center at Eisenhower Medical Center, this tournament boasts an atmosphere that harks back to the golden days of the desert, when seeing a movie star on the golf course was just par for the day. Please check the Web site for low-cost spectator and big-buck supporter prices.

MCCORMICK'S PALM SPRINGS EXOTIC CAR SHOW & AUCTION
Downtown Palm Springs
(760) 320-3290
www.classic-carauction.com
This three-day show and auction of rare and vintage automobiles held in late Feb is a good excuse to daydream and then grouse because dad didn't put you through Wharton so you could afford one of the beauties. Another identical event is held in downtown Palm Springs in Nov. Admission for the event is $10 per day or $15 for both days. On-street parking is free nearby.

THE DESERT CLASSIC CONCOURS D'ELEGANCE
LaQuinta Resort & Club
49-499 Eisenhower Dr., La Quinta
(760) 766-2824
www.desertconcours.com
A three-day event held the last weekend in Feb, the concours moved in 2010 to La Quinta. Some 150 of the finest examples of classic auto design will be on hand, with other displays of art, jewelry,

and watches. There is live music and food and beverage. The event features a tour of classic vehicles through the valley on Sat; check the Web site route map and to find out how to personally participate. Sunday's concours admission is $25 in advance, $30 at the gate, and kids under 12 are admitted free. Proceeds from the event benefit local charities.

MARCH

HIKE FOR HOPE
Indian Canyons
(760) 202-3885
www.hike4hope.com
A family-oriented, noncompetitive hiking event in the beautiful Indian Canyons, this benefits the City of Hope National Medical Center and its research on women's cancer. There are 10 different routes for easy, moderate, and strenuous hikes. The event brings as many as 1,000 women and their families together for a fun and exhilarating morning of hiking and companionship in early Mar, typically the first Sunday. People can participate individually, or as teams, and non-participants always can sponsor a person or team in the event.

FESTIVAL OF NATIVE FILM & CULTURE
2300 East Belardo Rd.
(760) 778-1079
www.accmuseum.org
Held over several days the first part of the month, the festival screens features, documentaries, and shorts by and about Native peoples.

BNP PARIBAS OPEN
Indian Wells Tennis Garden
78-200 Miles Ave., Indian Wells
(800) 999-1585
www.bnpparibasopen.org
Begun more than 30 years ago as a small-scale tennis tournament at the stadium at the Hyatt Grand Champions resort, this event has morphed into one of the most prestigious events on the professional tennis circuit, settling in at the top

of the tier just below the four Grand Slam events, and like the Big Four, produce full men's and women's fields playing across the same fortnight in mid-Mar.

The adjoining grounds are set up with food, entertainment, and vendors. Bring a hat, some sunscreen, and money for food, drink, and some trinkets; and be prepared for an exciting day up close with the best tennis players in the world.

There's a bewildering array of ticket options available, from cheap to obscene if going for a catered suite, so please consult the Web site for rates and dates.

CABAZON INDIO POWWOW
Fantasy Springs Resort Casino
84-245 Indio Springs Parkway, Indio
(760) 342-5000, (800) 827-2946
www.fantasyspringsresort.com

A three-day festival in Mar that celebrates Native American dance, music, culture, and food, the powwow attracts hundreds of the best Indian dancers from all over the country, as well as artisans displaying and selling beadwork, paintings, pottery, leather crafts, jewelry, and more. Designed to bridge the Indian and non-Indian cultures, the event encourages visitors and invites everyone to join in the intertribal dancing. Another three-day powwow is held here in Nov, with much the same format and details. Admission is free. The powwow is held adjacent to the Fantasy Springs Casino, and parking is free.

LA QUINTA ARTS FESTIVAL
La Quinta Civic Center
78-495 Calle Tampico, La Quinta
(760) 564-1244
www.lqaf.com

Established in the early '80s, this open-air festival held in mid-Mar has become known as one of the most noteworthy juried art events in the country. Several hundred artist-finalists selected from close to 1,000 entrants, sell and display sculpture, paintings, photography, drawings, prints, jewelry, and fine crafts in a nicely designed garden setting with live entertainment and food and beverages.

INDIAN WELLS ARTS FESTIVAL
Indian Wells Tennis Garden
78-200 Miles Ave., Indian Wells
(760) 346-0042
www.indianwellsartfestival.com

This three-day event at the end of Mar is a judged and juried show with arts and crafts from more than 200 artists across the country. Refreshments, wine tasting, a beer garden, and live entertainment are offered from 10 a.m. to 5:30 p.m., with the last admission at 4:30 p.m. Admission is $10 for adults. Children 12 and under are admitted free.

> **i** If you can't afford an original piece of art from one of the many art fairs and festivals, consider picking up a signature poster. The La Quinta Arts Festival and the Palm Springs International Film Festival are noted for outstanding poster designs that change each year.

KRAFT NABISCO CHAMPIONSHIP
Mission Hills Country Club
34-600 Mission Hills Dr., Rancho Mirage
(760) 324-4546
www.kncgolf.com

Beyond the U.S. Women's Open, there is no tournament on the LPGA schedule that has more primacy than the "Dinah Shore," and it likely is the most loved. Any number of attributes set the Kraft Nabisco apart, and chucking out the weather and the other attributes of the desert, we're left with a great course that's been used every year of the event; the huge embrace the community gives the tournament and the players; and the dedication Dinah and then a solid following of corporate sponsors paid to an ideal and a batch of great athletes. All the greats have hoisted this trophy.

The LPGA draws nothing like the boys tour, and that's both a travesty and a boon. On the positive side, fans can get in tight in the deepest throes of competition, on Sunday when what matters is on the line, and see and be part of the action; try that at Torrey Pines when the crowd is

57 deep and you skip from the 3rd hole to 15 to catch another glimpse of a hat. Come out, be a part of history; going forward, looking back.

Daily tickets are $25 midweek, $35 for Sat and Sun; advance tickets may sell out the previous summer.

> **i** The week of the Kraft Nabisco Championship is a premier vacation and party time for thousands of lesbians, who come to the desert to play, dance, and enjoy the golf.

APRIL

EASTER EGG HUNT
Ruth Hardy Park
700 Tamarisk Rd.
(760) 323-8181
The men and women of the Palm Springs Fire Department have been hosting this event for more than 40 years now, and they do a magnificent job of keeping the Easter Bunny magic alive for kids up to age 9. Fire trucks for the kids to climb on, colored eggs to find, and simple contests make this a delightful morning. Admission and on-street parking are free. The hunt usually begins at 9 a.m. on Easter Sunday.

WHITE PARTY
Various venues throughout Palm Springs
(760) 322-6000
www.jeffreysanker.com
This is the premier happening on the country's gay dance/party circuit. Promoter Jeffrey Sanker's brainchild, the White Party virtually takes over the city for (typically) Easter Week, with events in hotels and nightspots all over Palm Springs. The Palm Springs Convention Center is one of the venues and home of the two-room/two-dance-floor main party. Gay men from all over the country make this extravaganza a part of their vacation plans each spring, and it seems to get larger every year. For packages, prices, and detailed information on individual events, check the Web site.

JOSHUA TREE NATIONAL PARK ART FESTIVAL
Joshua Tree National Park Visitor Center
74-485 National Park Dr., Twentynine Palms
(760) 367-5500
www.joshuatree.org
This is a nice little arts event in early Apr with a folksy feeling and an eclectic collection of art and crafts. There are usually around 20 artists, each presenting a different and very personal view of the park in different media. All the works are for sale at prices far below what you might expect to pay in a glitzy art gallery in Palm Desert or Palm Springs. Admission and parking are free.

COACHELLA VALLEY MUSIC AND ARTS FESTIVAL
Empire Polo Field
81-800 Avenue 51, Indio
www.coachella.com
This multiday, multimedia event toward the back end of Apr has become one of the hottest international music fests anywhere, showcasing young bands, groups on the cutting edge of alternative and rock music, and in recent years some of the biggest headliners of all time. Past groups have included Coldplay, Nine Inch Nails, Bauhaus, Weezer, Cocteau Twins, and some guy named Paul McCartney. Three-day passes start at $269, but please consult the Web site for applicable rates and packages.

STAGECOACH FESTIVAL
Empire Polo Field
81-800 Avenue 51, Indio
www.stagecoachfestival.com
Country music's response to Coachella is Stagecoach, which moves into Empire Polo Club not long after the rockers depart; one would assume it's easier to clean up ZigZag remnants and dead Monster cans than Skoal cans and manure. Previous acts included Kenny Chesney, Brad Paisley, Reba, Jerry Jeff Walker, Ricky Skaggs, Lynn Anderson, and for those in the audience who came of age in the '70s, Poco and Pure Prairie League. Stagecoach rolls for two days, and

general admission tickets are $129 for Sat and Sun, and $79 for a single day, with reserved seats running off from $300 to $700, but please check the Web site for current pricing.

MAY

PALM SPRINGS SMOOTH JAZZ FESTIVAL
Indian Canyons Golf Resort
1097 East Murray Canyon Dr.
(760) 323-6673
www.palmspringsjazz.com

This is a much-anticipated annual event, when major jazz artists entertain under the stars. The event was most recently held at Indian Canyons Golf Resort, but it was previously staged at historic O'Donnell Golf Club, so check the Web site for current information and pricing. The event benefits Hanson House, a facility for families of critically ill patients at Desert Regional Medical Center.

JUNE

PALM SPRINGS FILM NOIR FESTIVAL
2300 East Baristo Rd.
(760) 864-9760
www.palmspringsfilmnoir.com

This campy, fun festival in early June celebrates the dark, sinister "B" films of the 1940s and 1950s—films that are appreciated today for their innovative use of lighting and camera work and their dramatic character studies. Festival producer Art Lyons, a lifelong Palm Springs resident and author of several popular crime-detective novels, is a huge fan of the film noir genre. In researching his book *Death on the Cheap: The Lost B Movies of Film Noir*, he formed the concept for a film festival and spent years scouring the country for original movie footage. Each year fans can expect to see films that were thought to have vanished, view a few familiar classics, and visit with some of the actors and actresses who starred in the original films. Tickets range from around $11 to $13 and an all-access pass is $120. The all-access pass includes admission to parties and other special star events.

PALM SPRINGS DESERT RESORTS RESTAURANT WEEK
Various restaurants across the valley
(760) 770-9000, (800) 967-3767
www.palmspringsrestaurantweek.com

Coordinated by the desert's convention and visitors bureau, Restaurant Week is actually a 10-day run in which some 70 of the valley's best restaurants put together prix fixe dinner menus at two price levels, $24 and $36 per person. A complete list of participating restaurants is on the Web site. Reservations are not required but often recommended. No pre-purchased tickets or passes are required; just show up at the restaurants that interest you and ask what's special.

i Get CDs of past Jazz in the Pines festivals at Idyllwild online at www.parkhillmusic.com. Recorded and mixed by Park Hill Music in Hemet, these capture the energy and verve of the live performances. Part of the proceeds goes to the Idyllwild Arts Scholarship Fund, (951) 652-8742.

AUGUST

IDYLLWILD JAZZ IN THE PINES
Idyllwild Arts Academy
52-500 Temecula Dr., Idyllwild
(951) 500-4090
www.idyllwildjazz.com

Taking a 45-minute drive up the winding mountain road from the desert to the little town of Idyllwild is a favorite escape when summer temperatures start hitting the 100-degree mark. Hiking in the pines, shopping in charming boutiques, and dining at a couple good restaurants are reasons enough. When Idyllwild Jazz is on, there's just no excuse to stay in the desert. A two-day weekend festival in late Aug, this party on the Idyllwild Arts Academy campus attracts some of the world's top modern jazz masters to benefit the school's scholarship fund. Arts and crafts, great food, beer, wine, and dancing are a big part of the fun. Rooms in Idyllwild are scarce all through the summer, so book yours early if you don't want to drive down the mountain in the dark.

The event is held the weekend before Labor Day weekend. Tickets are $65 per person but this of course is a moving target annually so please call or check the Web site for current pricing on tickets and ticket packages. The gates open at 9:30 a.m. on Sat and 10:30 a.m. on Sun, and music plays continuously up to about 6 p.m. both days. There is no reserved seating in the amphitheater. Seats are on the ground, so take a low chair or a pile of blankets.

Check the Web site for driving directions. Parking is available on campus for a small fee, and a shuttle runs from several locations in town. Limited reserved parking on-site accommodates vehicles with valid handicap plates. You are allowed to bring in food, but not alcohol.

SEPTEMBER

FALL CONCERTS IN SUNRISE PARK
Sunrise Park
401 South Pavilion Way
(760) 323-8272
On Tues nights from mid-Sept through mid-Oct, the City of Palm Springs hosts a weekly series of free fall concerts, featuring all types of music—from Big Band to rock, country and western, and bluegrass. Concerts start at 7 p.m. Food and drink vendors sell hot dogs and snack-type foods, but many concertgoers opt to bring their own picnic baskets and lawn chairs. Call for information.

OCTOBER

AGUA CALIENTE CULTURAL MUSEUM DINNER IN THE CANYONS
Andreas Canyon
(760) 778-1079
www.accmuseum.org
The primary fund-raiser for the museum, this annual party in Oct has the best setting of any event all year—a natural rock plateau in Andreas Canyon, with a canopy of stars overhead and a grove of stately palms as a backdrop. This is the only time when the Indian Canyons are open at

night for an event, and it's truly special. Native American music, a silent auction, a brief awards program, and a gourmet dinner catered by the Spa Resort Casino are part of the evening. Suggested attire is desert festive/aloha wear, and there's nothing wrong with a high-brow affair being cool casual. Tickets are $300 per person and a variety of sponsor packages are available.

AMERICAN HEAT BIKE WEEKEND
Downtown Palm Springs
(775) 329-7469
www.road-shows.com
This event in mid-Oct began as a motorcycle fest, then added hot rods and vintage cars. Thousands of motorcyclists fill the streets during the three-day weekend, and for all the leather, most are professional people who love the open road and their bikes. There's a competition ride-in show, bike games, stunt shows, live music, and lots of vendors. Despite the noise, this is usually a very well-behaved crowd that adds a great deal of color and spice to the usually serene downtown. There is no admission charge for any of the events. Parking is free on the street.

PALM DESERT GOLF CART PARADE
El Paseo Drive, Palm Desert
(760) 346-6111
www.golfcartparade.com
The Palm Desert Chamber of Commerce started the Golf Cart Parade in 1964 as a lark for the locals. Today they take it pretty seriously—more than 100 fantastically decorated golf cart "floats" parade down the toney El Paseo shopping district and attract around 25,000 spectators. Marching bands, jugglers, clowns, and other entertainers join the carts.

It's a pretty old-fashioned event in many respects, beginning with a Rotary Club pancake breakfast and ending with a street festival that offers live entertainment and children's activities. Entry proceeds benefit local charities. Usually held in Oct, the hosting month has over the years been somewhat of a moving target, so please call or check the Web site.

PALM SPRINGS TRAM ROAD CHALLENGE 6K
Tramway Road
(760) 324-7069
www.kleinclarksports.com
Billed as the world's toughest 6K, this race is uphill every step of the way, with 2,000 feet in vertical gain over 3.7 miles. Ouch. A desert tradition—2010 marks a quarter-century for the event—it's gotten the better of many hardy runners, particularly if the weather is still in summer mode, as it can be in mid-Oct. Organizers stress it's not just for runners, as well, and welcome all walkers to participate. The registration fee ranges from $20–$30 depending on age and if you planned ahead and booked early. Parking is free, with shuttle service along Tramway Road.

DESERT AIDS WALK
Downtown Palm Springs
(760) 323-2118
www.desertaidsproject.org
Now its second decade and held in late Oct, this annual walk to benefit the desert organizations caring for AIDS patients is a festive affair for all ages and genders. It's pretty casual, meaning anyone can join in, though most walkers are there with their pledge cards in hand. Sign-up is at 7:30 a.m., followed by an easy walk downtown starting at 9:30 a.m. There is no admission charge, but pledges are accepted. Parking is free on the street.

ℹ️ Golf carts are a big deal in the desert, and they're street-legal in Palm Desert. For the true aficionado, local dealers sell carts built to resemble Rolls Royces, Jaguars, Hummers, and other prestige autos.

HOWL-O-WEEN HARVEST HAPPENING
The Living Desert
47-900 Portola Ave., Palm Desert
(760) 346-5694
www.livingdesert.org

A full day of fun where kids can learn how animals collect food and prepare for winter, before heading over to the pumpkin patch or the corn-shucking contest, and concluding at the scavenger hunt. For the older "kids" there are cooking demonstrations and seasonal fruit and vegetable sampling courtesy of local growers. Regular admission applies: $12.50 for adults, and $7.50 for kids. Don't forget to wear your Halloween costume. Typically held the last Sat of the month.

NOVEMBER

RANCHO MIRAGE ART AFFAIRE
Whitewater Park
71-560 San Jacinto Dr., Rancho Mirage
(760) 324-4511
www.ci.rancho-mirage.ca.us
Around 100 fine arts and crafts exhibits, jazz entertainment, food, and wine are the highlights of this two-day juried arts fair in early Nov. This is the city's biggest community event, and it attracts upward of 10,000 visitors each year. With its creation, the valley is well on the way to becoming a year-round venue for arts festivals and events. Admission and parking are free.

GREATER PALM SPRINGS PRIDE FESTIVAL
Downtown Palm Springs
(760) 416-8711
www.pspride.org
This early Nov weekend festival celebrating gays and lesbians centered around a celebratory parade, a festive, lighthearted event that always packs the sidewalks with spectators and supporters. The fair in the Palm Springs Stadium is equally packed with vendors, food, and entertainment. No pets, coolers, or backpacks are allowed in the festival.

Admission is $15 for one day or $20 for both. The event runs from 10 a.m. to 8 p.m. on Sat and 10 a.m. to 6 p.m. on Sun. The parade is held Sun morning. Parking is free on nearby streets.

this is a two-day affair in mid-Nov that features professional and amateur dance companies and choreographers competing for cash prizes. Tickets range from $10 to $30. Parking is free.

MCCORMICK'S PALM SPRINGS EXOTIC CAR SHOW & AUCTION
Downtown Palm Springs
(760) 320-3290
www.classic-carauction.com
This is the Nov counterpart to February's popular car show and auction. If you can't make it to the venue, check out the excellent Web site, where you can preview and bid on the vehicles. Admission for the event is $10 per day or $15 for both days. On-street parking is free nearby.

CABAZON INDIO POWWOW
Fantasy Springs Resort Casino
84-245 Indio Springs Parkway, Indio
(760) 342-5000, (800) 827-2946
www.fantasyspringsresort.com
This three-day festival in late Nov is much the same as the one held here in late Mar. Visitors are encouraged to attend and are invited to join in intertribal dancing. The festival celebrates Native American dance, music, culture, and food. Artisans display and sell beadwork, paintings, pottery, leather crafts, jewelry, and more.

DECEMBER

INDIO INTERNATIONAL TAMALE FESTIVAL
Old Town Indio
(760) 391-4175
www.tamalefestival.net
Held the first weekend in Dec, the festival takes place on Sat and Sun from 10 a.m. to 6 p.m. and kicks off with a parade on Sat morning. Live entertainment, mariachis, a carnival, fireworks, and more varieties of tamales than you thought existed make this one of the country's top 10 "All-American Food Festivals," according to the Food Network. It also reputedly holds the Guinness World Record for largest tamale—a foot in diameter and 40 feet long. Be prepared for crowds. It

The [Insert Revolving Corporate Name] Skins Game

All but three of the Skins Games held annually since it was started in 1983 have been contested in the Coachella Valley, and most recently at Indian Wells Golf Resort. The event went into the cooler in 2009 when its latest corporate underwriter, LG, pulled out. Tournament officials talk as if it's a one-year hiatus, but time will tell if this one-time Thanksgiving weekend staple has gobbled its last gobble; don't bet on the turkey unless you get great odds. Organizers have tried various tricks to keep it compelling, from a thankfully short-lived tinkering with how skins were won to asking Annika to take the tee. Tinkering might not be enough. It was way cool when Lee Trevino nailed an ace on PGA West's "Alcatraz" island par 3, or when the participants were named Palmer, Nicklaus, Player, and Watson, but when the last three winners go by Ames, Ames, and Choi, and you had a Wetterich playing in there somewhere, it just doesn't drive the needle. And the $1 million purse quit being real money a number of presidential administrations ago.

DANCE UNDER THE STARS CHOREOGRAPHY FESTIVAL
McCallum Theatre for the Performing Arts
73-000 Fred Waring Dr., Palm Desert
(760) 341-9508
www.mccallumtheatre.com
Hosted by the McCallum Theatre Institute, the City of Palm Desert, and College of the Desert,

attracts well over 100,000 people, so get ready to mingle and chow down some masa. Admission and parking are free.

PALM SPRINGS FESTIVAL OF LIGHTS PARADE
Palm Canyon Drive, from Ramon to Tamarisk Roads
(760) 325-5749
www.paradesofpalmsprings.com
Held on the first Sat in Dec, this parade features lighted floats and displays of all kinds, marching bands, horseback riders, and lots of holiday spirit. It begins at 5:45 p.m.

TREE LIGHTING AT THE TOP OF THE TRAM
Mountain Station, Palm Springs Aerial Tramway
One Tramway Rd.
(760) 325-1391
www.pstramway.com
A great desert holiday tradition that began back in the '60s, the tree lighting at the top of the tram somehow makes the 70 degree days and all those palm trees recede to the background. Held on the first Sun of Dec, the lighting itself is at 5:30 p.m. Carolers, hot chocolate, and a jolly holiday atmosphere just add to the experience. Tram tickets are $22.95 for adults, $15.95 for children 3 to 12, and $20.95 for adults 60 and older. Parking is free.

WILDLIGHTS AT THE LIVING DESERT
The Living Desert
47-900 Portola Ave., Palm Desert
(760) 346-5694
www.livingdesert.org
This is a wonderful holiday event, with huge light sculptures of different animals lining the Living Desert's pathways, and there's hot chocolate, cider, and cookies, as well as a jolly Santa to delight the small ones. Wildlights usually begins on the last Sat in Nov and goes through the New Year's holiday, and is open on specific days; please consult the Web site. This is one of the desert musts for all ages, and when you're there, be sure to stop by the nocturnal exhibit to get in the mood for exploring the desert at night. Admission is $7.75 for adults and $5.50 for children ages 3 to 12. Parking is free.

ARTS AND ENTERTAINMENT

Art is almost as big in the everyday life of the valley as are golf and shopping—a distant third, perhaps, but important in a big way for such a small area. Most cities now have an Art in Public Places (AIPP) program, following the lead of Palm Desert, which created the first AIPP back in 1986. That program requires developers to either install art in a public place or pay a fee for the arts program. The fee structure applies to every building project in the community and has become a national model for other cities.

From that program 100 works of art decorate the public places around Palm Desert and add to the already considerable beauty of the city. One of the largest collections of these pieces is installed every year on the grassy median that divides the two sides of El Paseo Drive. Sculptures of every genre decorate this strip, and a new exhibit is set up each January and is lighted at night—a nice accompaniment to dinner and drinks.

The city also has put together a sculpture walk as part of the visual landscape in the 72-acre Civic Center Park adjacent to City Hall and near College of the Desert. Palm Springs' AIPP program has its own particular flavor, which nicely ties the major pieces into the city's history and personality. The bronze statue of Lucille Ball on a park bench downtown at the corner of Tahquitz Canyon Way and Palm Canyon Drive is a must-stop for tourist photos, as is the larger-than-life statue of Sonny Bono next to the fountain a few blocks south on Palm Canyon Drive. Palm Springs tends to go with large, statement pieces, such as the enormous Cahuilla Woman that stands on the median across from the Spa Resort Casino. Elegant classical bronze works and edgy modern pieces dot the downtown area and well-trafficked public places. Outside City Hall, Frank Bogert, the city's "cowboy mayor," is immortalized on his horse—a pose taken from a photo of the young wrangler when Palm Springs was just beginning to become known to the outside world. A fabulous construction by internationally famous glass artist Dale Chihuly hangs inside the Palm Springs Airport. Another Chihuly piece is the star attraction in the clubhouse for Palm Desert's public golf course, Desert Willow.

The desert hosts a number of art events and festivals throughout the year. For listings, check the Annual Festivals and Events chapter.

GALLERIES

ADAGIO GALLERIES
193 South Palm Canyon Dr.
(760) 346-1221
www.adagiogalleries.com
This spacious, airy gallery in downtown Palm Springs is known as the center for one of the country's finest collections of Southwestern contemporary art. Modern masters with extensive representation include R. C. Gorman and Miguel

Martinez. Paintings, sculpture, and watercolors are the predominant media.

A GALLERY FINE ART
73-956 El Paseo Dr., Palm Desert
(760) 346-8885
www.agalleryfineart.com
This contemporary-arts gallery has been around for more than 10 years. The collection of paintings, glass, sculpture, and jewelry features color-

ful, accessible pieces that highlight a few favorite returning artists as well as a changing roster of emerging, "trendy" ones.

BUSCHLEN MOWATT GALLERIES
45-188 Portola Ave., Palm Desert
(760) 837-9668
www.buschlenmowatt.com

One of the most prestigious galleries in the desert, this is an 8,500-square-foot showcase for leading contemporary artists in fine painting and sculpture. This is truly a collector's gallery, and many of the works would be at home in the Palm Springs Art Museum. A select number of emerging artists are featured. The opening events for new exhibitions draw the wealthy and wannabes from all over the desert and are an entertainment worth attending.

CODA GALLERY
73-151 El Paseo Dr., Palm Desert
(760) 346-4661
www.codagallery.com

Coda is a riot of color, featuring whimsical furniture, sculpture, paintings, glassworks, and jewelry. This is the place to go for the statement piece with a sense of fun and for a warm and casual atmosphere that never intimidates. Regular artists include Bye Bitney, E. David Dornan, Kent Wallis, and John Kennedy.

i If you fall in love with an art piece but are intimidated by shelling out the full price all at once, ask the gallery owners if they do payment plans. Many offer layaway arrangements that let you make regular payments over time until the piece is fully paid for.

DENISE ROBERGE ART GALLERY
73-995 El Paseo Dr., Palm Desert
(760) 340-5045
www.plazaroberge.com

A part of the Denise Roberge "empire" that includes Augusta restaurant and the Roberge jewelry salon, this large space always has a fine selection of well-known artists represented in painting and sculpture. Styles run from traditional to contemporary and postmodern.

DESERT ART CENTER
550 North Palm Canyon Dr.
(760) 323-7973
www.desertartcenter.com

Located in what was the valley's first elementary school, this homey little place offers workshops, art classes, twice-yearly art fairs, and a small gallery featuring works by local artists. The selections are strictly beginning and a bit above, but there are still some charming pieces and the occasional stunner.

DEZART ONE GALLERY
2688 South Cherokee Way
(760) 328-1440

This forward-thinking gallery is at the heart of the desert's emerging interest in representative and abstract modern-art. The artist-owners have cultivated an outstanding roster of emerging and mid-career contemporary artists. They are the staff here and, as such, offer an unusual depth of warmth and knowledge for the novice or experienced collector. Their regular open studio exhibitions in their next-door workspace have a hip, bohemian feel and always draw lively crowds to meet the artists and see how the works come together.

EDENHURST GALLERY
73-660 El Paseo Dr., Palm Desert
(760) 346-7900
www.edenhurstgallery.com

This amazing gallery is a godsend for aficionados of early 20th-century American and California Impressionist art, and it shows particular affection for the Golden State and region with works by Granville Redmond, Paul Grimm, Galen Doss, and Maynard Dixon, among others. Included on the walls are historical and contemporary European works and a broad-genre selection of living artists working in traditional styles.

ELONORE AUSTERER FINE ART
73-160 El Paseo Dr., Suite 6, Palm Desert
(760) 346-3695
www.austererfineart.com
Modern masters and international contemporary art are the focus here. The gallery specializes in original works on paper and rare graphic work by well-known 20th-century artists.

GALLERY 1000
73400 El Paseo Dr., Suite 1, Palm Desert
(760) 346-2230
www.gallery1000.com
Noted European artists are represented here, with an emphasis on quality across a variety of media, including Impressionistic oil paintings, dry-point engravings, sculptures, and bas-relief. Major artists include Marcel Demagny, Duaiv, Anatoly Dverin, and Karl Jensen.

THE HART GALLERY
73-111 El Paseo Dr., Palm Desert
(760) 346-4243
www.hartgallery.com
This gallery specializes in fine prints, with a mixture of contemporary artists and acknowledged masters. This is the place to find rare and beautiful works by Pablo Picasso, Henri Matisse, Marc Chagall, and Joan Miró, as well as pieces by their peers.

IMAGO GALLERIES
45-450 Hwy. 74, Palm Desert
(760) 776-9890
This avant, block-and-angle edifice caused a stir locally when it popped up behind the much more traditional El Paseo Drive; bully to 'em. Outside, the sculpture garden and terrace exhibit outsize works that tend to unhinge jaws. Inside the 18,000-square-foot gallery, there are major exhibits of internationally recognized artists in

painting, sculpture, glass, and photography, as well as artists' quarters where visiting artists can relax and make themselves at home. Like Buschlen Mowatt and Dezart, this place is known for its very upscale and energetic openings.

i The Palm Springs Art Museum usually offers at least one free day each month and may have special discount promotions, depending on the time of year. Check the Web site (www.psmuseum.org) to get the latest information.

JONES & TERWILLIGER GALLERIES
73-375 El Paseo Dr., Suite A, Palm Desert
(760) 674-8989
The focus is on original, traditional art with a strong talent pool drawn from well-respected American, Italian, Chinese, and Spanish artists. A vast variety of styles is showcased in the paintings and sculpture, and a very knowledgeable staff will help you find the perfect piece.

MELISSA MORGAN FINE ART
73-040 El Paseo Dr., Palm Desert
(760) 341-1056
Cutting-edge international art spanning media are featured here, with an emphasis on sculpture, Latin American art, and California movements.

R. E. WELCH GALLERY
73-680 El Paseo Dr., Palm Desert
(760) 341-8141
www.rewelch.com
Welch has been described by some as art-with-training-wheels. That's harsh. The gallery takes a more open approach to art, with an understanding that its clients' aspirations and interest levels might have less to do with zeroes on the left side of the decimal point or who's sizzling in Soho than what speaks to them and the many interests in their lives. To them art is not life, it's part of living, and it exists on many levels, and this gallery's collections touch many points.

ART MUSEUMS

PALM SPRINGS ART MUSEUM
101 Museum Dr.
(760) 322-4800
www.psmuseum.org
From a one-room facility in 1938 to today's 125,000-square-foot facility, the museum has greatly expanded its collections and programs. It now houses a collection of over 7,000 objects, including a significant collection of pre-Columbian artifacts and Native American baskets and tools, western American paintings and sculptures, and major pieces from respected international artists in every media.

Each year the museum mounts several major exhibitions and has become known for its focus on bringing a multifaceted overview of the art world to the desert's residents.

PERFORMING ARTS

ANNENBERG THEATER
In the Palm Springs Art Museum
101 Museum Dr.
(760) 325-4490
Located in the art museum, the Annenberg Theater is an intimate 433-seat space with near-perfect acoustics and an excellent line of sight from every seat. The programmers try to mix it up with scheduling, combining comedy, jazz, classical, dance, and lectures each season.

One of the city's biggest events is the night when the theater opens for the season, usually in early Nov. Its black tie and glitzy, with a rising young performing star to draw the crowds. A number of different series run through the year, with package prices that can make admission very reasonable. The Musical Chairs series features celebrity guests, who join a revolving company of top local and national professionals to salute composers and musical themes. The small stage is an excellent showcase for winners of national and international competitions in voice, piano, violin, and other instruments, as well as small jazz and classical groups and standup comedians.

The valley's best value for performing arts is often the theater's Sunday Afternoon Concerts series, which presents outstanding chamber music by soloists and groups. Dress at the Annenberg runs the gamut from shorts to very presentable evening attire.

> **i** Both Palm Desert and Palm Springs publish maps to the public art installations in their cities. Check the Web sites of both to get the latest version: www.palmdesertart.com and www.palm-springs.org.

THE FABULOUS PALM SPRINGS FOLLIES
The Plaza Theater
128 South Palm Canyon Dr.
(760) 327-0225
www.psfollies.com
Riff Markowitz, a theatrical impresario of the old school, came up with the idea for this vaudeville-style revue, and he's been packing them in since 1991. The Follies features perhaps the country's most unusual live entertainment premise. The elaborate shows are a modern-day, very slick version of old-time vaudeville, complete with what Riff calls the "signature line of long-legged lovelies" decked out in fabulous costumes and headdresses that rival the best in Vegas. Musical numbers call for these hoofers to dance, sing, and strut for as many as nine shows a week, typically Wed through Sun, with sporadic Tues performances, Nov through May. The show also highlights vocal groups, acts like ventriloquists and performing animals, and there's a special holiday production, as well.

All of the performers have had professional careers on Broadway and in musicals, movies, and live entertainment shows—and are now reviving those careers on the stage of the historic Plaza Theater, the valley's first movie house. The catch (and the draw) is that all of the performers are also what many producers would term "over the hill"—they're between the ages of 56 and 86. The show is an inspiration for anyone who has doubts about what their golden years might

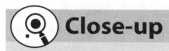 **Close-up**

Riff Markowitz

Some say that Riff Markowitz is the very incarnation of Broadway showman and impresario Flo Ziegfeld. That may be, but Flo had the Great White Way as his territory and the most beautiful and talented young performers in the country vying for a spot in his shows. Riff has the distinction of breathing new life into a moribund downtown and doing it with performers whose stage days are far in the past.

The Fabulous Palm Springs Follies, a vaudeville-style show with dancers and performers over the age of 55, was a concept that had a lot of doubters when Riff proposed it to Palm Springs in 1991. Riff wanted to put his show into the old Plaza Theater, a historical building with a lot of charm and a fabulous location downtown. But the Plaza was old, and refitting it to show modern movies just didn't make economic sense to any of the developers being wooed by the city's redevelopment people. It turned out to be the perfect venue for a variety show that, years later, has been written up in every major newspaper and magazine in this country and abroad and featured in dozens of broadcast programs.

Riff's background as a risk taker and entertainment genius stood him in good stead with the Follies. When he was just 15, he ran away from home and joined the circus as a tramp clown, moving on to become a radio DJ in northern Canada. He soon moved on to television and spent 30 years writing, producing, and directing variety TV shows, working with such big stars as Crystal Gayle, George Burns, Wolfman Jack, Abba, Tom Jones, Lauren Bacall, and Raquel Welch. In addition, he produced a number of specials starring cherished comedian Red Skelton, culminating in a Royal Command Performance at London's Royal Albert Hall. He also produced and cocreated HBO's award-winning dramatic hit series, *The Hitchhiker*.

He took early retirement in Palm Springs and sold his entertainment interests, including a Canadian pay television network and state-of-the-art postproduction studio. Quickly becoming restless without the excitement of producing, he came up with the Follies—an old-style stage show with Las Vegas-quality costumes and production values, and a cast of "a certain age."

Today his original pledge guides the seasonal shows: "To remain true to the spirits of the '20s, '30s, and '40s, keeping alive and well the music, comedy, and dance of those eras. As well, you have our pledge of providing a world-class entertainment experience at every performance."

Many in the city of Palm Springs give Riff and the Follies credit for bringing new life into downtown, attracting new shops, restaurants, and nightclubs, and revitalizing the whole feel of the city. The show has earned international fame and is still packing the house for every performance. And Riff himself has become as well known in live entertainment circles as Ziegfeld was in his day. The onetime tramp clown and DJ produces, directs, and emcees one of the most enduring and popular live shows in the nation, astounding audiences with the agility, beauty, and talent of performers whose ages start at 55 and go well past 80.

hold—and it's a remarkably well-done and entertaining creation. Tickets sell out fast, so if you're planning to attend when you visit, buy them online before you go.

THE HI-DESERT CULTURAL CENTER
61-231 Hwy. 62, Joshua Tree
(760) 366-3777
www.hidesertculturalcenter.com

There's more to the high desert than Europeans seeking out a desert park, U2 seeking awakening, and the tin-foil set seeking UFOs; there's performance art for those seeking it. The Hi-Desert Cultural Center is comprised of two venues, the Blak Box Theater and the rehabilitated Kay Ballard Playhouse, the former Hi-Desert Playhouse with the old west look that had more than one passerby pondering if they'd just missed something unique or the world's tackiest tourist trap/gift shop. But the cultural center is real world, putting on a slate of performances showcasing pianists and violinists, ancient Greek comedies, the best in local music—and there is a thriving art and music culture in the high desert—musicals, holiday specials, bluegrass, jazz, really the entire spectrum of performance arts. Please call or check the Web site for current performances and prices.

> **i** Bring a little extra cash for Champagne or sparkling wine and treats during intermission at the McCallum Theatre for the Performing Arts. This is a see-and-be-seen time, and it's great fun to people-watch with a glass of bubbly in hand.

MCCALLUM THEATRE FOR THE PERFORMING ARTS
73000 Fred Waring Dr., Palm Desert
(866) 889-2787
www.mccallumtheatre.com
Barry Manilow has been a common sight here, though more so before he started headlining at the Las Vegas Hilton, and that says a lot about the age group of the audience. With Bill Maher, Penn & Teller, Bill Cosby, Vince Gill, Dana Carvey, Stomp, Dave Koz, Tim Conway, and Andy Williams, no one is pushing this as a cutting-edge venue for entertainment and music. Where the McCallum excels is in being a Jack of Many Trades—and ages—and in its symphonic and occasional stage productions.

A desert institution, the McCallum had its beginning in 1973 with a group that called itself Friends of the Cultural Center, Inc. They had a vision of creating a year-round permanent home for performing arts of all types for all residents. Named for a longtime desert family and supported with funding from all the desert cities, the McCallum opened in 1988 and has been expanding and improving its space and offerings ever since. The McCallum Theatre Institute intro-

duces thousands of young people and adults to the joys of the performing arts, filling a void created by the elimination of arts programs in public schools. Each year the McCallum offers free performances and arts education programs to 43 local schools, involving almost 35,000 kids and teachers.

With a growing reputation as one of the country's most beautiful and prestigious small theaters, the McCallum attracts more than 150,000 theatergoers annually, with an average occupancy rate of 86 percent, versus a national average of 60 percent.

The theater is a striking midsize venue with continental-style seating on three levels, a carpeted floor to improve acoustics, and a top seating capacity of 1,100-plus. This is the desert, and it's a stretch to find any place where the crowd is consistently well dressed for evening events, so for those folks for whom such public demeanor is a treat, arriving at the McCallum and seeing that most of the crowd took the same care in choosing their clothing and buffing up their appearance should produce a smile. The McCallum's performances can be fairly pricey, so be sure to check for matinee tickets, which are often substantially cheaper than those at night.

PALM CANYON THEATRE
538 North Palm Canyon Dr.
(760) 323-5123
www.palmcanyontheatre.org
A nonprofit professional Actor's Equity theater, this little troupe is the essence of community theater. And because it's in the desert where a lot of professional actors live in retirement or semiretirement, the cast tends to have some serious acting chops. The plays are known classics of many eras—*The Music Man, Oliver, Gypsy, Miss Saigon,* and the like. The setting is small and intimate, and the price is right, a fraction of what you'll pay at the McCallum or Follies. The season runs from Oct through May, with a two-plus-week run of a different play each month.

KIDSTUFF

Not so long ago, families visiting the Palm Springs area with small children would be hard-pressed to find entertainment beyond the pool and the movies. The destination was not only adult-oriented but also a place where people came to "just do nothing," and even the grown-ups found themselves pretty much limited to golf, sunning, and the odd game of tennis.

Today the desert's year-round residents as well as its visitors are younger than they were just 10 years ago, and that has not escaped the attention of the area's tourism businesses, which are increasingly careful to tailor at least some of their offerings to families traveling with children.

When you're in the desert with children, make sure to spend at least some of your time outdoors. In addition to its international reputation as a spa retreat and golf capital, the Coachella Valley has become rightfully known for its wealth of natural resources. The mountains all around the valley are largely protected wilderness areas, with miles of hiking trails that go from the dusty desert into the cool pines, and lower there are lush palm oases. The beauty of it all is that the wilds are just a few minutes from wherever you are in the desert. Very few tourist destinations offer such varied opportunities to really experience nature, from watching the lizards scamper over the rocks in the Indian Canyons to tickling toes in a stream weaving through a mountain meadow.

Price Code

Price ranges apply to a regular season admission for one. Unless noted otherwise, assume that major credit cards are accepted at all locations.

Attractions:
$................ Less than $15
$$ .... $15 to $30
$$$ .... More than $30

Restaurants:
$................ Less than $10
$$ .... $10 to $20
$$$ .... More than $20

ATTRACTIONS

BIG LEAGUE DREAMS SPORTS PARK $–$$
33-700 Date Palm Dr., Cathedral City
(760) 324-5600
www.bigleaguedreams.com
The big attraction here is baseball and softball—

three of the fields are small replicas of Fenway Park, Wrigley Field, and Yankee Stadium—and pickup games are available if you call ahead. Among the activities and facilities are batting cages, sand volleyball courts, a mini-soccer field, and a tot lot for the little ones, as well as a covered in-line hockey facility and a restaurant. Outside food and drinks are not allowed. It's a clean, safe, and well-run facility.

The park typically opens at 8 a.m. and closes after the last game is played. Call for exact hours. Admission is free for spectators 12 and younger, and it's only a few bucks for older spectators and sports-participating kids; however, all activities require tokens, and these can add up quickly.

i Tour companies, particularly those that tour in jeeps, have age requirements, and many do not allow young children. Check for specifics before you book.

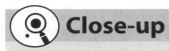 **Close-up**

Children's Discovery Museum of the Desert

The desert was not always a family place. In the early days of Palm Springs, those who could afford it sent their children off to boarding schools. Those who could not had to work to make sure their kids grew up with a sense of discovery and curiosity about the world. For working parents without the time to spend exploring the mountains and deserts, there were few places to go for a solid learning experience that was also fun.

Twenty years ago a group of concerned valley residents took up the challenge of creating a place where kids could learn and express themselves through play and without commercialism. These visionary founders could see the time when arts and music programs would drop off the public schools' list of necessities, and they set to work. The City of Palm Desert, long the valley's leader in quality-of-life issues, put up money for a needs assessment in 1987, and by 1990 the museum opened its office and first exhibits and started an exciting school outreach program.

The museum always has been a collaboration with kids and their families, schools, and communities. In 1991 Rancho Mirage and Indian Wells joined Palm Desert to create a $1.6-million building trust fund, and in 1992 the organization won the California Teachers Association State Gold Award.

Innovative programs with Scholastic, Microsoft, Crayola, and the *Los Angeles Times,* a family theater series, and a constantly changing smorgasbord of hands-on exhibits and activities have kept the museum fresh and kept the kids coming back. Before the permanent building opened in 1998, more than 20,000 children and their families took advantage of the fun. A look at the most recent statistics shows that this has grown to almost 100,000 a year.

Private and public donations paid for the current building, an elegantly designed 18,000 square feet of fun and learning. It sits on four acres donated by the Honorable Walter Annenberg and another two and a half acres that were also donated. In addition to the exhibit gallery, the campus includes a multipurpose facility named the Dinah Shore Center, an outdoor covered performance area/amphitheater, horticultural gardens, and a "logo grove." In its first six years of operation, the museum has served over 350,000 visitors, including 60,000 children on school field trips. Held regularly are summer and holiday camps; toddler, art, and dance programs; classes; performances; family fun days; birthday parties; museum store events; and more.

In 2001 the Children's Discovery Museum of the Desert was ranked number 20 in the nation and number 2 in California, important recognition on a wide scale that its mission of generating a "spark of lifelong learning" is being fulfilled.

BOOMERS! FAMILY FUN CENTER $$
67-700 East Palm Canyon Dr., Cathedral City
(760) 770-7522
www.boomersparks.com

More the typical amusement park/arcade setup than anything else, Boomers has miniature golf, go-Karts, bumper boats, batting cages, a rock wall for climbing, and a noisy video arcade plus snack bar. This is not the best-kept place, but it's safe and may be a good option for the kids to let off steam on a slow summer night. Unless you have teenagers and they just have to get away for a bit, this is a parent-with-child facility, so plan on scrunching into those bumper boats and acting like a kid yourself.

Boomers opens at noon every day for miniature golf and games, and closes at 11 p.m. (9 p.m. Sundays). The outside attractions fire up at 4:30 p.m. daily. You can choose an all-day admission pass or enter and pay for activities on an a la carte basis. Check the Web site for particular day-of-week, seasonal, and other pricing specials that can save you a lot of money.

i The Palm Springs Art Museum offers classes and special events for kids all summer. You can sign your kids up for a one-time class or movie and tour the museum while they're occupied.

CHILDREN'S DISCOVERY MUSEUM
OF THE DESERT $
71-701 Gerald Ford Dr., Rancho Mirage
(760) 321-0602
www.cdmod.org

You and your young children can easily spend most of the day here, playing and learning. There are scores of hands-on exhibits, including a kid-scale archaeological dig where children dress up like little Indiana Joneses and search for "artifacts." There's a child-size grocery store where the kids can shop, act as cashiers, move the stuff around, and play grown-up. Vintage clothes and props are another fun make-believe activity. Everything here is geared to a child's imagination, and nothing is hands-off.

This is not a place where you can drop off the kids for a few hours, but rather a spot where the entire family is encouraged to play together. The gift shop is full of fun and educational gifts and toys that are perfect for entertaining small ones back at the hotel. Outside, there's an outdoor amphitheater where special events and activities are held, community gardens, and a covered picnic area.

Check the Web site for such events as free family fun nights, toddler parties, and holiday activities. Classes and special programs for ages one through four are planned throughout the week. For more details, see the listing in the Attractions chapter.

The museum is open Mon through Sat 10 a.m. to 5 p.m. and on Sun noon to 5 p.m. It is closed on Mon from May through Dec, and on some holidays.

DESERT IMAX THEATRE $
68-510 East Palm Canyon Dr., Cathedral City
(760) 324-7333

This is a typical IMAX, which means lots of amazing nature and adventure documentaries, and animated films, some in 3-D, shown on staggeringly large and lifelike screens, with resonating sound systems. Be sure to check *The Desert Sun*'s movie listings, as this facility regularly runs specials and offers discount coupons that can save a lot for a large family.

THE INDIAN CANYONS $
38-500 South Palm Canyon Dr.
(760) 323-6018
www.indian-canyons.com

TAHQUITZ CANYON $
500 West Mesquite Ave.
(760) 416-7044
www.tahquitzcanyon.com

The Indian Canyons are the ancestral home of the Agua Caliente Band of Cahuilla Indians, the original Palm Springs residents. Thousands of years ago they developed complex communities here, relying on the abundant water, plants, and animals that flourished in these natural palm oases. Today many remains of that ancient society—rock art, house pits, foundations, irrigation ditches, trails, and food preparation areas—still exist in the canyons.

The three canyons at the south end of Palm Springs, the so-called "Indian Canyons"—Andreas, Murray, and Palm—are listed on the National Register of Historic Places. They are among the small number of places where the California fan palm grows naturally, and they are quiet spots from which you can escape the diversions of resort life.

Located on Agua Caliente tribal land, just a few minutes' drive from downtown, Andreas, Murray, and Palm Canyons are true, natural palm oases, with waterfalls, streams, and cool canopies of towering palm trees. Palm Canyon and Andreas Canyon also have what is said to be the world's largest stand of naturally occurring

Golf for Kids

The vast majority of valley golf courses and clubs have junior golf programs of some type. It may be as simple as an instructor who is good with kids or it could run into a full-blown schedule of clinics, tournaments, and other kid-specific golf events.

Desert Willow Golf Resort
38-995 Desert Willow Dr., Palm Desert
(760) 346-7060
www.desertwillow.com

One of the most extensive junior programs can be found at this city-owned facility. FairwayKids is an after-school program of clinics, focused instruction, and supervised play, and the club offers seasonal vacation camps, too. The adjoining Palm Desert Golf Academy is one of the leading instructional centers in the desert and can tailor a program for aspiring kids of any ability. Call or check the Web site for special events or more information.

College Golf Center
73-450 Fred Waring Dr., Palm Desert
(760) 341-0994
www.college-golf-center.com

Located at College of the Desert, this is perhaps the busiest driving range in the valley. Junior instructional and competition programs are offered.

The First Tee of Coachella Valley
74-945 Sheryl Ave., Palm Desert
(760) 779-1877
www.thefirstteecoachellavalley.org

The First Tee, an award-winning nationwide endeavor, is a multi-pronged educational and developmental program the goal of which is to help kids become strong, responsible, empowered, self-sustaining students, individuals, and future adults. Golf is one of the vehicles used in this process, and it is hoped the game becomes a lifelong passion, but no one is setting out to build the next Tiger or Annika, specifically. If you'd like to help or to see what the First Tee can do for your kids, please contact your local chapter; www.thefirsttee.org.

---

palm trees. Pack a picnic and wear your walking shoes because you'll want to spend the day here, exploring, hiking, or just dreaming.

To reach the canyons, follow South Palm Canyon Drive in Palm Springs until it dead-ends, just a few minutes from downtown. Andreas Canyon is the easiest spot to access, just steps from a paved parking lot. About a half mile away is Murray Canyon, with unusual rock formations, and Andreas Creek, which runs year-round.

At the end of the canyons road is majestic Palm Canyon, one of the most beautiful wild areas in the country. At the top of the canyon, the trading post sells maps, refreshments, Native American arts and crafts, and books. A lovely little waterfall is a short walk away. A paved, moderately graded footpath winds down into the canyon and its 15 miles of hiking trails, waterfalls, and picnic areas.

Ranger-led interpretive hikes provide a wealth of information about the canyons and the Agua Caliente Band of Cahuilla Indians. The hikes are usually about a mile in total and will accommodate most ages and abilities. Call for the daily hike schedule and register at the trading post.

Tahquitz Canyon is just a few blocks from downtown Palm Springs and is famous for its spectacular 60-foot waterfall, rock art, wild setting, and amazing view of the city. The only access to Tahquitz is on a ranger-led hiking tour over rocky trails. The hike takes up to two and a half hours total and is not appropriate for very young children, who may have a hard time keeping up. For families with active kids older than about eight or nine, though, it is a wonderful adventure, as the transition from bustling city to cool canyon is a stunner and the rangers do an excellent job bringing to life the desert flora and fauna, and Native practices. For more details, see the listing in the Attractions chapter.

The Indian Canyons are open daily from 8 a.m. to 5 p.m. Oct through June and 8 a.m. to 5 p.m. Fri through Sun during the summer months. Tahquitz Canyon is accessible 7:30 a.m. to 5 p.m. daily Oct through June, and the same hours Fri, Sat, and Sun during the heat of summer. Reservations are required.

i Sacred to the local tribe, Tahquitz Canyon is said to be home to an evil spirit who will snatch up wandering children. The "Witch of Tahquitz" appears as a shadow in the shape of a witch on a broomstick in the early morning or late afternoon. Look west from the intersection of Farrell Drive and Vista Chino.

JOSHUA TREE NATIONAL PARK $
74485 National Park Dr., Twentynine Palms
(760) 367-5500
www.nps.gov/jotr/index.htm

Located to the north and northeast of the Coachella Valley starting just about at the top of the crestline of the mountains that rim that part of the desert, Joshua Tree National Park is a pristine desert wilderness area covering 794,000 square miles. The park's enormous boulder formations draw rock climbers, photographers, and visitors from all over the world, and those who have spotted UFOs here say that the park is attracting visitors from other galaxies, as well (What is it about deserts and conspiracy/alien theorists?). This is an ideal spot to watch the ballet of the Milky Way as there is little light pollution from the lower desert and the skies are clear virtually all year.

i Rangers at Joshua Tree National Park conduct free guided hikes and presentations on desert animals and plant life. This is also the best spot to view the stars in the night sky, and the locals often come out for free, family-oriented "star-watching parties." Contact the park for more information: (760) 367-5500; www.nps.gov/jotr/index.htm.

In the spring the park can be carpeted overnight with dozens of species of wildflowers, and if the rains have been particularly propitious in the winter, the many cacti and Joshua trees will be showing off blooms that range from white through brilliant fuchsia. Hikers, equestrians, and off-roaders will find miles of trails, and campgrounds dot the park.

Home to the Pinto Native Americans hundreds of years ago, the area saw an influx of explorers, cattlemen, and miners in the late 1800s. Though gold was discovered and mined here, there was never a big "strike," and the lack of water made life too rough for most settlers.

Bill and Francis Keys were hardy types, though, homesteading 160 acres in the early part of the last century and building the Desert Queen Ranch on the site of the defunct Desert Queen Mine. Park rangers lead tours of the ranch grounds, which include the ranch house, schoolhouse, store, workshop, orchard, and piles of mining equipment that help tell the story of life almost a hundred years ago. Whether you're coming to climb, shoot photos, hike, or picnic, Joshua Tree is worth at least a day of your time. Permits are required for backcountry camping. Pets must be on a leash and attended at all times and are not allowed on nature trails.

The park is open year-round. The several visitor and interpretive centers are open daily, generally from 8 a.m. to 5 p.m.

For more information on Joshua Tree please refer to the listing in "Attractions."

KNOTT'S SOAK PALM SPRINGS $$
1500 South Gene Autry Trail
(760) 327-0499
www.knotts.com

Admission to the Knott's Soak City water park includes unlimited use of all water rides and attractions. There's an additional charge for parking and locker rentals. If you're going for the day and want to splurge, cabana rentals give you a large private cabana and your own private, relatively uncrowded sunning area to use as home base in between rides and swimming.

There are 18 or so major water "attractions," including big and little water slides and an 800,000-gallon wave pool that mimics the ocean surf well enough to call for boogie boards. For future surfers there's Gremmie Lagoon, a kids' water playground, and Kahuna's Beach House, a family-interactive water playhouse.

You are not allowed to bring in food or beverages, so budget for some burgers and soft drinks. Men's and women's changing rooms offer lockers for a small fee. Life vests and tubes are provided free. This isn't the beach; so don't bring chairs, barbecues, or much of anything extra besides standard swimwear and towels. Other rules ban long pants, denim, and swimwear with metal or plastic ornamentation in the pool and activity areas. Soak City is a well-kept, orderly family attraction. If you've got kids longing to cut loose from the quiet of the hotel pool, this is the place where they can scream and giggle to their heart's content.

For more details, see the Attractions chapter. Knott's is open from Mar through Sept.

i **Knott's Soak City often offers discounted admissions. Some of the deals in the past have included lower prices for later-in-the-day arrivals and "four-pack" pricing—four admissions at a reduced cost for each person. And AAA discounts are standard procedure. So with the late-setting sun you can still get in a lot of fun for less money. But remember, old sol can still burn you late in the day, so wear sunscreen.**

THE LIVING DESERT $
47-900 Portola Ave., Palm Desert
(760) 346-5694
www.livingdesert.org

Established in 1970, the Living Desert today is one of the most successful zoological parks in the country, attracting more than 275,000 visitors each year. At the Living Desert you'll discover nearly 400 fascinating desert animals representing more than 150 species, including coyotes, bighorn sheep, Arabian oryx (also known as the "unicorn of the desert"), zebras, cheetahs, and meerkats.

One of the facility's many strong points is its organization. Depending on your available time and attention span, you can tour the entire park or focus on one or two special areas, such as Eagle Canyon, with its streams, mountain lions, bobcats, Mexican wolves, and golden eagles. The African exhibit, Village WaTuTu, is an authentic replica of a 19th-century Nigerian village, with mud huts, an Elders Circle, and a storyteller's area. Little children will be thrilled with the Petting Kraal, where they can feed and pet sheep, goats, and Ankole cattle. Other animals here include leopards, camels, hyenas, giraffes, and ostriches. The Living Desert has a full schedule of activities and events planned especially for children. The golden eagle exhibit is amazing and allows kids to get up close to these magnificent birds.

Because there are so many different activities and events going on, it's a good idea to call before you visit or check the daily schedule on the excellent Web site for updated events, programs, special tours, demonstrations, or lectures. Regular tram shuttles, guided tours, gift shops, first aid stations, restaurants, baby-changing stations, and ATMs make this a full-service attraction for the family. For additional information, check the Attractions chapter.

The Living Desert is open daily from 9 a.m. to 5 p.m. Sept 1 through June 15, with the last admission at 4 p.m.; it is closed on Dec 25. It's open daily from 8 a.m. to 1:30 p.m. June 16 through Aug 31, with the last admission at 1 p.m. Regular, non-narrated shuttle service is available throughout the park for an extra charge. Parking is free.

The best time to see the animals at the Living Desert is when the park opens in the cool morning hours. Most of the animals are at their most active before noon; in the afternoon the intense sun drives them to seek shade and rest. Also check for special evening programs, as many desert dwellers are nocturnal.

PALM SPRINGS AERIAL TRAMWAY   **$$**
One Tramway Rd.
(760) 325-1391, (888) 515-8726
www.pstramway.com
A trip to the top of the tram in Palm Springs is like a ride on the Staten Island Ferry in Manhattan—you've just got to do it. This is one of the world's longest tram rides, and as for its vertical rise, it is the steepest in the world, starting not far from the desert floor and reaching 8,516 feet at the Mountain Station in very short order. The ride up is in a very stable, 80-person car that rotates 360 degrees over the course of the 15-minute ride, giving everyone a stellar view of the desert below.

At the top, the views are even more breathtaking from the balcony and dining areas, both inside and outside. There's an acceptable cafeteria-style eatery, a good restaurant, a gift shop, and a short educational film, plus viewing platforms with telescopes. A short walk down a steep incline leads you right into the Mount San Jacinto State Park and Wilderness, a cool pine forest with lovely meadows that are dotted with flowers in the spring and covered with snow in the winter.

In the colder months (the tram top is always 30 to 40 degrees colder than the desert), the Winter Adventure Center rents snowshoes and cross-country skis. Free guided hikes are held daily, and the trails are gentle and clearly marked, though the altitude does rob the air of a good bit of its oxygen. It's a great place for a cool picnic in the summertime and a bracing snowball fight in the winter. Overnight camping and backpacking are by permit only. For additional information, check the Attractions chapter.

Tram cars depart at least every half hour, starting at 10 a.m., Mon through Fri, and starting at 8 a.m. on weekends and during holiday periods. The last car up is at 8 p.m., with the last car down being at 9:45 p.m. Ride 'n' Dine specials that give a discount for a ride and a meal are available after 3 p.m.

Guided hikes at the Palm Springs Aerial Tramway are easy enough for all skill levels and an excellent way to introduce your children to this mountain wilderness. But if granny has a breathing problem it is best to have her stick to the Mountain Station given the altitude.

RESTAURANTS

Several of these eateries are featured in the "Restaurants" section above and being replicated down here means they're good spots for the kids, and yet parents won't be consigned to enduring weenie-beanie fettuccine. Prices as indicated are for a standard menu item, not the cheapest, not the Ft. Knox one, for a typical diner, regardless of age. Most places will, of course, have special kids offerings and prices.

CALIFORNIA PIZZA KITCHEN   **$–$$**
73-080 El Paseo Dr., Palm Desert
(760) 776-5036

123 North Palm Canyon Dr.
(760) 322-6075
www.cpk.com
A chain with a massive national reach, CPK has consistently good food, good prices, and a fun, friendly atmosphere that's a lot more civilized than the usual noisy pizza place. The CPKids Menu features kid-size pizza, pastas, and desserts, so everyone gets his own choice of the many different toppings. As goes with the brand, both CPKs in the desert are sparkling clean, offer quick service, and have enough of a variety that they're good for much more than one or two stops. Open for lunch and dinner, with a small but good offering of beer and wine. No reservations.

i Afternoons are bargain matinee times at most area movie theaters. With kids in tow, you can save a lot by seeing a matinee, then eating during the ubiquitous "early-bird dinner" time, usually before 6:30 p.m. in area restaurants.

CHEESECAKE FACTORY $$
71-800 Hwy. 111, Rancho Mirage (The River)
(760) 404-1400
www.thecheesecakefactory.com

Like CPK, the Cheesecake Factory is a chain, and one that knows how to do a moderate-priced menu well, though on a much more grand scale. In this case, there are more than 200 menu items, with some excellent burgers, sandwiches, salads, and children's items. The big draw is the dessert menu. Cheesecakes and other sweets aren't inexpensive, but the portions are huge. You may decide that this is the place to go for a special treat, particularly if you've been eating at the more humdrum spots or cooking in your condo. There's also an extensive bakery section, so keep that in mind when you're planning picnics. Open for lunch and dinner. No reservations.

i Summer is not only value season in the desert but also family season. Most of the large resorts have special children's programs that offer supervised activities in the day, movie nights, and on-call child care.

DON & SWEET SUE'S CAFÉ $-$$
68-955 Ramon Rd., Cathedral City
(760) 770-2760
www.donandsweetsues.com

Breakfast at Don & Sweet Sue's is a desert tradition, and lines are very long on the weekends. It's a big place, though, and the service is spot-on, so you won't be waiting long. When you have the yen for great platters of fluffy pancakes, crispy waffles, fresh egg and slabs of ham, homemade biscuits and gravy, a side of spicy salsa, fresh grapefruit picked locally, steaming coffee—well, it's all here, from early in the morning until late at night. The lunches and dinners are also beautifully cooked and reasonably priced, but the breakfast is legendary. It's a friendly, noisy place with a lot of bustle and a high tolerance for restless kids. Kids menu prices are a fraction of the already reasonable main menu prices. No reservations.

KEEDY'S FOUNTAIN GRILL $
73-633 Hwy. 111, Palm Desert
(760) 346-6492

Keedy's in Palm Desert, a joint in every perfect aspect of that word, serves real breakfasts and real lunches that are real inexpensive. Everyone in town eats here, from the country club sophisticates in designer sweats stacking lox, tomatoes, red onion, and a few capers on a cream-cheesed bagel to the passel of kids fueling up on flapjacks and hashbrowns and scrambled eggs in preparation for the day's energy burn. And treat the family to a milkshake.

KOBE JAPANESE STEAK HOUSE $$-$$$
69-838 Hwy. 111, Rancho Mirage
(760) 324-1717
www.koberanchomirage.com

Kobe Japanese Steak House is a good place to go "fancy" without the fuss and bother that often comes when trying to dine somewhere beyond burgers and the corner pasta shop. The draw here is teppan, which means a variety of meats at least one of which is likely to please everyone in the group. Vegetables are involved—and grilled—which isn't a bad thing for growing bodies. There's a built in show that will amuse all. And you sit in a nice community format, so there's a lot going on. This isn't the cheapest eat in town but for the quality and the show, it's worth the extra money, and there's a special kids menu (and sushi for those averse to flamed food). Open for dinner only.

LAS CASUELAS—THE ORIGINAL $$
366 North Palm Canyon Dr.
(760) 325-3213

LAS CASUELAS CAFÉ $–$$
73-703 Hwy. 111, Palm Desert
(760) 568-0011

LAS CASUELAS NUEVAS $$
70-050 Hwy. 111, Rancho Mirage
(760) 328-8844
www.lascasuelasnuevas.com

LAS CASUELAS QUINTA $$
78-480 Hwy. 111, La Quinta
(760) 777-7715
www.lascasuelasquinta.com

LAS CASUELAS TERRAZA $$
222 South Palm Canyon Dr.
(760) 325-2794

Las Casuelas started as a small lunch and dinner spot in downtown Palm Springs. The Delgado family, under the inspired cooking tutelage of matriarch Mary, went on to open Terraza a few blocks from the original, then Nuevas in Rancho Mirage, Quinta in La Quinta, and Cafe in Palm Desert. The cafe is the only one to offer breakfast, and it's the most reasonably priced, although they are all firmly in the moderate range.

This is the place to go for good, solid, border Mexican food—fajitas, fattening platters of nachos with guacamole and cheese, traditional enchiladas and burritos, and so on. A family can eat very well here, and even the pickiest eater will find something yummy, as there's a nice selection of chicken, burgers, and salads, and the kitchen is happy to tone down or spice up anything on the menu. All the restaurants except for the cafe also have mariachi music during happy hour and outside dining areas that let you enjoy the fabulous weather. Open for breakfast (the cafe only), lunch, and dinner. No reservations.

i Bring the swimsuits, no matter the time of year. If there's a desert motel or hotel without a swimming pool, it's keeping itself a secret. Be aware, though, that few pools offer lifeguards, so you should plan on being with your children or arranging for adult supervision.

MURPH'S GASLIGHT $$
79-860 Avenue 42, Bermuda Dunes
(760) 345-6242

73-155 Hwy. 111, Palm Desert
(760) 340-2012
www.murphsgaslight.com

A big part of the fun of travel is finding new things. When it comes to eats, sometimes the chains are a needed antidote to a brood clamoring for the familiar. Yet you have to branch out. Murph's is part of the very fabric of the desert. It's old school, it's clientele is old, and one of its restaurants is based in an old social/athletic club, and the tennis courts and the swimming pool are still there to prove it. But Murph's serves big piles of "American" favorites, the most favorite of which is the family-style all-you-can-eat fried chicken dinner. Available nightly, and it's the only thing on the menu on Sundays, it's a steal at under 20 bucks for adults and $8.95 for the kids. You get all the sides, which admittedly are of variable quality, and then you get the CHICKEN. Massive piles of wonderful juicy fried chicken. And they even give you another plate at the end so you have chicken to take back to the hotel. There can be a wait to get in so try the Bermuda Dunes Murph's and while Parent #1 is in the throwback lounge having one of the stiffest pours in the valley, Parent #2 can parade the kids across the parking lot to check out the airplanes at the private airport or run 'em about the "country club" grounds.

RED ROBIN $–$$
78-722 Hwy. 111, La Quinta
(760) 777-1111

72-797 Dinah Shore Dr., Rancho Mirage
(760) 324-8310
www.redrobin.com

Beloved by Zagat raters, Red Robin is a nationwide maker of burgers that will make you happy you sat down with the kids rather than buzzing through BurgerMeisters drive-thru. With burgers done more ways than most pizzerias do pizza, chicken sandwiches, wraps, salads, all grilled up hot and tossed fresh, it's food everyone loves and when you get done the arteries want to say thank you almost as much as your belly. Red Robin is festive, the kids can cut loose a bit, sports fans can catch the game out of the corner of their eye—what's not to like?

SHERMAN'S DELI & BAKERY $$
401 East Tahquitz Canyon Way
(760) 325-1199

73-161 Country Club Dr., Palm Desert
(760) 568-1350
www.shermansdeli.com
A kosher-style family restaurant, Sherman's in Palm Springs has been packing in the locals since 1953. The Palm Desert Sherman's also is much younger, though building a reputation, but if you want to give the family a feel for the old-time desert and an old-school deli, find a table in Palm Springs and watch the kibitzing among the locals and out-of-towners. As should be expected of any good deli, the waitresses don't take any guff, and they really know the menu. Fresh-baked breads, pies, and cakes, full dinners, and a truly massive sandwich menu mean that everyone gets what they want. You can easily spend $20 on a simple meal here, or you can save with the early-bird and daily specials. And the sandwiches are massive, so you can turn at least two kids loose on one. Open for breakfast, lunch, and dinner. No reservations.

DAY TRIPS AND WEEKEND GETAWAYS

Afffter decades of being a day trip and weekend getaway destination itself, the desert is also becoming the home base for vacationers who want a reliably warm and sunny spot and a relaxed lifestyle to be the center of their "hub and spoke" ventures in Southern California. Those who live in the desert year-round usually have their favorite day trips and getaways, and the choices are plentiful, encompassing city life, the beaches, mountains, and major tourist attractions.

The Coachella Valley is an ideal location to use as a hub for exploring Southern California, with everything from coastal Los Angeles to the San Gabriel Mountains and then on to San Diego and the Mexican border a two- to three-hour drive away, depending on Southern California traffic, of course. This means that every destination can be a day trip as well as a weekend getaway—the choice is up to you.

The chapter is organized into broad geographic areas, such as Los Angeles, Santa Monica, and Long Beach; Orange County, Laguna Beach, and Newport Beach; San Diego; and nearby mountains and deserts. Within each area, we'll take a look at major attractions, activities, and any special annual events of note.

Freeways were born in Southern California and many from outside the state think all of us were born in our cars given our close attachments to them. Driving is the major mode of travel throughout the state, and the public transportation system—buses, trains, and rapid transit—is very good in spots yet sketchy at best as a way to move throughout the region. A car here means freedom, even if that freedom involves the right to sit on the 91 freeway for hours. If you do not want to drive or cannot do so, there are still ways to get where you want to go, primarily with tour companies and a combination of commuter airline and taxi. If this is your choice, you will have to do a lot of homework on your own, plan ahead, and be patient.

i Always take a cell phone and map with you, even when you're driving to the most urban of areas.

LOS ANGELES, SANTA MONICA, AND LONG BEACH AREA

You could spend the entire year doing day trips and weekend getaways in this broad area and never repeat yourself. There are hundreds of events, some of the country's most famous tourist attractions, world-class shopping and museums, movie and TV studios, sports, gardens, and zoos. It's not possible to list them all here, so we're picking out highlights that will appeal to a wide variety of ages and tastes.

Los Angeles is a sprawling community—more a concept than a sharply defined geographic area. There's downtown LA, the "Westside" and Santa Monica, Burbank and Long Beach, all distinct areas but referred to as "the LA area."

Downtown is the oldest section, and over the years it's become a bit gritty around the edges, as new communities grew up on all sides. Many of California's most important architectural treasures are here, home to everything from banks to run-down bodegas and trendy restaurants. A move toward containing Southern California's urban sprawl is behind what many residents hope will be a renaissance of the downtown, and a few intrepid developers are finding an eager market for lofts and condos in renovated buildings.

The famed **Jewelry District** is downtown, as is the heart of California's diminishing retail apparel industry. The Jewelry District is renowned for wholesale prices on precious gems, watches, and all types of fine jewelry. If you have the stamina and persistence to visit dozens of shops to compare and bargain before you buy, you can take advantage of huge savings by purchasing from the source and cutting out the middleman.

The LA **Fashion District** covers dozens of blocks in the downtown area. Access to the high-end fashion offices is reserved for wholesale buyers, but there's plenty on the street to keep you amazed and shopping. From bridal accessories to flip-flops, flowers to thousands of bolts of silk, this area has it all. The action is fast-paced and bargaining is expected, even though the prices are already quite good.

Both the Jewelry District and the Fashion District close up early—usually around 5 p.m.—and are not open on Sundays or major holidays.

Also downtown is **Olvera Street,** a touristy Mexican marketplace offering mostly cheap trinkets and the like, yet it is where El Pueblo de Nuestra Señora la Reina de los Angeles del Río de Porciúncula was founded. That's the long-hand name for LA.

Greater downtown attractions include Chinatown, Dodger Stadium, the University of Southern California, the historic Los Angeles Memorial Coliseum, the Natural History Museum of Los Angeles County, Staples Center and L.A. Live, Cathedral of our Lady of the Angels, Union Station—a stunning example of the art-deco movement—Walt Disney Concert Hall, Griffith Observatory, Los Angeles Zoo, and the Autry National Center of the American West.

i **Most TV shows offer free tickets to their tapings. A painless way of getting tickets to be in the live audience at your favorite show is to go to the Web site www.tvtix.com. All tickets are free.**

Heading west through Mid-Wilshire, on to **Westside** and up to the hills, this is the LA of legend, taking in Hollywood, Beverly Hills, Bel-Air, and Westwood, and the richest assemblage of museums, theaters, restaurants, shopping areas, and celebrity hangouts in the state. One not to be missed is the **Farmers' Market,** which celebrated 75 years in 2009. Open every day and selling fresh meats, poultry, seafood, produce, flowers, bakery goods, and specialty foods, the market really comes to life on weekends. Other must-see sites near the market are the stunning Los Angeles County Museum of Art, Pedersen Automotive Museum, George C. Page Museum at the La Brea Tarpits, where for tens of thousands of years tar has been pooling in bubbling pits, trapping all manner of Ice Age and later critters—saber-toothed cats, dire wolves, giant ground sloths, mammoths—many of whom are now kindly giving scientists a bony but insightful look into the basin's prehistory. For diners, head straight to Canter's Deli or Mario Batali's side-by-side greats, Osteria Mozza, and Pizzeria Mozza. The truly breathtaking hilltop Getty Center has an extensive collection of art, but the building and the views are an equal draw. The Museum of Tolerance, with high-tech, interactive exhibits that explore the dynamics of discrimination, the legacy of the Holocaust, and current human rights issues, is moving and disturbing.

As you might expect, the shopping on the Westside is extraordinary. Two Rodeo, and its neighbor, Rodeo Drive, is a pedestrian area that includes such shops as Gucci, Gianfranco Ferre, Versace, Tiffany, and more. Melrose Street, with its jumble of small retailers selling apparel, jewelry, gifts, and souvenirs, is in this area, as is the glitzy **Hollywood & Highland Center.** A destination unto itself, Hollywood & Highland includes the Kodak Theatre, Renaissance Hollywood Hotel, a six-screen cinema, 12 bowling lanes, some excellent restaurants, and more than 60 specialty shops

To the north, over the hills, **Burbank** and the **San Fernando Valley** are home to the motion picture studios, including Universal and Warner

Brothers. **Universal** has become an attraction in itself, with theme rides and what they call "full sensory" experiences built around blockbuster movies. At **Warner Brothers,** tours include behind-the-scenes looks at working studios.

ℹ Major attractions do not allow outside food or drinks. Given the steep prices for everything inside a park's gates, you may want to plan to eat a hearty breakfast and dinner outside and just have a snack or two while you're playing.

Also in the San Fernando Valley is the Los Angeles Equestrian Center, a huge facility with horse shows and events, a riding academy and rental stables, retail shops, and a restaurant/bar.

On the shopping end, Universal has also developed the Universal Citywalk shopping/entertainment complex, with dozens of restaurants and specialty shops, an 18-screen multiplex, an IMAX 3-D theater, and several nightclubs. Shopping in the LA area doesn't get any more varied than at the upscale Glendale Galleria, with five major department stores and 250 specialty stores.

In the **San Gabriel Valley,** star attractions include San Gabriel Mission, Santa Anita Park, with spring and winter sessions; the Norton Simon Museum of Art and its far-ranging European art collection; and the Los Angeles County Arboretum & Botanic Gardens. The Huntington Library, Art Collections, and Botanical Gardens is 200-plus acres featuring art galleries and a library, gorgeous gardens, a bookstore, and daily English tea. Pasadena, of course, is home to the annual Tournament of Roses New Year's Day parade and the granddaddy of them all, the Rose Bowl (stadium and same-named game).

Farther west—right on the ocean—is **Santa Monica,** a beautiful, friendly little city that's just made for walking. It's home to zillion-dollar movie star beach retreats, excellent shopping, and a lovely little beach that's more urban than any other beach along the Southern California coast.

If you're going for the day, look for a pay lot near the beach and head to the walk-in Visitor Information Center at 1920 Main St., where you can pick up a special events schedule and a trip schedule for the Big Blue Bus, a locally run bus system that is all you'll need to get around for the day. There's also a visitor information kiosk in the stretch of beachfront that runs right between the Pacific Ocean and Ocean Avenue.

A pedestrian shopping/dining area a few blocks from the beach, **Third Street Promenade** is the heart of the town. Major retailers such as Abercrombie & Fitch, Banana Republic, Borders Books & Music, Anthropologie, Levi's, and Old Navy share space with independent boutiques selling everything from motorcycle gear to jewelry and designer clothing. Fred Segal, the upscale men's, women's, and home boutique that is the star of the city, also has its main store and several mini-boutiques on and around Third Street. Street entertainers of all types lend a festive air, and most shops stay open late—until 9 p.m. on weekdays, 10 p.m. on Fri and Sat, and 6 p.m. on Sun. There's also an excellent farmers' market adjacent to Third Street on Wed and Sat mornings. The Third Street promenade is anchored by Santa Monica Place, a traditional indoor shopping mall with Macy's and the usual assortment of mall specialty stores and kiosks.

Another good shopping/dining district is the more laid-back **Main Street,** a few blocks from the beach and a haven of beautiful old buildings that have been converted into boutiques, restaurants, and sidewalk coffee shops. This is the place where locals go to read the paper and lounge around on a weekend morning.

Mid-City is a growing art hub, with the renowned 18th Street Arts Complex and Bergamot Station Arts Center, the latter of which houses the Santa Monica Museum of Art as well as the largest collection of art galleries on the West Coast. You'll need the bus to get here, but it's a short ride and well worth it if you love browsing in galleries.

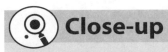

Close-up

The High Desert

Pick a crisp, sunny day, pack a lunch, and leave the Saks card and golf clubs at home. You're on an expedition beyond "Palm Springs," venturing into the High Desert, where bikers, space aliens, orchid growers, rock climbers, U.S. Marines, and Old West gunfighters spin out their days under wandering clouds. In this vast, dusty landscape, a lawn- and Starbucks-free zone, personal eccentricities and dreams flourish to an astonishing degree.

Start from the west end of the valley, going 14 miles north on Indian Avenue from the heart of Palm Springs. Indian Avenue curves to the west and intersects with Highway 62 (29 Palms Hwy.). As you drive up the hill, you'll spot antiques shops, small diners, and a "dig your own cactus" nursery. A good way to weave together the threads of this town, Morongo Valley, and the ones to follow, Yucca Valley, Joshua Tree, and finally Twentynine Palms, and then start exploring on the return trip.

At first sight Twentynine Palms is just another modest little highway town, nothing special. But its heart beats with a rare patriotism fueled by its neighbor, the Marine Air Ground Combat Center, the world's largest Marine combat training center and a complete town unto itself. With today's heightened security, individual and group visits are tightly scrutinized.

In Twentynine Palms itself, the Mural Project has been busy creating huge outdoor murals on business building walls since 1994. The murals depict the city's history since 1910 and showcase the work of world-famous artists. Most are on buildings located on 29 Palms Hwy., and all are well worth a look.

The North Entrance Station for Joshua Tree National Park is also in Twentynine Palms, just off the highway on Utah Trail, which becomes Park Boulevard directly past the Oasis Visitor Center. This is the best path to take for a "quick" look at a serenely beautiful expanse of 800,000 acres where the ecosystems of the Colorado Desert and the Mojave Desert come together. There's often snow in the winter, and spring can bring spectacular displays of wildflowers.

Five different palm oases, "forests" of Joshua trees and cholla cactus, granite monoliths, and immense mosaics of boulders dot the landscape. A few miles in from the North Entrance you'll pass through Jumbo Rocks and Hidden Valley, both spectacular spots for exploring, having a picnic, and watching the climbers who come here from all over the world.

i Expect to encounter "June gloom" at the beaches through late June. This is a thick layer of fog that settles overnight and usually lingers until early afternoon. Dress in layers you can peel off when the sun comes out.

At the northern edge of town but still an easy walk from downtown is **Montana Avenue,** perhaps the quintessential Southern California shopping/dining experience. On 10 blocks in the middle of an upscale family neighborhood,

luxury boutiques, high-priced home furnishing stores, bakeries, restaurants, wine bars, and cafes are populated by a distinctly upscale crowd of locals and celebrities. Shops here close around 6 p.m., and the restaurants and bars become the hub of the action.

Santa Monica is a big dining-out town, and you'll find just about every type of food and price point here, from inexpensive Mexican to very high-end concept cuisine. This is the city where "California cuisine" was born, and the competition for the newest, most popular, best, most exotic fare is fierce.

Head back out of the park on the continuation of Park Boulevard past the West Entrance Station and into the town of Joshua Tree. Continue to the middle of Yucca Valley and turn north on Old Woman Springs Road (Highway 247). Keep on this road for 10 miles, turn right on Reche Road, drive another 2.5 miles, and then turn left on Belfield Boulevard, an easy-to-miss road that leads to the Integratron. Three miles north of that building is Giant Rock. These two spots have made the High Desert legendary among those who believe in extraterrestrials, UFOs, and all things unseen. For a closer look at the Integratron, see the chapter on Attractions.

Right across the road is Gubler Orchids. A world-famous orchid grower, Gubler also grows and ships bromeliads, ferns, and carnivorous plants. Tours are always free, and there are some great spots outside to loll around on picnic benches in the sun.

The real goodies, of course, are the orchids. Dozens of varieties are for sale, each perfect and perfectly tempting, from the vanilla-scented "dancing ladies" to the lusty magenta "prom corsage" flowers. The prices are outstanding, and the quality is superb. Even if you've already consumed a picnic lunch, you can still make room for real barbecue on the way back. Take Pioneertown Road north from the middle of Yucca Valley, travel 4 miles, and slow way down— the speed limit on Pioneertown's wide dirt streets is 5 miles per hour.

When it was built as an all-inclusive movie location in the late 1940s, the adobe and wooden storefronts along Mane Street housed cast and crew. A sound stage for interiors, the Golden Stallion Restaurant, The Red Dog Saloon, and a bowling alley made it a very practical movie town.

Because most of the buildings there were built to last, the town looks much as it must have in 1950. The storefronts now house a film production studio and sound stage, Web services company, post office, church, photo studio, and homes for many permanent residents.

The undisputed star of Pioneertown and the one "must stop" on a visit here is Pappy and Harriet's, a little adobe bar and grill that serves as local watering hole. It's been the center of town for almost 30 years and remains the place of choice on Saturday and Sunday afternoons (www.pappyandharriets.com).

Motorcycles, pickups, and sleek sports cars surround the building on weekends, their drivers drawn here for the cold beer, backyard barbecue, and live music. Eric Burdon, Donovan, and Eddie Vedder of Pearl Jam are a few of the singers who have dropped in to jam and entertain.

The **Santa Monica Pier** and adjacent **Pacific Park** are worth a day's trip in themselves. The Santa Monica Aquarium offers hands-on fun for children, and the Carousel at the Pier is a beautifully restored 1922 ride for everyone. Pacific Park is the West Coast's only amusement park on a pier, so come on down and hop on the famous roller coaster and the nine-story, solar-powered Ferris wheel. The park also has a lot of smaller rides and games, as well as typical amusement park food and souvenir shops.

Nearby **Venice Beach,** long famous for its artist hangouts and Muscle Beach, is definitely worth a side trip. The various street entertainers and artists on the beach promenade are friendly, funky, and frenetic—this is California people-watching at its best.

Just off the coast is lovely little **Catalina Island,** just 18.5 miles long and 7 miles wide. It's edged with beautiful sandy beaches, and the town is a gem of small shops and cafes. Take a ferry ride over and rent a golf cart to tour around—no cars are allowed.

Back on land but still by the ocean, **Long Beach** is home to the famous *Queen Mary* ocean liner, as well as the Long Beach Aquarium, a fabulous place with more than 12,500 creatures in 50 different exhibits. A highlight is the Shark Lagoon, with more than 150 sharks, some of which you can actually touch. Also check out the Museum of Latin American Art.

i Even if you're staying at an independent boutique hotel, it pays to ask if they have connections or reciprocal relationships with hotels in your weekend destination. The California tourism industry is close-knit, and you just may find an excellent value.

ORANGE COUNTY, LAGUNA BEACH, AND NEWPORT BEACH

Anaheim in Orange County is home to Disney's **California Adventure Park** and the **Disneyland Park,** the Adam, Eve, and Eden of all American man-made tourist attractions. California Adventure concentrates on the Golden State, re-creating elements of California's past and its psyche: the gold rush, wine country and agriculture, the moviemaking magic of Hollywood. Rides and beachfront carnivals go on all the time. And everyone knows of Disneyland, the original: the themed lands, pirates and haunted spirits, bobsledding an icy mountainside, rocketing into space, getting that idiotic doll song stuck in your head for weeks. So many California memories are wrapped up in Walt's Magic Kingdom And not far away, in Buena Park, it's Knott's Berry Farm. Pretty much most of the berries and all of the farm are out of Knott's, a place that in our childhood's was more cobbled together Americana as attraction than what is it today. Now it's all amusement park all the time, with a bevy of coasters, the most tame of which might still give the average Disneygoer a bit too much of a rush. Just a little south of all this excitement is some of the country's best shopping in two very different "malls." The first, South Coast Plaza, is compact, almost like a neighborhood, albeit one that's enclosed.

Department stores include Macy's, Nordstrom, Saks Fifth Avenue, and Sears. There's a concierge, valet and taxi services, tons of ATM machines, a carousel, and a staggering array of shops. You'll find European couture, American athletic gear, fine jewelry, exquisite home furnishings, art, and much more.

Fashion Island, in Newport Beach, replicates most of South Coast's big national retailers, and adds more than 100 other shops. It's an open-air "village," laid out in nine different sections that encourage wandering, browsing, and often getting lost. This is the place to go for people-watching and it's a lovely excursion on a sunny day.

In nearby **Newport Beach** and **Laguna Beach,** the atmosphere is just made for vacationers. Like Santa Monica, these are mostly walking towns, with the main shopping and dining districts stretched out along Pacific Coast Highway, which is just a few steps away from the sandy beaches. Both towns are noted for their fine art galleries and laid-back, casual atmosphere. In the summer the Laguna Arts Festival, Sawdust Arts Festival, and Pageant of the Masters pack in visitors from all over. It's a crush, but never hectic or stress-inducing. If you're in the area around the holidays, the Newport Beach Christmas Boat Parade is a magical collection of lighted and decorated yachts and small boats that goes on for several evenings. In 2008 the tradition celebrated its 100th birthday.

Heading south, crossing over into San Diego County, you'll find **Del Mar** and **La Jolla,** two more lovely and very upscale beach communities. Del Mar is most famous for the summertime Del Mar races. Opening day in July can be an elegant, dress-up affair, especially if you have tick-

i According to the experts at South Coast Plaza, the best days to shop, whether you go to an outlet mall or a big department store, are Tuesday and Thursday. If you get your shopping done by early afternoon, you'll really avoid the crowds.

ets to the much-coveted box seats; heck, we just thought it was about betting on the ponies.

The Birch Aquarium at Scripps features a tide-pool center, revolving exhibits, a live coral reef, dive shows, a simulator ride, and, best of all, seasonal full-moon walks on the La Jolla Pier, which is closed to the public except for these evenings. Art galleries abound in La Jolla, as do excellent bars and restaurants. And La Jolla is home to one of the nation's greatest publicly-owned golf facilities, Torrey Pines Golf Course.

SAN DIEGO

Down in **San Diego,** a visit to the historic Gaslamp Quarter, or old downtown, is a must. This is a lively entertainment and dining district full of wonderful old buildings that have been restored to their original beauty, and home to the Padres and their Petco Park, about as slick of a place in all of baseball to take in a game. Downtown San Diego, once a seedy and forgotten neighborhood surrounded by the high-tech companies in the suburbs, is coming into its own as a vibrant, fun place to eat and play all week long.

Seaworld San Diego has seen more than 100 million visitors since it opened in 1964. It's a full day of rides, shows, and attractions such as the world-famous Shamu.

In the heart of the city, Balboa Park is home to 15 museums, various arts and international cultural associations, and the San Diego Zoo, making it one of the nation's largest cultural and entertainment complexes. The **San Diego Zoo** is one of the country's biggest and best, with more than 100 acres, in addition to its sibling San Diego Wild Animal Park 30 miles north just outside Escondido.

Beaches around San Diego are clean and crowded—it seems like everyone in the city is an ocean lover—with generally calm surf. One of the nicest spots for a stroll on a Sun morning is the strand by the historic **Hotel Del Coronado.** The "Del," as locals call it, was built as a luxury resort in 1888 and has since been designated a National Historic Landmark. If you go to San Diego, this is

a must, whether you stop in for tea or dinner or just amble through the lobby and look into the gift shop.

i **December through May is the season for whale-watching, and there are several tour companies that arrange regular boat trips to view these extraordinary creatures. Check the local paper or do an Internet search for "whale watching."**

NEARBY MOUNTAINS AND DESERTS

With their pine forests and winter sports, Idyllwild to the west in the San Jacinto Mountains and Big Bear and Lake Arrowhead a bit farther north in the San Bernardino Mountains offer a complete change from the desert and make fun little excursions just about any time of year.

Idyllwild is a rustic mountain village where many "flatlanders" have purchased summer homes or cabins. The downtown is small, with pretty little art galleries, shops selling crafts, and several good restaurants. The big draw here is a summer escape from the desert heat, and the August music festival is always packed with smooth-jazz aficionados.

Lake Arrowhead and **Big Bear** are even more popular summer "escape" destinations. Because the lake in Lake Arrowhead is privately owned, visitors have very limited use. If you have a friend who belongs to a beach club or owns a house there, you can water-ski and loaf around on the lake as much as you like. If not, you'll be limited to taking a boat out and gazing at the lakeside mansions from a distance.

i **Most museums have frequent free days, and some will offer reduced admission if you go late in the day. This can be a considerable savings if you're going in a family group and want to see several museums. Check each museum's Web site for details.**

It's a different story in Big Bear, which is more of a "real world" place and also happens to have an excellent-for-these-here-parts downhill skiing facility at Bear Mountain. Big Bear Lake is public and open to power boating, and it is an excellent fishery, kicking off some monumental trout at times. The town itself is better stocked than other So Cal mountain communities in terms of retail, eats, and just things to do in general. Outdoor recreation is the attraction here, whatever the season, with camping, a maze of hiking trails, and even a little golf course for summertime use.

Desert natives say that **Borrego Springs** is "Palm Springs 50 years ago." Stretching that out to 75 years might not be a bad idea. Located in the middle of the Anza-Borrego desert around 60 miles from Palm Springs, this little town is the ultimate "relax and do practically nothing" hideout. You'll find golf, a couple of chic-fun resorts, horseback riding, four-wheel exploring, a few good restaurants, and perhaps the most lovely desert canyons and palm oases in the state, and it's all wrapped up in Anza-Borrego Desert State Park. This is a place where you can hear the coyotes howl every night and soak up the silence and beauty of the desert away from lights and traffic. If you go in the spring, the wildflower shows are peerless.

RETIREMENT AND RELOCATION

Making the decision to relocate, whether for retirement or a different lifestyle, involves considering a lot of factors, from the availability of health care to the cost of living and quality of life. Many a desert visitor has fallen in love with the Palm Springs area and become a permanent resident. If you're thinking about moving here, take your time. Visit at all times of the year, not just in the lovely winter months. Talk to people who have lived here for a few years and can give you the good and not-so-good—the real "insider" information. Some of the happiest retirees and relocatees are those who, over the course of several years, spent months at a time in the desert, getting used to the rhythm of life in the different seasons and learning the quirks of each city.

This chapter gives you the basic information you'll need to start your research. Here, we give you a brief overview of each city, moving from Palm Springs in the west to Indio in the east; touch on the general "personality" of each; and give some pros and cons to consider if you are thinking of relocating. This is followed by sections that round up information on the desert's health care, libraries, police and fire service, senior centers, utilities, child care, schools, media, and worship; we invite you to supplement with material you pick up during your Web searches and visits. You'll find a lot of variation in all of these amenities from city to city, and some may be the "deal breakers" or "deal makers" you're looking for.

THE COMMUNITIES

Palm Springs

Incorporated in 1938, Palm Springs is the flagship of the desert, carrying the famous name that is often used to refer to the entire valley. It's got a lot of depth going for it, including the Palm Springs International Airport, Palm Springs Art Museum, Palm Springs Aerial Tramway, Moorten Botanical Garden, Mizell Senior Center, Desert Regional Medical Center, Spa Resort Casino, Indian Canyons, and the valley's most "downtown" downtown. The city has very little buildable land left, and property values jumped during the past decade as investors, visitors, and even some locals "rediscovered" Palm Springs. Following Palm Desert's lead, the city established an excellent Art in Public Places program, installing a large selection of important sculptures in public areas. Developer fees pay for this program, and as the new condos go up, the fees go up as well.

Palm Spring's population is about 46,000—2008 figures provided by the Coachella Valley Economic Partnership—and some claim seasonal "residents" equal a like number. In terms of household income, Palm Springs ranks above Indio and Cathedral City and below Palm Desert, Rancho Mirage, and La Quinta.

i When you're buying a house, make sure you know whether it's "lease land," which means it is Indian-owned. Homes on lease land may appear to be less expensive as the land-lease costs are a separate animal from the selling price (and eventually whatever PITI costs go into your mortgage payment). On fee-owned land you are buying the dirt below, along with the house, pool and termites, as part of the purchase price. When lease terms expire, it can get dicey and costly for whoever owns the sticks above the land.

Palm Springs has a decidedly more liberal and varied population and attitude than most of the other valley cities, as evidenced by the large gay population and the increasingly diverse ethnic makeup. It's still rather homogeneous, as the desert always has been, but compared to Rancho Mirage, Palm Springs is a virtual United Nations.

Despite budget woes that have plagued the city since the retail migration to the east began more than 20 years ago, the city still fights to keep the parks, library, and public services at the top of the quality scale, and it succeeds very well. It's a very easy city to navigate, compact and logically laid out, with a lot of neighborhood centers that offer such necessities as groceries, cleaners, movies, and more within a walkable distance.

Cathedral City

Cathedral City is more similar to Indio than it is to its next-door neighbors, Palm Springs and Rancho Mirage. Originally developed as a planned subdivision in 1925, the city grew up in the shadow of Palm Springs and incorporated in 1981. For years it was known as a blue-collar place, with few amenities for its residents, and it was far behind its neighbors in the development of the type of resorts and golf courses that brought in budget-sustaining tourist dollars. The absence of a central downtown area meant it had the feeling of a bedroom community.

With an estimated population of 52,000, Cathedral City is the desert's second-largest city, behind Indio. In recent years Cathedral City has become one of the hotspots for the valley's automotive businesses and has worked hard to leverage tax dollars and redevelopment funds to clean up and modernize neighborhoods, downtown, and other public spaces. The biggest improvement is in the area around City Hall, just off Highway 111, where an entertainment complex of restaurants, shops, and theaters is coming together

Housing in Cathedral City is among of the most affordable in the valley, and more than half of the housing units are rentals. With its convenient location close to the middle of the valley and the large hotels, this is a popular spot for the many service workers who keep the hotels and restaurants running. Like all towns, there are family neighborhoods full of well-kept homes and streets filled with playing children, and areas that are a challenge. Cathedral City also has space in which to develop new housing, and office, commercial, and retail. The city is still struggling with its blue-collar image, though, and the city's amenities for residents—parks, public arts, and recreation programs—are pretty skimpy when compared to other cities in the desert.

Rancho Mirage

Rancho Mirage is a retail and dining dynamo, with a small but prestigious group of golf and spa resorts. As the community grew up with a land-use pattern determined, largely, by private residential-golf communities and the urban retail-commercial core along Highway 111, and not much else, it lacks the "neighborhoods" feel of the adjoining cities. Perhaps that's part and parcel of being a city that calls itself the "playground of millionaires." The tax rolls keep the public spaces and infrastructure in top condition, and though parks are in small supply and of limited scope, like the city's library, they are nattily dressed up. The River retailtainment complex, Children's Discovery Museum of the Desert, and Eisenhower Medical Center all call Rancho Mirage home. Rancho Mirage's population was 17,000 in 2008.

Palm Desert

Palm Desert incorporated in 1973, as did Rancho Mirage. It began as a general-law municipality but subsequently changed over to be a charter-governed city (1997). Functionally, the charter allows the city, its public officials, and its resident-voters to better fine tune the city's structure and governance than is possible under general state law. Like many other valley cities, it has a council-manager government, with five citizens elected to staggered four-year terms, and the mayor is drawn from the council on a rotating one-year basis. The city's permanent population is 50,000 and an estimated 30,000+ are seasonal residents.

Palm Desert prides itself on its balance—in business, real estate, education, and quality of life. Apartments, condos, single-family homes, and luxurious golf country clubs are in the real estate mix. Like many other cities, Palm Desert struggles with the state's requirements for a certain amount of affordable housing. It was the first city in the desert to create an Art in Public Places program, which requires developers to either pay a fee for public art or install significant pieces.

The Palm Desert Community Garden opened its gates in the spring of 1999 and was the first in the Coachella Valley. Open to novice as well as experienced gardeners, the gardens are aimed at strengthening community ties as well as providing fresh, inexpensive produce for those who share their time and work. The city is an active partner in the whole garden program, bringing in speakers to teach about design, nutrition, cooking, and soil, and sponsoring field trips to local farms.

Palm Desert also has an excellent public parks and recreation program. For details, check the Parks, Recreation, and Sports chapter.

Indian Wells

Incorporated in 1967, Indian Wells has a full-time population of 5,000, and a small footprint of just 15 square miles, almost exclusively given over to extremely high-end housing and private clubs. An additional 5,000 to 6,000 part-time residents call the city home during the winter months. The population is older—63 on average—well educated and with the highest median family income in the county at $135,000. Home to the Indian Wells Golf Resort, a compelling 36-hole complex completely reworked in 2006–07, Indian Wells Tennis Garden, and a great supporter of cultural events and institutions throughout the valley, Indian Wells has established itself as the conservative culture hub of the desert. There is virtually no buildable land in the city, a modicum of higher-end retail, and virtually no affordable housing. In many ways the city is much like a very large, very exclusive country club.

La Quinta

The fastest-growing city in the desert and one of the most rapidly expanding in California, La Quinta is becoming known as an attractive family community. PGA West and the La Quinta Resort are the undisputed economic engines of the city, attracting thousands of visitors each year. A lot of those visitors return to relocate or retire, or just to invest in the lifestyle and beautiful setting.

i | **Earthquake insurance? Most would tell you not to get it, even if you can.**

When it incorporated in 1982, La Quinta had a population of just over 5,200. Today the population has grown to approximately 41,000. Retail and commercial have exploded along Highway 111, and the city is working to bring vitality and business back to its historic heart down in "the cove." A variety of housing stock is available, and single-family residential tends to cluster in exclusive residential-golf developments and more standard but still mid-high tracts.

Indio

Indio was the Coachella Valley's first incorporated city, taking this step in 1930, when it had a population of 1,875. The city now boasts nearly 80,000 residents. Indio experiences a much smaller percentage of seasonal change than its valley siblings, owing to its more working-class roots and the absence until recent years of the kind of high-end residential-golf developments that fuel that market segment. It's a young city, age-wise, of low- to moderate-incomes, and heavily Hispanic. The economic demographic started shifting dramatically in the first decade of this century as single-family residential leapfrogged I-10, filling in the valley floor below the Indio Hills with some of the desert's nicest new tracts. Mixed-grade retail is clustered along Highway 111 and the downtown core, and new regional commercial centers have followed the housing northward.

HEALTH CARE

For such a small population, the desert's medical facilities are outstanding, owing in large part to the many famous and wealthy men and women who have retired here and donated time and money to make sure they are cutting edge.

Hospitals

DESERT REGIONAL MEDICAL CENTER
1150 North Indian Canyon Dr.
(760) 323-6511
www.desertmedctr.com

This 367-bed acute care facility houses the only designated trauma center in the Coachella Valley. It has the distinction of being located at the site of the old El Mirador Hotel, once the most famous "hot spot" in the Palm Springs social scene.

The Comprehensive Cancer Center here provides patients with outpatient surgery facilities, a radiation oncology treatment area, a medical oncology infusion center, a "stat" laboratory for quick processing of treatment related labwork, physician offices and exam rooms, a pharmacy, a comprehensive breast center, a research department, a patient resource center, psychosocial and nutritional support services, and financial counseling services. Satellite facilities are located in nearby Yucca Valley and Indio.

Other special services and facilities include treatment for low- and high-risk obstetrical patients at the Women and Infants' Center, including central fetal monitoring; the Orthopedic Institute; weight-loss surgery; and a community fitness program at the Wellness Center. A free club for desert residents age 50 or older provides health and education programs, a referral service, claims application assistance, discounted preventive health screenings, and hospital pre-registration.

EISENHOWER MEDICAL CENTER
39-000 Bob Hope Dr., Rancho Mirage
(760) 340-3911
www.emc.org

Dolores and Bob Hope donated the original 80 acres of land for this hospital and Dolores spearheaded the formation of the Eisenhower Medical Center Auxiliary when ground was broken in 1969. The hospital opened in 1971. Over the years Dolores has been president, chairman of the board, and chairman emeritus of the board of trustees.

In the last 30 years the medical center campus has grown tremendously, and has been recognized as one of the country's top hospitals.

Eisenhower Medical Center is now home to a number of world-class facilities, including: **Annenberg Center for Health Sciences (760-773-4500; www.annenberg.net).** This accredited center provides continuing education for health care professionals and includes a 500-seat auditorium. Professional video production as well as graphic design, videoconferencing, and satellite uplink/downlink services are available.

Barbara Sinatra Children's Center (760-340-2336; www.sinatracenter.org). This nonprofit facility has received international recognition for being an advocate for abused children and provides help regardless of a family's ability to pay for services. The Sinatra Center address issues of child abuse detection and prevention, as well as counseling, through its Web site, outreach programs, and a speakers' bureau.

Betty Ford Center (760-773-4111; www.bettyfordcenter.org). Founded in 1982, the Center is a licensed 100-bed recovery hospital that has treated thousands of patients and family members from all over the United States and throughout the world. All aspects of drug and alcohol dependency are addressed in residential, outpatient, family, and children's programs so that patients' physical, spiritual, and psychological needs can be met.

The Hearing Institute of the Desert (760-341-3188; www.hearing-institute.com). The staff of this independent facility that is located on the Eisenhower Medical Center campus evaluate and treat hearing loss, tinnitus, and dizziness. This was the first Coachella Valley clinic to provide cochlear implants.

Additional special centers at Eisenhower include the **Eisenhower Lucy Curci Cancer Center,** providing full cancer care and support services; the **Eisenhower Smilow Heart Center** for advanced cardiac care services; and the **Eisenhower Orthopedic Center** for care and surgery in sports medicine, total joint replacement, and spine, as well as hand and foot, disorders.

Educational services are offered through the **Diabetes Program,** the first program in the Coachella Valley to achieve recognition by the American Diabetes Association and the **Phillip & Carol Traub Center,** for help with Parkinson's disease. The **Center for Healthy Living** is a free club for permanent and seasonal desert residents aimed at promoting healthy lifestyles. The center offers education, information, screening, and wellness programs. Members can receive discounts on services at local businesses and Eisenhower Medical Center, counseling on how to file Medicare and supplemental health insurance claims, and help in filling out advance health care directives.

i The desert has excellent traditional medical facilities. On the flip side, it has only recently started warming to alternative medicine providers such as acupuncturists, naturopaths, and the like.

JOHN F. KENNEDY MEMORIAL HOSPITAL
47-111 Monroe St., Indio
(760) 347-6191
www.jfkmemorialhosp.com
This 158-bed acute care hospital has a 24-hour emergency room and a daily express care center. There is a 16-bed intensive care unit and a 24-bed medical surgical unit. Specialties include maternity and obstetrical services, with prenatal classes and private labor and post-partum rooms; the multidisciplinary Arthritis Institute; neurosurgery and spine care; orthopedic, general, and vascular surgery; urology services; and an array of standard radiology and laboratory services.

The hospital, a part of Tenet-California, also has a pediatric asthma management program, which educates individuals about asthma in both English and Spanish. The program serves both inpatient and outpatient children.

Urgent Care Centers

These are stand-alone clinics for urgent but not life-threatening health situations and are used frequently when individuals don't have a regular doctor or can't get in to see one. All are open 24 hours. They are not emergency rooms. Each clinic does routine physical exams, vaccinations, and other routine medical office procedures.

BERMUDA DUNES IMMEDIATE CARE
41-120 Washington St., Suite 202,
Bermuda Dunes
(760) 360-3193

DESERT URGENT CARE
74-990 Country Club Dr., Suite 310,
Palm Desert
(760) 341-8800

EISENHOWER EXPRESS CLINICS
67-780 East Palm Canyon Dr., Cathedral City
(760) 328-1000

74-785 Hwy. 111, Suite 100, Indian Wells
(760) 837-8953

78-822 Hwy. 111, La Quinta
(760) 564-7000

39-000 Bob Hope Dr., Rancho Mirage
Uihlein Building, 1st Floor
(Eisenhower Medical Center)
(760) 674-3844

INDIO IMMEDIATE CARE
81-800 Dr. Carreon Blvd., Indio
(760) 775-9641

PALM SPRINGS IMMEDIATE CARE
275 North El Cielo, Suite C-1
(760) 320-8814

STAT URGENT CARE
73-211 Fred Waring Dr., Suite 101,
Palm Desert
(760) 837-0321
www.staturgentcare.com

Specialty Facilities

BRAILLE INSTITUTE
70-251 Ramon Rd., Rancho Mirage
(760) 321-1111
www.brailleinstitute.org
A local chapter of the national organization, this offers free educational, social and recreational programs, low vision rehabilitation consultations, a Vistas shop, a youth program, and library services.

PALM DESERT VA CLINIC
41-990 Cook St., Building F, Palm Desert
(760) 341-5570
This is an medical clinic under the auspices of the VA's Loma Linda Healthcare System in Loma Linda, California. It's services are for veterans only and it is not an urgent care center. To establish qualification, please call the center and schedule a qualification appointment.

LIBRARIES

The following libraries are operated under the Riverside County Library System. Go to www .riverside.lib.ca.us for hours, directions, general information and holdings, or call the individual libraries.

COACHELLA VALLEY BOOKMOBILE
Various locations
(760) 347-2385

DESERT HOT SPRINGS
11-691 West Dr., Desert Hot Springs
(760) 329-5926

INDIO
200 Civic Center Mall, Indio
(760) 347-2383

LA QUINTA
78-275 Calle Tampico, La Quinta
(760) 564-4767

PALM DESERT
73-300 Fred Waring Dr., Palm Desert
(760) 346-6552

i All of the local libraries have borrowing privileges within the larger county-wide system, so you can order and enjoy materials that aren't actually on the shelves of your local branch.

THOUSAND PALMS
31-189 Robert Rd., Thousand Palms
(760) 343-1556
Three of the desert cities operate their own libraries, Cathedral City, Palm Springs, and Rancho Mirage:

CATHEDRAL CITY
33-520 Date Palm Dr.
(760) 328-4262

PALM SPRINGS
300 South Sunrise Way
(760) 322-7323
www.palmsprings-ca.gov

RANCHO MIRAGE
71-100 Rancho Mirage
(760) 341-7323
www.ranchomiragelibrary.org

POLICE AND FIRE

Five of the nine cities in the valley contract with the Riverside County Sheriff's Department for law enforcement protection; Cathedral City, Desert Hot Springs, Indio and Palm Springs are the exceptions. There are advantages and some would say disadvantages with either approach. Contracting for service can lower costs—personnel, administration/legal, equipment and maintenance, facilities. Proponents of home-grown departments counter that while contract cities have personnel dedicated to their "police departments," with designated line and command officers, authority still ultimately passes through to the county agency, it's elected sheriff, and the county Board of Supervisors. Who is correct? The four cities above think they have a formula that works best for their residents. Coachella, Indian Wells, La Quinta, Palm Desert, and Rancho Mirage think the county service is just fine. The county also provides fire protection services to all desert communities and cities except Cathedral City and Palm Springs.

As always in the case of an emergency, call 9-1-1. For non-emergency calls or general law enforcement inquiries, please call:

CALIFORNIA HIGHWAY PATROL
(760) 772-8900

CATHEDRAL CITY POLICE DEPARTMENT
(760) 770-0300

DESERT HOT SPRINGS POLICE DEPARTMENT
(760) 329-6411

INDIAN WELL/PALM DESERT/RANCHO MIRAGE POLICE DEPARTMENT
(760) 836-1600

INDIO POLICE DEPARTMENT
(760) 391-4051

LA QUINTA POLICE DEPARTMENT
(760) 863-8990, (760) 771-3320

PALM SPRINGS POLICE DEPARTMENT
(760) 323-8116

RIVERSIDE COUNTY SHERIFF'S DEPARTMENT
(760) 836-1600

SENIOR CENTERS AND SERVICES

THE COMMUNITY CENTER AT TIERRA DEL SOL
4537-171 West Buddy Rogers Ave.,
Cathedral City
(760) 321-1548
www.thecommunitycenterattierradelsol.com
Dubbed an "Outreaching Oasis for Seniors," the center provides a raft of health, recreational, educational, counseling, ombudsman, and other services to residents of the several-year-old Tierra del Sol senior housing project, and area seniors. Among the not-so-usual offerings are "meet the pharmacist day" for one-on-one counseling on meds usage, an archaeological society, an Apple/Mac users group, and the ever-popular pet vaccination and micro-chipping day.

INDIO SENIOR CENTER
45-222 Towne St., Indio
(760) 391-4170
www.indio.org
The center's programs are available to anyone age 50 and older, and the building is open on weekdays from 7:30 a.m. to 4:30 p.m. Resources include the Meals on Wheels program, information and referral services, health screening, exercise, arts and crafts classes, bridge, a variety of counseling, educational programs and workshops, bingo, a library, and a program of catered lunches and breakfasts.

JEWISH FAMILY SERVICE OF THE DESERT
801 East Tahquitz Canyon Way
(760) 325-4088
www.jfsdesert.org
JFS is a social service agency serving the needs of seniors and all ages, regardless of faith, across the valley. Services and programs include counseling, outpatient services, meal and transportation assistance, and spiritual health. The agency has a satellite operation in Palm Desert, available by appointment (same phone number).

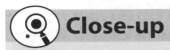 **Close-up**

Palm Springs Art Museum

The history of the Palm Springs Art Museum, the oldest cultural establishment in the desert, says a lot about the quality of life for those who choose to retire or relocate here from more urban areas.

The Palm Springs Art Museum was founded in 1938 as the Palm Springs Desert Museum, a one-room showcase for Native American artifacts and the natural sciences, specializing in the environment of the surrounding Coachella Valley. Soon the growing museum found temporary new quarters in a section of the town's library; it then expanded again in 1947 into a section of a converted wartime hospital.

With the war over, the desert started experiencing its first population boom. New residents were looking for a sunny, beautiful place to spend at least half of the year, and many of them hungered for the art and culture that were a part of their lives in Chicago, New York, or Los Angeles.

A modern 10,000-square-foot structure was built in downtown Palm Springs in 1958, and in 1962 it expanded to include an auditorium and galleries for contemporary art exhibitions.

A significant fund-raising effort marked by large donations from all manner of celebrities, business tycoons, and everyday people built the museum's first modern home on Museum Drive, in the middle of downtown and right up against the foothills of the San Jacinto Mountains.

E. Stewart Williams, a Palm Springs resident and internationally famous architect, was the mastermind behind the new facility. Williams, one of the country's most renowned mid-century architects, captured the magic of the desert with references to sand dunes and liberal use of the rocks from the surrounding mountains. The soaring space is filled with light at all hours and somehow manages to create a feeling of intimacy and openness at the same time.

In 1960 Williams designed a new theater for the site, and in 1976 he added a wing for art, one for natural science, and the expanded Annenberg Theater. He was back again in 1982 to design the administration building so that staff could free up museum space for the western American art wing.

As his latest achievement for the museum, Williams came out of retirement to design a major expansion to incorporate the Steve Chase Art Wing and Education Center, which opened in 1996. Every addition came together seamlessly—visitors can't tell where the original building ended and the new parts began.

JOSLYN SENIOR CENTER
73-750 Catalina Way, Palm Desert
(760) 340-3220
www.joslyncenter.org
Joslyn provides programs, services and activities for those 50 and better in Indian Wells, Palm Desert, and Rancho Mirage. Some 500 people visit the center daily, which is open from 8 a.m. to 5 p.m. weekdays. Offerings include a wellness center and health screenings, fitness and dance classes, all types of games from mah-jongg to bridge and lawn bowling, language lessons, art classes,

bingo, legal counseling, and a vast array of excursions and special events year-round. Membership is just $30 a year and the "best" of the better-than-50 crowd is reportedly a spry 105.

LA QUINTA SENIOR CENTER
78-450 Avenida La Fonda, La Quinta
(760) 564-0096
www.la-quinta.org
This facility for folks 55+ offers a variety of classes and seminars, special events, and weekly programs. The city's list of services and activities

Williams is just one of the extraordinary people who have made the desert their home and have given huge amounts of time and skill to make it a better place to live. When the expansion to the museum opened in 1996, he said it would not be complete until the building, the art, and the people came together. To him, the vitality of the museum and its role in enriching the lives of everyone in the desert were the crowning achievements.

From a one-room facility in 1938 to today's 125,000-square-foot facility, the museum has greatly expanded its collections and programs. It now houses a collection of over 7,000 objects; the Marks Administration Building is home to the administrative staff and library; Frey House II was a bequest to the museum in 1999; and the Buddy Rogers Box Office opened in 2000. Buddy Rogers, Albert Frey, and Walter Marks all had homes in the desert, loved it, and contributed significantly to the museum, in both time and money.

Nine active councils—devoted to Architecture and Design, Artists, Contemporary Art, Docents, Museum Associates, Museum Service, Performing Arts, Sunday Afternoon Concerts, and Western Art—attract an amazing talent pool from current community leaders and those who have retired and now spend their days improving the valley's quality of life. A major fund-raising arm of the Board of Trustees, the Museum Associates Council boasts exceptional success in planning and carrying out innovative fund-raising events.

In April 2004 the museum made a major shift in its focus, from a multidisciplinary museum to a world-class art museum with a vibrant theater program. It became clear that the art collections were growing and that the art audience was expanding—primarily in the areas of architecture, photography, and contemporary glass. In April 2005 the museum officially changed its name from the Palm Springs Desert Museum to the Palm Springs Art Museum, to reflect its emphasis on the visual and performing arts.

Accredited by the American Association of Museums, Palm Springs Art Museum has 28 galleries, two sculpture gardens, four classrooms/resource centers, an artists' center, five storage vaults, a 90-seat lecture hall, a 433-seat theater, a 1,000-square-foot store, and a locally popular cafe.

The museum has more than 4,000 members, and the institution has come to be one of the most egalitarian cultural organizations in the valley. Exhibitions, education programs, and performing arts productions at the museum are constantly changing and improving, made possible by admission fees, private funds, donations, memberships, grants, and volunteer efforts from all over the desert and the nation.

reads like the rap sheet for the NBA and NFL combined, which means a LOT of entries. Consult the Web site or call to inquire about current offerings. If a class or activity is not fully booked one day prior to its run date, adults under the magic 55 number will be accepted.

MIZELL SENIOR CENTER
480 South Sunrise Way
(760) 323-5689
www.mizell.org
A top-notch facility supported heavily by local

donors, Mizell offers a wide range of activities and programs, including daily lunch, support and counseling groups, exercise and dance, excursions, music, special-interest groups, computer instruction, table games and bridge, bingo, and special events.

RIVERSIDE COUNTY OFFICE ON AGING
73-750 Catalina Way, Palm Desert
(760) 341-0401
www.indio.org
Think of the office on aging as the master clear-

inghouse and service provider for seniors across the county. The office works as partner, ombudsman, and overseer at the level of the public and private agencies that provide services, as well as operating program, facilities and services of its own. It's kinda watchdog and friend.

UTILITIES

WATER: Desert Water Agency serves Palm Springs and approximately one-third of Cathedral City. The Coachella Valley Water District serves approximately two-thirds of Cathedral City and all of Rancho Mirage. Imperial Irrigation District, a community-owned utility, supplies water to Palm Desert and communities to the east.

GAS: Southern California Gas Co. serves the entire valley.

ELECTRIC: Electricity rates are a huge sore point for desert residents, most of whom are served by Southern California Edison, which charges one of the highest rates in the nation. It's not uncommon for summer electric bills to run into the hundreds of dollars, some customers even see four-figure bills. Edison serves Palm Springs, Cathedral City, Rancho Mirage, and part of Palm Desert. Imperial Irrigation District, with far lower rates, services part of Palm Desert and all areas east through Indio.

COACHELLA VALLEY WATER DISTRICT
(760) 398-2651
www.cvwd.org

IMPERIAL IRRIGATION DISTRICT
(760) 335-3640 (electricity)
(760) 339-9322 (water)
www.iid.com

SOUTHERN CALIFORNIA EDISON
(800) 655-4555
www.sce.com

SOUTHERN CALIFORNIA GAS CO.
(800) 427-2200
www.socalgas.com

i If you're retiring and want to make sure your grandkids are welcome in your new home, be diligent about researching the rules for condo or planned community developments you're considering. Many are downright uptight about allowing kids in for more than a hug and a fast adios.

CHILD CARE

For the past decade-plus, the population of all of the desert cities has increased significantly and more and more families are part of the explosion. In turn, the new younger families have created a demand for dependable, professional child care services. Where once this was limited to a neighbor's home, there are any number of full-service facilities offering care for infants to preteens. Desert churches also offer child care during school-holiday times.

To help you sort through the mass of providers, with some sense of comfort as to the results, check out www.desertdaycares.com, which lists all the desert day care facilities that are licensed by California's Community Care Licensing Division.

EDUCATION

Public Schools

DESERT SANDS UNIFIED SCHOOL DISTRICT
47-950 Dune Palms Rd., La Quinta
(760) 777-4200
www.dsusd.k12.ca.us
This school district serves part of Palm Desert, plus La Quinta and Indio. It contains 20 elementary schools, seven middle schools, seven high schools, and one alternative school.

PALM SPRINGS UNIFIED SCHOOL DISTRICT
980 East Tahquitz Canyon Way
(760) 416-6000
www.psusd.us
This school district serves the communities of Palm Springs, Cathedral City, Desert Hot Springs, Rancho Mirage, Thousand Palms, and parts of

Palm Desert. There are 16 elementary schools, five middle schools, three high schools, and five alternative learning venues.

Private Schools

CHRISTIAN SCHOOL OF THE DESERT DESERT CHRISTIAN HIGH SCHOOL (PRE-K–12)
40-700 Yucca Lane, Bermuda Dunes
(760) 345-2848
www.csod.org

DESERT CHAPEL CHRISTIAN (K–5)
630 South Sunrise Way
(760) 327-2772
www.desertchapel.org

DESERT TORAH ACADEMY (PRE-K–6)
73-550 Santa Rosa Way, Palm Desert
(760) 341-6501
www.chabadpalmsprings.com

THE LEARNING TREE (PRE-K–2)
42-675 Washington St., Palm Desert
(760) 345-8100
www.thelearningtreecenter.com

MARYWOOD-PALM VALLEY (PRE-K–12)
35-525 Davall Rd., Rancho Mirage
(760) 328-0861
www.mwpv.org

SACRED HEART SCHOOL (K–8)
43-775 Deep Canyon Rd., Palm Desert
(760) 346-3513
www.sacredheartpalmdesert.com
This is a traditional Catholic school, with around 300 students from kindergarten through grade 8. Academic instruction is aimed at preparing students to go into a standard college prep program in high school.

ST. MARGARET'S EPISCOPAL SCHOOL (PRE-K–8)
47-535 Hwy. 74, Palm Desert
(760) 346-6268
www.stmargarets-school.org

ST. THERESA SCHOOL (K–8)
455 South Compadre Rd.
(760) 327-4919
www.stsps.org

XAVIER COLLEGE PREPARATORY HIGH SCHOOL
34-200 Cook St., Palm Desert
(760) 601-3900
www.xavierprep.org

Colleges and Universities

CALIFORNIA STATE UNIVERSITY, SAN BERNARDINO PALM DESERT CAMPUS
37-500 Cook St., Palm Desert
(760) 341-2883
www.pdc.csusb.edu
CSU offers a dozen undergraduate degrees, an MA in public administration, teaching/educational certification and Master's program, and several professional credential options, all aligned closely with the curriculum at the local community college, College of the Desert. The curriculum is structured for both mainline, full-time students and working professionals, and as a branch of CSUSB, students can take classes on the main campus in San Bernardino. The campus slowly started popping up out of the desert in the mid-2000s, and the buildings are gorgeous—institutional architecture as art. It's an important part of the city of Palm Desert's master plan and sits on several acres donated by the city.

BRANDMAN UNIVERSITY, COACHELLA VALLEY
42-600 Cook St., Suite 134, Palm Desert
(760) 341-8051
www.chapman.edu
Brandman is the multi-campus satellite system of Orange-based Chapman University. The desert branch offers both online and on-campus program in a myriad of disciplines, granting Bachelor's and Master's degrees, and professional credentials. A two-year general education Associates Degree is offered as well. The curriculum is principally

focused on students who work full-time. Interestingly, the entire library system is a virtual one, with online access to a large research database.

COLLEGE OF THE DESERT
43-500 Monterey Ave., Palm Desert
(760) 346-8041
www.collegeofthedesert.edu
Enrollment in this community college is almost 12,000, a mix of both full- and part-time students working for associate degrees or certificates. Campus facilities include a gym/pool complex, athletic facilities, library, golf driving range, a student center, and use of the McCallum Theatre for the Performing Arts. The College of the Desert Alumni Association puts on the highly successful weekend street fair and farmers' market, with booth rentals benefiting the college. Nursing and education are top certificate programs, and the curriculum is designed to allow students to get the standard classes required by four-year colleges at a very affordable tuition rate.

UNIVERSITY OF CALIFORNIA, RIVERSIDE
Palm Desert Graduate Center
75-080 Frank Sinatra Dr., Palm Desert
(760) 834-0800
www.palmdesert.ucr.edu
UCR is part of a shared higher education and research campus in Palm Desert. The school offers two graduate degrees: Executive MBA and Master of Fine Arts in creative writing and writing for the performing arts. The university also has a number of outreach programs in the desert community.

MEDIA

There's a selection of local daily newspapers as well as home delivery and newsstand availability of the *Los Angeles Times, USA Today, Wall Street Journal,* and even the *New York Times.* The county's largest paper, the *Riverside Press-Enterprise,* ceased desert delivery several years ago and devotes little to no editorial coverage of the region, though

that has been an on-again, off-again prospect over the years. The local business news publication, *Public Record,* is available to subscribers only. The free *Desert Post Weekly,* available every Thurs at paper boxes throughout the valley, provides the latest in movies, restaurants, club openings, theater, music, and everything fun. The local daily, *The Desert Sun,* is a Gannett publication and has excellent local sections as well as general national and international coverage. If you really want to call yourself a "local," *Palm Springs Life Magazine* is a must-read. This glossy publication is packed with the latest in fashion, art, home, and the local gossip/social scene.

The electronic media are also well represented in the valley, with more than two dozen radio stations broadcasting the gamut from news/talk and sports to classic rock and jazz. All three of the major television networks also have affiliates in the desert. Public access television is available in each city so locals can keep up with city hall.

i If you're hungering for a culture fix and don't want to negotiate the drive to Los Angeles or San Diego, check into the many day trips and overnight excursions offered by local travel agencies.

Publications
THE BOTTOM LINE
(760) 323-0552
www.psbottomline.com
This glossy monthly, targeting the gay and lesbian market, has been around for about 30 years, with a circulation of more than 100,000. This is the bible for everything to do with the GLBT scene in the desert, from parties to politics.

DESERT GOLF
(760) 324-2476
www.desertgolfer.com
This publication is devoted to desert golf and the golf lifestyle in the valley.

DESERT POST WEEKLY
(760) 322-8889
This is a weekly publication of *The Desert Sun* and is aimed at the 20- to 30-something group, with in-depth pieces on local music and independent entertainment, as well as some spicy opinion columns.

THE DESERT SUN
(760) 322-8889
www.thedesertsun.com

PALM SPRINGS LIFE MAGAZINE
(760) 325-2333
www.palmspringslife.com

THE PUBLIC RECORD
(760) 771-1155
www.desertpublicrecord.com

i Earthquakes are a fact of life in the desert—in fact, they give the desert some of its truly unique attributes—and you don't have to be here long to feel a good shaker. It's always a good idea to be prepared, so give yourself a solid footing by checking out the info on the state Office of Emergency Services' Web site: www.oes.ca.gov.

Radio
KPSC 88.5 FM
www.kusc.org
Classical.

KCRI 89.3 FM
Public radio.

KHCS 91.7 FM
www.joy92.org
Christian.

KQCM 92.1 FM
Top 40.

KKUU 92.7 FM
www.927kkuu.com
Top 40.

KCLB 93.7 FM
www.937kclb.com
Rock.

KLOB 94.7 FM
Spanish.

KXCM 96.3 FM
Country.

KUNA 96.7 FM
Spanish.

KRCK 97.7 FM
www.krck.com
'80s rock.

KWXY 98.5 FM
www.kwxy.com
Easy listening.

KMRJ 99.5 FM
www.995theheat.com
Alternative rock.

MIX 100.5 FM
www.mix1005.fm
Adult contemporary.

KATY 101.3 FM
www.1013katy.com
Adult contemporary.

KJJZ 102.3 FM
www.102kjjz.com
Smooth jazz, Palm Springs-style.

KEZN 103.1 FM
www.ez103.com
Soft rock.

KDES 104.7 FM
www.kdes.com
"Oldies" rock.

KPLM 106.1 FM
Country.

THE EAGLE 106.9 FM
www.theeagle1069.com
Classic rock; Mark & Brian.

KPSI 920 AM
www.newstalk920.com
News/talk.

KXPS 1010 AM
www.1010kxps.com
Sports.

Television

KPSP (2), CBS
www.kpsplocal2.com

KESQ (3), ABC
www.kesq.com

KMIR TV (6), NBC
www.kmir6.com

WORSHIP

With more than 100 places of worship through-out the valley, you certainly can find what you're looking for. Some of the more famous ones are St. Theresa's in Palm Springs, the site of Sonny Bono's funeral, and St. Louis Catholic Church in Cathedral City, home to the Sinatra clan. Whatever you choose, from nondenominational Christian-based teaching to Jewish temples or Episcopalian churches, you will be at home.

The best way to locate the service of your choice is either by reading the Saturday edition of *The Desert Sun*'s Religion Section or, of course, by looking in the Yellow Pages or online.

INDEX

ABOUT THE AUTHOR

Travel and golf writer Ken Van Vechten was born in Riverside, CA, and after a couple of decades bouncing around across the bottom quarter of the Golden State and various locales in Oregon, he again resides in Riverside. From his first childhood trip up the Palm Springs Aerial Tramway not long after its opening to his most recent round of golf at Desert Willow Golf Club, the Coachella Valley has been like a second home. The one-time newspaper editor and columnist, political hack, and corporate flack is the author of several guidebooks, including GPP's *Las Vegas EAT!*, and a contributing editor to the most recent edition of Zagat's *America's Top Golf Courses*. His work appears in the *Los Angeles Times, Alaska Airlines Magazine, Westways,* and other publications.